HISTORICITY
···· and the ····
LATTER-DAY SAINT SCRIPTURES

Edited by Paul Y. Hoskisson

VOLUME EIGHTEEN
IN THE RELIGIOUS STUDIES CENTER MONOGRAPH SERIES

Religious Studies Center
Brigham Young University
Provo, Utah

Cover design by Covenant Communications, Inc.

Distributed by Covenant Communications, Inc.
American Fork, Utah

Printed in the United States of America
First Printing: October 2001

08 07 06 05 04 03 02 01   10 9 8 7 6 5 4 3 2 1

ISBN 1-57734-928-8

HISTORICITY
···· and the ····
LATTER-DAY
SAINT
SCRIPTURES

RELIGIOUS STUDIES CENTER PUBLICATIONS

BOOK OF MORMON SYMPOSIUM SERIES

The Book of Mormon: The Keystone Scripture
The Book of Mormon: First Nephi, The
Doctrinal Foundation
The Book of Mormon: Second Nephi, The
Doctrinal Structure
The Book of Mormon: Jacob through Words of
Mormon, To Learn with Joy
The Book of Mormon: Mosiah, Salvation Only
through Christ

The Book of Mormon: Alma, The Testimony of
the Word
The Book of Mormon: Helaman through
3 Nephi 8, According to Thy Word
The Book of Mormon: 3 Nephi 9–30, This Is
My Gospel
The Book of Mormon: Fourth Nephi through
Moroni, From Zion to Destruction

MONOGRAPH SERIES

Nibley on the Timely and the Timeless
Deity and Death
The Glory of God Is Intelligence
Reflections on Mormonism
Literature of Belief
The Words of Joseph Smith
Book of Mormon Authorship
Mormons and Muslims
The Temple in Antiquity
Isaiah and the Prophets

Scriptures for the Modern World
The Joseph Smith Translation: The Restoration
of Plain and Precious Things
Apocryphal Writings and the Latter-day Saints
The Pearl of Great Price: Revelations from God
The Lectures on Faith in Historical Perspective
Mormon Redress Petitions: Documents of the
1833–1838 Missouri Conflict
Joseph Smith: The Prophet, the Man
Historicity and the Latter-day Saint Scriptures

SPECIALIZED MONOGRAPH SERIES

Supporting Saints: Life Stories of Nineteenth-
Century Mormons
The Call of Zion: The Story of the First Welsh
Mormon Emigration
The Religion and Family Connection: Social
Science Perspectives
Welsh Mormon Writings from 1844 to 1862:
A Historical Bibliography
Peter and the Popes
John Lyon: The Life of a Pioneer Poet
Latter-day Prophets and the United States
Constitution

View of the Hebrews: 1825 2nd Edition
Book of Mormon Authors: Their Words and
Messages
Prophet of the Jubilee
Manuscript Found: The Complete Original
"Spaulding Manuscript"
Latter-day Saint Social Life: Social Research on
the LDS Church and Its Members
From Jerusalem to Zarahemla: Literary and
Historical Studies of the Book of Mormon
Religion, Mental Health, and the Latter-day
Saints

OCCASIONAL PAPERS

Excavations at Seila, Egypt
Christopher Columbus: A Latter-day Saint
Perspective
Church History in Black and White: George
Edward Anderson's Photographic Mission
to Latter-day Saint Historical Sites
California Saints: A 150-Year Legacy in the
Golden State
A Woman's View: Helen Mar Whitney's
Reminiscences of Early Church History

Joseph Smith Portraits: A Search for the
Prophet's Likeness
A Descriptive Bibliography of the Mormon
Church
Brigham Young: Images of a Mormon Prophet
Prophets and Apostles of the Last Dispensation
The Restored Gospel and the Message of the
Four Gospels
Finding God at BYU

Contents

Introduction

When I lived in Waltham, an old industrial town on the Charles River near Boston, Massachusetts, I would take a shortcut through the woods to my classes at the nearby university. There were no paths or markers, so my course each day took a different route. I never ceased to marvel at the beauty of the deciduous forests of New England, especially early in the spring of the year. I would inhale the air, heavy with moisture and with the odor of rich humus, damp tree bark, and decaying leaves. If I treaded lightly over the matted leaves covering the damp soil, it seemed to me that I hardly left a trace behind of my intrusion. Yet for the trained eye I did leave telltale signs that I had passed that way. Here and there I would have crushed a stubborn leaf that had refused to fuse into the mat of the previous fall's leaves.

On the morning of a beautiful, clear, early spring day in 1820, the young lad Joseph Smith walked into such woods seeking divine guidance. Somewhere along his path he would have crushed just such a leaf. If we had walked along that same path an hour later, we might have found the crushed leaf, and we would have concluded that someone had walked this way before us. We might have recognized the imprint of his shoe sole on the fertile earth. We might even have seen the Prophet leaving the woods. Therefore, even though today we cannot empirically demonstrate that he had been in the woods, the imprint of his sole on a crushed leaf, or any other such sign at the time, would have demonstrated his presence in the grove that momentous spring day of 1820.

The title of this volume, *Historicity and the Latter-day Saint Scriptures,* introduces the theme. Historicity is the study of the authenticity of recorded past events and as such is a narrow subfield of the broad discipline of history.[1] This volume will address the issue of historicity as it relates to the scriptures that the Latter-day Saints accept as canon. Some articles discuss historicity, others discuss scripture, and some treat both. All the articles contribute to a more complete picture of historicity and Latter-day Saint scripture.

The topic is of special interest to Latter-day Saints for several reasons. Since the beginnings of the Church, those who participated in the Restoration were commanded to keep a history (see D&C 21:1). Latter-day Saints are known to go to extraordinary lengths to capture the history of our predecessors. We have an abiding interest in the history of God's dealings with this earth. We reverence the history of scripture because our faith is grounded in events that took place in the space and time of this world.

It is no longer sufficient, however, that Latter-day Saints simply take for granted the necessity for a historical basis of our faith. For over two hundred years now the historical faith of our brothers and sisters among other faiths, and more recently our Latter-day Saint faith, has been under siege. Some vociferous scholars and a few clamorous armchair theologians have attempted to convince those who believe in scripture that holy writ is not historical. An even smaller minority have argued that the scriptures need not be historical to produce faith because the stories in the scriptures, though not historical, are nevertheless inspired fiction.

Latter-day Saints must reject these ideas. For us, historical events and historical people do form the basis of our faith. Therefore, with growing concern for what is happening in the secular world of scripture study and its possible overflow into Latter-day Saint spheres, it was decided to hold a conference on Latter-day Saint scriptures and historicity. A call for papers was issued, presenters were selected, and the conference took place 23–24 February 1996 on the campus of Brigham Young University. Those who presented at the conference were invited to submit papers for publication, the results of which appear in this volume. In addition, this volume contains two articles that were not presented at the symposium. Elder Dallin H. Oaks's piece on Book of Mormon historicity had been presented earlier at a Foundation for Ancient Research and Mormon Studies (FARMS) banquet and subsequently made available through FARMS as a typescript offprint. It was decided to include his article in this volume for two reasons. The content fits very well within and adds to the theme of this volume, and it is hoped that through its inclusion Elder Oaks's valuable contribution may reach an additional audience. Permission to include it was graciously granted. Sometime after the symposium, James Faulconer approached me with a draft of some ideas he had been wrestling with and asked if I might consider including it in the final publication. After reading the manuscript, I was enthusiastic about his contemporary approach and encouraged him to submit a final draft. The felicitous and carefully reasoned result appears herein.

It is my desire as editor that with the articles in this volume we, the authors, have added reason to our hope and substance to our faith. This volume, therefore, is dedicated to proclaiming our Latter-day Saint faith through exploring historicity and scripture.

Note

1. In general, if a story has historicity it is also historical; if it is not historical, then it lacks historicity. For example, the story of the Good Samaritan may be historical without having historicity. That is, the story may be accurate in presenting material that is true to the historical period in which the story took place. In fact, every detail of the story of the Good Samaritan could have been drawn from actual incidents in the New Testament period, and therefore every detail would be historical. Yet the story as Jesus told it may never have happened. Therefore, the story may be historical but lack historicity. Another way to explain this is that not all stories that are historical also have historicity. Conversely, a story may have historicity, that is, it actually happened, but through the recording and transmission process some of the details may have been garbled and therefore are not historical. Thus, we can talk about the degree of historical facts in a story that has historicity. But a story that is not historical at all cannot have historicity.

The Latter-day Saint Concept of Canon

1

Elder Alexander B. Morrison

Traditional Christianity struggled for many years to define its canon, to determine which of its writings were sacred, inspired, and authoritative. The Latter-day Saint concept of canon differs from that of other Christians. In addition to the Bible, the Latter-day Saint canon includes the Book of Mormon, the Doctrine and Covenants, and the Pearl of Great Price. These "standard works" provide a measuring rod by which we can judge other texts and statements. But while we have a canon, we nevertheless believe that God continues to make known His will through the First Presidency and the Quorum of the Twelve Apostles—men we sustain as prophets, seers, and revelators. Inspired by the Holy Ghost, their decisions are to be made in unity (D&C 107:27). We as Church members also need the Holy Ghost in order to recognize scriptural power in their words, and we can be comforted in the Lord's promise that the President of the Church will never lead us astray.

I begin my remarks today with a caveat and a conclusion. I speak to you not as a scholar, but as one—albeit the least—of those who are called to be "especial witnesses unto the Gentiles and in all the world" (D&C 107:25). Mine is the voice of witness and testimony, not of scholarship. I do not come as an apologist for the Latter-day Saint canon, its historicity, or contents, but rather as a "witness of the sufferings of Christ" (1 Pet. 5:1), of His Resurrection and Atonement, and of the Restoration through the Prophet Joseph Smith of Christ's gospel in its fulness.

In the final analysis, the truth of our canon will not be discovered by scholarly examination alone. I am reminded of Winston Churchill's words: "History with its flickering lamp stumbles along the trail of the past trying to reconstruct its success to revive the echoes and kindle with pale gleams the passions of former days."[1] Flickering lamps and pale gleams will not, cannot, illuminate the face of God. The writer of Ecclesiastes put it well: "When I applied mine heart to know wisdom, and to see the business that is done upon the earth . . . then I beheld all the work of God, that a man cannot find out the work that is done under the sun: because though a man labour to seek it out, yet he shall not find it; yea further; though a wise man think to know it, yet shall he not be able to find it" (Eccl. 8:16–17). In the book of Job we read, "Canst thou by searching find out God? canst thou find out the Almighty unto perfection? It is as high as heaven; what canst thou do? deeper than hell; what canst thou know? The measure thereof is longer than the earth, and broader than the sea" (Job 11:7–9).

If history is an inadequate tool in our search for religious truth, so too is logic. Despite the grandeur of the logic of the medieval philosophers and theologians, despite the genius of men such as Augustine, Anselm, Abelard, or Aquinas, logic—while it may buttress—can never prove the existence of God, nor the facticity of the canon that we espouse.

With great respect, in a sense then, the conclusions of this or any other learned symposium are irrelevant. God will not be found through scholarly analysis alone. To find Him is primarily a journey of faith. The options open to the seeker of religious truth are stark and simple. Either God is or He is not. The Prophet Joseph Smith either saw Him, conversed with Him, and learned from Him, or he did not. Either President Hinckley is a prophet or he is not. The truth of the matter supersedes history and transcends human logic. The Lord does not think as man thinks. "But the natural man receiveth not the things of the Spirit of God: for they are foolishness unto him: neither can he know them, because they are spiritually discerned" (1 Cor. 2:14).

Canon

Against the background of that caveat and conclusion, permit me to make a few observations about the Latter-day Saint concept of canon. As you all know, the word *canon* is of Latin and Greek origin. Though it has numerous meanings, for our purposes it denotes "a collection or authoritative list of books accepted as holy scripture."[2] I leave to others the task of defining—insofar as the Bible is concerned—the content of that list of books, but note in passing that the traditional Christian world has had a long and hard struggle throughout its history to define which writings are sacred, inspired, and binding on believers. Protestant Bibles (including the King James Version), which Latter-day Saints accept as "the word of God as far as it is translated correctly" (A of F 8), do not include some books accepted as canonical by the Roman Catholic and Orthodox churches. Even within Protestantism, the question of canon is perhaps not yet unanimously resolved. Martin Luther characterized the epistle of James as an "epistle of straw," apparently because it did not substantiate his teaching of justification by faith alone, and he mistrusted the book of Revelation.[3]

Latter-day Saint views on canon, in the minds of some Christians, are so extreme as to deny us the right to even refer to ourselves as Christians. We are simply unacceptable to some of our Christian brethren, gone beyond heresy to anathema. While that may be regrettable, what others label us, or even think about us, is of far lesser importance than what is true and thus acceptable to God.

Basic to the Latter-day Saint concept of canon are two eternal principles. The first is that compared to the rest of the Christian world, ours is an expanded canon. In addition to the Bible, we accept as canonical three other books of holy scripture—the Book of Mormon (531 pages), the Doctrine and Covenants (294 pages), and the Pearl of Great Price (61 pages).[4] These four books make up the "standard works" of the Church, a term first used a century ago by Elder James E. Talmage. The Book of Mormon: Another Testament of Jesus Christ has as one of its purposes "the convincing of the Jew and Gentile that Jesus is the Christ, the eternal God, manifesting himself unto all nations" (Title Page). Of it the Prophet Joseph Smith declared, "I told the brethren [the Twelve Apostles and Joseph Fielding] that the Book of Mormon was the most correct of any book on earth, and the keystone of our religion, and a man would get nearer to God by abiding by its precepts, than by any other book."[5] When that statement is coupled with our assertion that the Bible is the word of God as far as it is translated correctly, it must be concluded that even within the written canon, there are gradations of inerrancy and spiritual power.

The Doctrine and Covenants, we affirm, is a collection of divine revelations and inspired declarations given for the establishment and regulation of the kingdom of God on the earth in the last days. The Pearl of Great Price is a selection of inspired writings touching the faith and doctrine of The Church of Jesus Christ of Latter-day Saints, including, in the present edition, selections from the Book of Moses, the Book of Abraham, Joseph Smith's history, and his translation of chapter 24 of the book of Matthew from the Bible, as well as the Articles of Faith.

Not only is ours an expanded canon, but it is also open and unended. We do not subscribe to the finalist and minimalist views of other Christians with regard to holy writ. We believe in continuing and unending revelation, ever augmented by living prophets.

The scriptures of the past are not sufficient for us today. I quote President Joseph F. Smith on this matter:

> Are we to understand, then, that God does not, and will not further make known his will to men; that what he has said suffices? His will to Moses and Isaiah and John is abundant for modern followers of Christ? The Latter-day Saints take issue with this doctrine, and pronounce it illogical, inconsistent, and untrue, and bear testimony to all the world that God lives and that he reveals his will to men who believe in him and who obey his commandments, as much in our day as at any time in the history of nations. The canon of scripture is not full. God has never revealed at any time that he would cease to speak forever to men. If we are permitted to believe that he has spoken, we must and do believe that he continues to speak, because he is unchangeable.
>
> His will to Abraham did not suffice for Moses, neither did his will to Moses suffice for Isaiah. Why? Because their different missions required different instructions; and logically, that is also true of the prophets and people of today. A progressive world will never discover all truth until its inhabitants become familiar with all the knowledge of the Perfect One.[6]

That is not to say, of course, that every word the Brethren speak is scripture. The scriptures inform us on how to answer the crucial question: When are the writings and sermons of Church leaders entitled to the claim of being scripture? The answer is found in D&C

68:2–4, a revelation given through the Prophet Joseph to brethren who were to engage in missionary work: "And, behold, and lo, this is an ensample unto all those who were ordained unto this priesthood, whose mission is appointed unto them to go forth—and this is the ensample unto them, that they shall speak as they are moved upon by the Holy Ghost. And whatsoever they shall speak when moved upon by the Holy Ghost shall be scripture, shall be the will of the Lord, shall be the mind of the Lord, shall be the word of the Lord, shall be the voice of the Lord, and the power of God unto salvation." The burden of proof for what is scriptural thus rests on the reader or hearer. This rule or principle, President J. Reuben Clark Jr. noted, has no exceptions. It is universal in its application. Having thought deeply about how we know if things spoken by the Brethren are said as they are "moved upon by the Holy Ghost," President Clark concluded: "I have given some thought to this question, and the answer thereto so far as I can determine, is: we can tell when the speakers are 'moved upon by the Holy Ghost' only if we, ourselves, are 'moved upon by the Holy Ghost.' In a way, this completely shifts the responsibility from them to us to determine when they so speak."[7]

Brigham Young's wise counsel comes to mind. He said, "Were your faith concentrated upon the proper object, your confidence unshaken, your lives pure and holy, every one fulfilling the duties of his or her calling according to the Priesthood and capacity bestowed upon you, you would be filled with the Holy Ghost, and it would be as impossible for any man to deceive and lead you to destruction as for a feather to remain unconsumed in the midst of intense heat."[8]

Our individual responsibilities to find out for ourselves what constitutes scripture and what does not are underlined by this additional comment from President Young: "I am more afraid that this people have so much confidence in their leaders that they will not inquire for themselves of God whether they are led by Him. I am fearful they settle down in a state of blind self-security, trusting their eternal destiny in the hands of their leaders with a reckless confidence that in itself would thwart the purposes of God in their salvation, and weaken that influence they could give to their leaders, did they know for themselves, by the revelations of Jesus, that they are led in the right way. Let every man and woman know, by the whispering of the

Spirit of God to themselves, whether their leaders are walking in the path the Lord dictates, or not."[9]

Are There Problems with an Open Canon?

Professor W. D. Davies has posed a fundamental question raised by the existence of an open canon. "Progressive and continuous revelation," he has noted, "is certainly an attractive notion, but equally certainly it is not without the grave danger of so altering or enlarging upon the original revelation as to distort, annul, or even falsify it."[10]

While it certainly is not in any sense a closed canon, the existence and acceptance of the standard works provides the Latter-day Saints with a core set of texts with which to judge or measure other religious writings or pronouncements. New light and knowledge is judged by its uniformity to "the things which are written; for in them are all things written concerning the foundation of my church, my gospel, and my rock" (D&C 18:3–4). In other words, new revelation must fit into the great framework of the plan of salvation as presented in the standard works.

It is important to note that the standard works support and sustain each other. Elder Bruce R. McConkie put it this way:

> Every book of scripture is a witness of the truth and divinity of every other volume of holy writ. No compilation of the divine word stands alone; all join in bearing the same witness and in teaching the same truths. Their settings vary; their miracles fit their own needs; their prophets have different names and speak the local languages. But the message of salvation is the same. Always the scriptures bear witness of Christ; always they teach the truths of salvation; always they call upon fallen man to forsake the world and be reconciled to God through the atonement of his Son; always they speak peace to sorrowing souls in this world and hold out to them the hope of eternal life in the world to come.[11]

Thus, the Bible and the Book of Mormon speak of, describe, and support each other. Indeed, in a revelation given through the Prophet Joseph Smith in April 1830, the Lord declared that the Book of Mormon came forth to prove "to the world that the holy scriptures [i.e., the Bible] are true" (D&C 20:11). Nephi saw in vision a book, the Bible, carried forth among the people. An angelic ministrant said to him: "Knowest thou the meaning of the book? . . . The book that thou beholdest is a record of the Jews, which contains the covenants of the Lord, which he hath made unto the house of Israel; and it also containeth many [but not all!] of the prophecies of the holy prophets; and it is a record like unto the engravings which are upon the plates of brass, save there are not so many; nevertheless, they contain the covenants of the Lord, which he hath made unto the house of Israel; wherefore, they are of great worth unto the Gentiles. . . . And when it proceeded forth from the mouth of a Jew it contained the fulness of the gospel of the Lord, of whom the twelve apostles bear record" (1 Ne. 13:21–24).

Then something happened to the Bible, which had "contained the fulness of the gospel"—something which goes beyond the inevitable errors and shortcomings of even the most accomplished and devoted translators and transcribers. As the Church, bereft of apostolic leadership by the end of the first century after Christ's death and resurrection, struggled to adjust to the philosophies of men, Christ's message to the world was altered. "Many plain and precious things" were taken away from the book, "which is the book of the Lamb of God," causing an "exceedingly great many" to stumble, "insomuch that Satan hath great power over them" (1 Ne. 13:28–29). Nevertheless, God in His mercy will not suffer "that the Gentiles shall forever remain in that awful state of blindness . . . because of the plain and most precious parts of the gospel of the Lamb which have been kept back by that abominable church, . . . which is the mother of harlots, saith the Lamb—I will be merciful unto the Gentiles in that day, insomuch that I will bring forth unto them, in mine own power, much of my gospel, which shall be plain and precious, saith the Lamb" (1 Ne. 13:32–34). "These plain and precious things," the Lord proclaimed, shall be written by the Nephites to come forth in the last days "unto the Gentiles, by the gift and power of the Lamb. And in them shall be written my gospel . . . and my rock and my salvation" (see 1 Ne. 13:29, 35–36). This record is the Book of Mormon, which not only supports and sustains the Bible but also restores many of the plain and precious truths lost from it by Satan-inspired perversion of the record.

Let us then deal squarely with Professor Davies' concern that continued revelation is in "grave danger of so altering and enlarging upon the original revelation as to distort, annul, or even falsify it." Distortion, annulment, and falsification of the revelations of God have, we readily concede, occurred. But The Church of Jesus Christ of Latter-day Saints is not responsible for them. We assert in boldness that uninspired men have "strayed from mine ordinances, and have broken mine everlasting covenant; they seek not the Lord to establish his righteousness, but every man walketh in his own way, and after the image of his own god, whose image is in the likeness of the world, and whose substance is that of an idol, which waxeth old and shall perish" (D&C 1:15–16). Thus we reject the Christ of the creeds and councils; we reject the doctrines of the Trinity as taught by most Christian churches; we assert that the creeds which set forth the view of "traditional" Christianity about the nature of the Godhead, and were adopted only after centuries of debate and political maneuvering, do not reflect accurately the doctrine or beliefs of the New Testament Church. For similar reasons, we reject the doctrines of original sin and of salvation by grace alone, asserting that they, too, are false doctrines which arose and were accepted by so-called "traditional" Christianity centuries after Christ.

Although the standard works provide canonical measuring rods against which additional revelation is to be judged, it is important to note the role of the spoken word as given by the living prophets. Continuing revelation for the Church and world comes through the First Presidency and the Twelve, who have a special spiritual endowment as prophets, seers, and revelators to declare the mind and will of God to the world. As Joseph Smith said, "Where the Oracles of God are not there the Kingdom of God is not."[12]

Every decision made by the Twelve, the revelations tell us, "must be by the unanimous voice of the same; . . . every member in each quorum must be agreed to its decisions" (D&C 107:27). The First Presidency also are as one, fully and completely united in the work of the kingdom. President Joseph F. Smith spoke of that unity as follows:

> I propose that my counselors and fellow presidents in the First Presidency shall share with me in the responsibility of every act which I shall perform in this capacity. I do not propose to take the reins in my own hands to do as I please; but I propose to do as my brethren and I agree upon, and as the Spirit of the Lord manifests to us. I have always held, and do hold, and trust I always shall hold, that it is wrong for one man to exercise all the authority and power of presiding in the Church of Jesus Christ of Latter-day Saints. I dare not assume such a responsibility, and I will not, so long as I can have men like these (pointing to presidents Winder and Lund) to stand by and counsel with me in

the labors we have to perform, and in doing all those things that shall tend to the peace, advancement and happiness of the people of God and the building up of Zion.[13]

President Gordon B. Hinckley has added his personal testimony that decisions of the First Presidency and the Twelve are made in unity. He said:

No decision emanates from the deliberations of the First Presidency and the Twelve without total unanimity among all concerned. At the outset in considering matters, there may be differences of opinion. These are to be expected. These men come from different backgrounds. They are men who think for themselves. But before a final decision is reached, there comes a unanimity of mind and voice.

This is to be expected if the revealed word of the Lord is followed. . . . I add by way of personal testimony that during the twenty years I served as a member of the Council of the Twelve and during the nearly thirteen years that I have served in the First Presidency, there has never been a major action taken where this procedure was not observed. I have seen differences of opinion presented in these deliberations. Out of this very process of men speaking their minds has come a sifting and winnowing of ideas and concepts. But I have never observed serious discord or personal enmity among my Brethren. I have, rather, observed a beautiful and remarkable thing—the coming together, under the directing influence of the Holy Spirit and under the power of revelation, of divergent views until there is a total harmony and full agreement. Only then is implementation made. That, I testify, represents the spirit of revelation manifested again and again in directing this the Lord's work.

I know of no other governing body of any kind of which this might be said.

This procedure obtains even in the absence of the President of the Church. I hasten to add, however, that the Brethren would not be inclined to do anything which they feel would be out of harmony with the attitude, feelings, and position of their beloved leader, the prophet of the Lord.[14]

The president of the Church, *primus inter pares* among the prophets, seers, and revelators, does, however, stand preeminent. He is "like unto Moses" (D&C 107:91), "having all the gifts of God which he bestows upon the head of the church" (D&C 107:92). His official statements in his time may take precedence over revelation in scripture pertinent to other times or other statements by previous presidents—though in fact this rarely occurs. When it does, it is because needs change over time; the word of God needed to answer the problems of our era may not be what is required in another. Speaking of the importance of the living prophet, President Ezra Taft Benson said, "God's revelations to Adam did not instruct Noah how to build the ark. Noah needed his own revelation. Therefore, the most important prophet, so far as you and I are concerned, is the one living in our day and age to whom the Lord is currently revealing His will for us. Therefore, the most important reading we can do is any of the words of the prophet contained each week in the Church Section of the *Deseret News* and any words of the prophet contained each month in our Church magazines. Our marching orders for each six months are found in the general conference addresses."[15]

The president of the Church will never be permitted to lead the people astray. President Wilford Woodruff stated: "I say to Israel the Lord will never permit me or any other man who stands as the President of this Church, to lead you astray. It is not in the programme. It is not in the mind of God. If I were able to attempt that, the Lord would remove me out of my place, and so he will any other man who attempts to lead the children of men astray from the oracles of God and from their duty."[16]

Beyond the prophet lies the consummate authority of God himself. The Prophet Joseph Smith counseled, "The best way to obtain truth and wisdom is not to ask it from books, but to go to God in prayer, and obtain divine teaching."[17]

The Process of Canonizing

The ways by which revelations become canonized, and hence binding on the faithful, provide an additional check and balance to the openness of the Latter-day Saint canon. The basic principle involved is that of common consent: "And all things shall be done by common consent in the church, by much prayer and faith, for all things you shall receive by faith" (D&C 26:2).

Scripture to be canonized is presented to the people assembled in conference for their sustaining vote. This occurred, for example, with Official Declaration 2, which was presented by President N. Eldon Tanner on behalf of the First Presidency at the semi-annual general conference of the Church on 30 September 1978. The revelation on the priesthood, received by President Spencer W. Kimball, had first been presented to the counselors in the First Presidency, who accepted it and approved it. It was then presented to the Quorum of the Twelve Apostles, who unanimously approved it, and was subsequently presented to all other general authorities, who likewise approved it unanimously. Finally, Official Declaration 2 was presented to all general and local priesthood officers of the Church throughout the world.

What would happen (and it never has and, I warrant, never will) if the people were to reject a proposal for canonization? Elder B. H. Roberts answered that questions as follows: "The truth remains. The action of the Church has not affected it in the least. The truth remains just as true as if the Church had accepted it. Its action simply determines the relationship of the members to that truth; and if they reject it, the truth still remains; and it is my opinion that they would not make further progress until they accepted the rejected truth. The truth remains."[18]

The Facticity of the Canon

The facticity of three of the standard works (Book of Mormon, Doctrine and Covenants, and the Pearl of Great Price) has been under almost constant attack by the enemies of the Church for 165 years. The adversary knows full well that if he can persuade people, both in and out of the Church, that the latter-day scriptures are false, he will momentarily win the day. He will, of course, not succeed. This work will go forth, as Joseph Smith said, "boldly, nobly, and independent, till it has penetrated every continent, visited every clime, swept every country, and sounded in every ear; till the purposes of God shall be accomplished and the great Jehovah shall say the work is done."[19]

But even the Bible's factual basis is under attack. Luke Timothy Johnson has recently written a scathing review of the work of the so-called Jesus Seminar, a group of individuals more learned than they are wise, who claim they wish to "liberate Jesus" from the Gospels, portraying him as less than the Son of God and by no means the risen Lord.[20] Interestingly enough, a publication of the Jesus Seminar entitled *The Five Gospels* includes the Gospel of Thomas together with the four canonized Gospels of the New Testament. The Gospel of Thomas, written in Coptic, is one of the compositions discovered at Nag Hammadi in 1947 and is considered by many scholars to be of Gnostic origin.[21]

11

This is not the place for a full review of the work of the Jesus Seminar. It will be difficult for many biblical scholars to disagree with Johnson's view that its work has a political agenda and is not responsible or even critical scholarship, but a self-indulgent charade.

Within The Church of Jesus Christ of Latter-day Saints, a classic example of a concerted attack on the facticity of our canon is the so-called modernism controversy of 1910–11 at Brigham Young University. The story of that dramatic event in our history, which had a profound import on this University, was told with his usual skill and spiritual insight by President Boyd K. Packer in an address given on 29 August 1995 to BYU's Annual University Conference.[19] Time permits only a brief recounting of the controversy. George Brimhall, president of BYU in 1911, had hired three well-trained professors to assist in transforming the institution into a full-fledged university comparable to the country's best. The professors determined that intellectual and scientific philosophies should take the place of the practicality and religion that had been paramount at the school. "The fundamentals of religion," they averred, "could and must be investigated by extending the (empirical) method into the spiritual realm." In other words, religion can and must be proven, like physics or mathematics.

The professors were popular, dynamic, and charismatic. The students flocked to their cause, and many of the faculty agreed.

The superintendent of Church schools, Horace Cummings, reported his deep concerns to the Church Board of Education. His anxieties included the following:

> "The teachers were following the 'higher criticism' . . . , treating the Bible as a 'collection of myths, folk-lore, drama, literary production, history and some inspiration.'"

> "They also taught that 'visions and revelations are mental suggestions. The objective reality of the presence of the Father and Son, in Joseph Smith's first vision, is questioned.'"

> "They rejected the flood, the confusion of tongues, the miracle of the Red Sea, and the temptation of Christ."

> "All truths change as we change. Nothing is fixed or reliable."[23]

Not much basis for religious faith there!

The school administration wavered at first, trying to keep the peace, hoping to smooth things over, not wanting to grasp the nettle and do what needed to be done. Eventually, the professors were let go and the affair subsided. But by that time the faith of many, both young and old, had been shaken and in too many instances lost.

The story has many morals, but one of the lessons to be learned from it is that those who, under the guise of scholarship, sneer at, question, and tear down the faith of others need not feel proud of themselves. They are as those spoken of by the Nephite prophet Jacob, who lamented the vainness, frailties, and foolishness of men: "When they are learned they think they are wise, and they hearken not unto the counsel of God, for they set it aside, supposing they know of themselves, wherefore, their wisdom is foolishness and it profiteth them not. And they shall perish. But to be learned is good if they hearken unto the counsels of God" (2 Ne. 9:28–29).

Doctrinal Essentials

I remind you of two statements by the prophets, seers, and revelators that define that core of truth that must be accepted by all who claim membership in The Church of Jesus Christ of Latter-day Saints.

Nearly sixty years ago, President J. Reuben Clark Jr. defined clearly those things that "may not be overlooked, forgotten, shaded or discarded" by each and all of the members of the Church. They are as follows:

> First—that Jesus Christ is the Son of God, the Only Begotten of the Father in the flesh, the Creator of the world, the Lamb of God, the Sacrifice for the sins of the world, the Atoner for Adam's transgression; that He was crucified; that His spirit left His body; that He died; that He was laid away in the tomb; that on the third day His spirit was reunited with His body, which again became a living being; that He was raised from the tomb a resurrected being, a perfect Being, the First Fruits of the Resurrection; that He later ascended to the Father; and that because of His death and by and through His resurrection every man born into the world since the beginning will be likewise literally resurrected. . . .
>
> The second of the two things to which we must all give full faith is that the Father and the Son actually and in truth and very deed appeared to the Prophet Joseph in a vision in the woods; that other heavenly visions followed to Joseph and to others; that the gospel and the Holy Priesthood after the Order of the

Son of God were in truth and fact restored to the earth from which they were lost by the apostasy of the primitive Church; that the Lord again set up His Church, through the agency of Joseph Smith; that the Book of Mormon is just what it professes to be; that to the Prophet came numerous revelations for the guidance, upbuilding, organization, and encouragement of the Church and its members; that the Prophet's successors, likewise called of God, have received revelations as the needs of the Church have required, and that they will continue to receive revelations as the Church and its members, living the truth they already have, shall stand in need of more; that this is in truth the Church of Jesus Christ of Latter-day Saints; and that its foundation beliefs are the laws and principles laid down in the Articles of Faith. These facts also, and each of them, together with all things necessarily implied therein or flowing therefrom, must stand, unchanged, unmodified, without dilution, excuse, apology, or avoidance; they may not be explained away or submerged. Without these two great beliefs the Church would cease to be the Church.[24]

President James E. Faust also has spoken of the essentials that must be believed by all Latter-day Saints:

1. That Jesus is the Christ, the Savior and the Redeemer of all mankind through His Atonement.

2. That through Joseph Smith, a prophet of God, the gospel of Jesus Christ was restored in its fulness.

3. That the Book of Mormon is another testament of Christ.

4. That all of the Presidents of the Church since Joseph Smith have successively possessed the keys and authority which was restored through Joseph Smith.

5. That Gordon B. Hinckley is the prophet, seer, and revelator to the world at this time.[25]

Conclusion

The Latter-day Saint concept of canon separates us from the rest of our Christian brothers and sisters. We believe not only in an expanded canon but also in an open canon resulting from continued revelation to God's living, authorized spokesman. At the same time, however, the standard works provide not only a core set of beliefs but also a yardstick against which to judge other religious texts and pronouncements. The process of canonization, involving the unique role of the president of the Church, the need of unanimity among the Twelve, and common consent by the members, combine to assure that additions to scripture are not only consistent with the written word contained in the standard works but also are significant and important. Perhaps of greatest importance is the view that Church leaders pronounce scripture when moved upon by the Holy Ghost, and that members can tell when leaders are so led only if they themselves are moved upon by the Holy Ghost. The burden of responsibility for spiritual discernment thus comes back to the individual. That is, I believe, one of the great strengths of this wondrous latter-day work.

Elder Alexander B. Morrison is a member of the First Quorum of the Seventy, The Church of Jesus Christ of Latter-day Saints.

Notes

1. James C. Humes, *The Wit and Wisdom of Winston Churchill* (New York: Harper Collins, 1994), 43.

2. *Webster's Third New International Dictionary of the English Language Unabridged* (Springfield, Mass.: Merriam-Webster, 1986), s.v. "canon."

3. Roland H. Bainton, *Here I Stand: A Life of Martin Luther* (New York and Toronto: Mentor, 1950), 138, 259–61.

4. Page totals in current English-language editions.

5. Joseph Smith, *Teachings of the Prophet Joseph Smith,* comp. Joseph Fielding Smith (Salt Lake City: Deseret Book, 1938), 194.

6. Joseph F. Smith, *Gospel Doctrine* (Salt Lake City: Deseret Book, 1986), 36–37.

7. J. Reuben Clark Jr., "When Are Church Leaders' Words Entitled to Claim of Scripture?" *Church News,* 31 July 1954, 9.

8. *Journal of Discourses* (London: Latter-day Saints' Book Depot, 1854–86), 7:277.

9. Ibid., 9:150.

10. W. D. Davies, "Reflections on the Mormon Canon," in *Christians among Jews and Gentiles: Essays in Honor of Krister Stendahl on His Sixty-Fifth Birthday,* ed. George W. E. Nickelsburg (Philadelphia: Fortress, 1986), 64.

11. Bruce R. McConkie, *A New Witness for the Articles of Faith* (Salt Lake City: Deseret Book, 1985), 418.

12. Andrew F. Ehat and Lyndon W. Cook, eds., *The Words of Joseph Smith: The Contemporary Accounts of the Nauvoo Discourses of the Prophet Joseph* (Provo, Utah: Religious Studies Center, Brigham Young University, 1980), 156.

13. Joseph F. Smith, *Gospel Doctrine,* 176–77.

14. Gordon B. Hinckley, *Conference Report,* April 1994, 74–75.

15. Ezra Taft Benson, *BYU 1980 Devotional and Fireside Speeches* (Provo, Utah: University Publications, 1981), 27.

16. Wilford W. Woodruff, *Conference Report,* October 1894.

17. *Teachings of the Prophet Joseph Smith,* 19.

18. B. H. Roberts, "Relation of Inspiration and Revelation to Church Government," *Improvement Era,* March 1905, 364.1.

19. *Times and Seasons* 3, no. 9 (1 March 1842): 709.

20. Luke Timothy Johnson, "The Jesus Seminar's Misguided Quest for the Historical Jesus," *The Christian Century* 113, no. 1 (3–10 January 1996), 16–22, esp. 17.

21. Robert W. Funk, Roy W. Hoover, and the Jesus Seminar, trans. and eds., *The Five Gospels: What Did Jesus Really Say?* (San Francisco: Harper San Francisco, 1993).

22. *Brigham Young Magazine* 49, no. 4 (November 1995): 46–52.

23. Ibid., 48.

24. J. Reuben Clark Jr., "The Charted Course of the Church in Education," *Charge to Religious Educators,* 3d ed. (Salt Lake City: The Church of Jesus Christ of Latter-day Saints, 1994), 3–4.

25. James E. Faust, "Joseph Smith and the Book of Mormon," *Ensign,* January 1996, 5–6.

Scripture as Incarnation

2

James E. Faulconer

Today the modernist view of history in which texts only represent events is so predominant that most Latter-day Saints automatically apply it to the question of scriptural historicity. Unfortunately, historical scholarship rarely lines up with our understanding of scripture as well as we would like. Problems arise when we use modernist tools to examine scripture written by premoderns, who considered their writing not as mere representation but as incarnation—an embodiment of the symbolic ordering of the world. The premodernist reading of the scriptures more accurately reflects Latter-day Saint beliefs: whereas modernism would use reason to understand history (and thus the Divine in history, i.e., scripture), premodernism uses divinely revealed scripture as well as ritual, ritual objects, and ritual language to give order to history. Instead of examining scripture as just another element of history, premoderns consider scripture to be the defining element in history.

The historicity of scripture is important to most Christians and especially to Latter-day Saints.[1] Christians disagree among themselves about how to understand scriptural history, but few deny that, in some important sense, Christian scripture is historical. However, given the challenges to scriptural history, challenges that are especially strong for Latter-day Saints who take the Book of Mormon to be historical, what are we to make of the claim that scriptures are history? Given those challenges, is it *possible* to understand scripture as literal history? The answer to that question—positive, I will argue—lies in answering the question of what we mean by *history*.

Christian Belief and the Historicity of Scripture

The way that academic historians have thought of history since the beginning of modernism (about 1500) is not the only way to think about it.[2] However, since the eighteenth century, and especially in the nineteenth and twentieth centuries, those approaching the Bible and, later, also Latter-day Saint scripture, have used some variation of the academic understanding of history as their entrée into the question of scriptural historicity. We understand scriptural interpretation to be a subset of scholarly historical understanding, but the science of history has raised and continues to raise a variety of questions about the historicity of scriptural accounts. For the Bible, some of those questions have been resolved to the satisfaction of believers, and others remain questions. Given the unique character of the Book of Mormon, work on defending its historicity has been much less decisive. As a result, believers, especially Latter-day Saints, find themselves having to answer the question of to what degree their scriptural accounts are historical.

In general, scholars, even believing ones, have been more or less skeptical of the historical character of scripture. However, believers (scholars and otherwise) have felt it necessary to defend the historicity of scripture with the historian's scholarly tools because most Christians believe that the religious claims of Christianity cannot be completely separated from its historical claims. They also believe that they have no way of understanding those claims except via the tools of historical scholarship. For example, few have been willing completely to give up the historicity of Jesus' life and, particularly, the historicity of his death. Even those who deny the physical character of the resurrection usually tie the idea of resurrection to a historical event, such as an experience of the first Apostles.[3] We seem faced with two options for understanding scripture. On the one hand, we can accept some variety of the academic historians' approach to scripture—we may opt for the more "liberal" approach of people such as Raymond Brown, or we may prefer the more "conservative" approach of Christian literalists, but we agree that scripture is historical. Believers have generally sought to show that the scriptures are to some degree accurate histories, and they have accepted some version of the canons of historical scholarship as the canons for understanding the historicity of scripture.[4]

A common alternative is to escape the problems created by accepting those canons by arguing that the scriptures are not essentially historical. In this view, rather than being accurate descriptions of historical events, the scriptures are writings that may often look like history and, in fact, may have historical elements, but they are really about something other than the events portrayed in them. These believers often argue that scriptures are not about history but about another reality, such as a reality of archetypical meanings. Given the problems of establishing the historicity of scripture, such believers want to reject that historicity but retain the truth of scripture: scriptures are not about historical truth, they are about religious truth, these people argue. Thus, according to them, though scripture takes the guise of history, it is actually about something else, such as a transcendent or archetypical reality.[5]

Most Christian believers find this ahistorical resolution of the problem of scriptural historicity unacceptable, and this is especially true for Latter-day Saint believers. For example, most Latter-day Saints find it difficult to explain and accept the Book of Mormon's account of itself and Joseph Smith's account of its origin if it is not substantially a historical document rather than an embodiment of a- or trans-historical truth. Most Latter-day Saints feel that if the Book of Mormon is not substantially historical, then much of its text—the narrative—is irrelevant to its meaning for us, and it is difficult to see how to avoid accusing Joseph Smith of fraud.

Perhaps one way to avoid that charge would be to understand the production of the Book of Mormon as the creation of myth, in the positive sense of that word, namely a discourse that purports to give the structure of reality. As will be apparent, I am sympathetic to that understanding. Nevertheless, I think it is flawed because, as usually argued, it gives up too much. Such an explanation gives up the claim of peculiar and unique truth—a truth inseparable from historical truth—that most Christians and (even more) most Latter-day Saints take to be essential to their religion and their religious experience. The historicity of origins has been an essential element of biblical religions from the beginning. To understand any of those religions *only* in terms of myth changes them and the religious experience within them to such a degree that it is not clear how those who take the mythic view can claim that they are Christians, or Latter-day Saints, or Jews, or Muslims.

For Latter-day Saints the problem of the mythic understanding of scripture is even more severe. It is difficult to understand such things as the hefting of the gold plates and the testimony of the various witnesses and the visits of the angel Moroni if they are only part of the construction of a myth.[6] Mythmakers account for their myths as things they have received.[7] To that degree Joseph Smith's account could be construed as mythic. However, mythmakers do not consciously create the kinds of detailed, first-person accounts of that reception that Joseph Smith gives. Mythmakers have received the story from someone who received the sacred objects; they have not themselves received the objects. Thus, if we explain Latter-day Saint scripture by saying that Joseph Smith was making myth *rather than* reporting historical experiences, it is still difficult to avoid coming to the conclusion that not only was he making myth, he was also committing fraud. The phenomenon of mythmaking and the phenomenon of the origins of the LDS Church are not consonant with each other.

However, I believe that there is a more difficult problem. Beside the existential and phenomenological problems of the mythmaking understanding of scripture, there is a theoretical problem: those who argue that the authors of scripture are mythmakers assume, with the apologists and the academics, that the canons of academic history are *the* canons of history. They do not consider the possibility that there are other ways of understanding history and that, on one of those understandings, scripture is historical, literally so.

As a result of such problems, believers find it necessary to insist on the historical character of scripture, though doing so is sometimes rationally difficult; historical scholarship seldom lines up with our understanding of scripture as well as most believers would like it to. We can take various positions on the historicity of scripture, but if we are to think about that historicity, we must ask ourselves what the word *history* can mean, and which of its possible meanings we can most accurately apply to scripture. I argue that our discomfort with the various alternative attempts to deal with the historicity of scripture results from using a concept of history that is inappropriate to scripture. As a result, though I believe that the historical part of scripture is genuinely historical, I do not think the canons of historical scholarship will be much help to us in understanding scripture as history. We must reconsider what history is.

The discussion of history and its meaning, and (especially in the eighteenth and nineteenth centuries) the discussion of the historicity of scripture, have been an important part of modern intellectual history. Much of the contemporary discussion of these issues owes its form and content to those earlier debates.[8] However, though the terms *premodern* and *modern* are not unproblematic, I believe that the understanding of history held by premoderns is quite different from our own, that it is a plausible understanding of history, and that a contemporary re-thinking of it gives us a better way to understand scripture than does a modern understanding.[9] Consequently, a brief comparison of modern and premodern history can serve as a starting point for thinking about alternative conceptions of history.[10]

The Modern Concept of History: Representation/Reference

Perhaps the first thing to be said about the difference between modern and premodern history is that modern history takes narratives and the events they describe to be separable from each other, but premodern history does not. The distinction is not an obvious one. In fact, even if we understand that distinction conceptually, we do not find it easy to think about scripture except by using the modern distinction. Though, in its origins, the separation of event and narrative is an academic distinction, it has become so "obvious," so "natural," that we have difficulty understanding the distinction or reading scripture in any other way. It seems inescapably true to us that there are two things: the event itself and what one can truthfully say about that event. But premodern thinking does not have that distinction, at least not in the way that modern history does.

To give an account of an event is to speak meaningfully of that event. For example, "The cat sat on the mat" is meaningful, but it doesn't say much. Though we can understand it lexically and syntactically, unless that sentence is correlated to an event in some way (whether negatively or positively), it lacks fullness of meaning. If I say "The cat sat on the mat" as a description of a particular event, then I find that event meaningful, and the meaning of the sentence is a presentation of a meaning of the event. Without such presentations, explicitly put into language or not, there are no events. Events without meaning are strictly inconceivable; *as events, events are meaningful.* Modernism's mistake was to think that the meaning of sentences and the events they describe is explained merely referentially. Modernism assumes that the truth of the sentence is a function of its reference to a particular event, but reference is not enough to explain the meaning of events. It isn't necessarily that reference is impossible. After all, we do speak of things in the world, and attempts to do away completely with talk about things in the world are self-refuting (if there are such attempts).[11] The modernist mistake is not necessarily in thinking that meaning requires reference but in thinking that reference is sufficient to explain meaning as truth. There is meaning, but it always goes beyond what one can account for merely referentially.[12]

The connection between a word and the thing it refers to—in other words, meaningful reference—exists only in an *act* of reference, but no theory of reference can give an account of that act. Among other things, a theory of reference cannot account for the particular thing to which the meaning-act points or for the fact that it does so point in this case. Language theories can tell us how words relate to each other (in an "endless chain of signification," to use a phrase from Jacques Derrida), but given the infinite variety of possible references in any particular act of meaning, language theories cannot fully account for the success of acts in which we talk about things in the world.

Most theories mark this inability by mentioning the importance of context. But such a remark illustrates Derrida's point, for context does not name something to which we can refer, though at first glance it may seem to. Each reference to a context is made possible by another context which is itself not referred to, making any attempt to refer to context itself endless. One cannot refer to context as such; context is beyond reference, though essential to it. This means that the invocation of context in a theory of reference shows that, besides whatever the theory proposes to explain meaning, something more is needed. What I mean in a putative referential act, such as the description of a historical event, is not completely decided by the sign system (such as a natural language) that I use to make that reference or by any theory of such sign systems. It is always also decided by "something more."

We may try to specify what that something more is by mentioning the speaker's intent, the particular audience she addresses, the history of the language, the social relations in force at the time of the event, and all of the other "things" to which rhetoric attends, including the relation of the referential object to the person making the reference (which begs the question of reference). However, though we can talk about context, about what else reference requires, there seems to be no possible science or theory of context. Beside that, the act of reference (which must, as an act, include both the object of reference and the particular, existent thing that corresponds to that object) exists within the system of signs in which the reference occurs. Thus, the referential act is not a simple connection of two autonomous things, the thing to which I refer and the reference.[13] We cannot leave language behind, even in our putative reference to what is outside language.

We must use language to speak of what is beyond language. Nevertheless, we necessarily say what is, strictly speaking, impossible to say, namely, that talk about the world and the things in the world always involves something more than language. Something more than/other than language, something that cannot be said directly, accounts for any successful talk about things. Contrary to a common American (mis)interpretation of Derrida, the point is not that there are only texts, but that, though we can deal with only texts and text analogues, there is necessarily something more than *any* text.[14] Ironically, modernism rather than Derrida insists that there is nothing other than the text. By assuming that, in principle, it is possible or at least desirable for human beings to give a final, complete description of the world, modernism makes an identity of its ultimate text and the world described by that text. In contrast, Derrida denies the possibility of that identification. Something always remains beyond the text, beyond explanation, something that explains the text in question but is not explained by that text.

The empiricism of modernism (not the only kind of empiricism) imitates the sophists of classical Greece, for it pins its hopes for understanding on a supposed ability to fix the connections between ideas and words, on the one hand, and things on the other. However, as Catherine Pickstock notes, it is not only impossible to achieve fixity in that connection, it is dishonest to seek for it: "Human life is always in the midst of things; the clarity of empiricist conclusions is an illusion fostered by the falsely isolated and inert nature of its artificial findings." In contrast, "the genuine 'fixity' parodied by the sophists can be attained only in the unshakeable conviction of a certain way of life."[15] In other words, as Aristotle argues in *Nichomachean Ethics,* the alternative to the fixity of ideas is fixity of character, the fixity of a lived life, a fixity that cannot be reduced to a fixed connection between ideas and things. By ignoring that alternative, when modernism discovers that it cannot nail things down as it wishes, that crucifixion is no more appropriate for ideas and values than it is for human beings, it concludes that nihilism is the only alternative.[16]

For history, as for any other discipline, the question that a nonmodern understanding of signs and reference raises is, "What else is involved in producing the 'text' of our understanding of history?" According to what we choose, we will get different ways of understanding history. And, though we can and must adjudicate between the various ways of understanding history, there is no way to do so "purely," in other words, without referring to such things as various authorities; our goals and traditions; social, scholastic, and other conventions; social relations; and so on. In other words, as Nietzsche saw clearly, we must take into account the lives and ways of life into which such histories enter.[17] We cannot name, once and for all, what the "what else" of language or even of an individual language act is. Contrary to the expectations of the Enlightenment, we have no Archimedean point from which we can leverage our decision for or against a particular understanding of the world, much less of history. It is important to note, however, that the consequence of the absence of such a risk-free leverage- or standpoint does not result in absolute relativity and, therefore, in the meaninglessness of our decisions. That relativist consequence would follow only if, contrary to fact, we have only two options: mathematical certainty or absolute relativity.[18] Philosophers such as Plato and Aristotle, among the ancients, and Hannah Arendt, in this century, have offered other options. However, we need not know the work of these philosophers to see that we can break the horns of the dilemma with other options. The necessity of faith (though not necessarily religious faith) shows that there are more than those two options.[19]

Since the eighteenth century, both those who criticize scripture as history and those who defend it have assumed the modernist understanding of the connection between history and meaning, though usually only implicitly. I argue that, in spite of themselves, eighteenth-century biblical critics (who, as previously mentioned, laid the groundwork for the discussion of biblical interpretation for the nineteenth and twentieth centuries, as well as much in literary criticism) give up the Bible as a sacred text—*even those who wish to defend it as such*. They assume that there *is* a universal, language-free view available to them (at least in principle) and that the scriptures should accurately refer to or depict that universal view.[20] They assume that events exist prior to and independent of the meanings of those events, and that the better a historical text is, the more accurately it describes the event. By agreeing to the modernist assumption about how meaning is fixed, even defenders of the Bible conflate historical understanding with an accurate, referential description of events. They assume that meaning, biblical or otherwise, is essentially referential/representative and that only a rational method can give us understanding of historical texts, such as the Bible. By making the question of biblical truth—biblical literalness—a merely referential question (in other words, by understanding meaning via a referential theory and by applying that understanding to scripture), both the religious and the critics of religion turn religion into a set of beliefs to which one assents because one takes them to be referentially valid. But to paraphrase James, the devils also refer, and tremble (James 2:19).

A Premodern Concept of History: Incarnation

In contrast, premodern thinkers take the Bible not as an accurate reference to either history or another reality (though they do not deny that we can speak of the world) but as the incarnation (or enactment) of a symbolic ordering.[21] Work in the anthropology of religion, such as that of Mircea Eliade, suggests that we misunderstand religion when we understand it as essentially a set of beliefs.[22] In contrast, when we see what such anthropological work shows us, we discover that religion is an ordering of the world in and through symbols. Beliefs are consequent on that ordering, not constitutive of it. Thus, a Catholic, a Southern Baptist, and a Latter-day Saint differ from one another, not so much because they hold different beliefs (though they do), but because they are involved in different ways of ordering the world symbolically (though, given that they are all Christians, there is considerable overlap in the orderings manifest in their lives).

The most obvious place to find symbolic ordering is in the rituals of religions and in their sacred objects, though symbolic ordering also encompasses more ordinary aspects of life, including such things as peculiar idioms and patterns of deference—and assertions of belief. Especially in religion, systems and sets of beliefs are part of the orders in question, but they are not foundational to those orders. To be religious, therefore, is not to assent to particular propositions or assertions, though that assent follows from the fact that one is religious. Instead, to be religious is to recognize—to reverence—the sacred and to live in a world of which the contents, including beliefs, are ordered by the sacred.[23] For the religious, the sacred is the ordering principle, the "form" of the world, to use a term important to Plato, Aristotle, and all of medieval philosophy.[24] For premodern thought, both religious and nonreligious, the real is primarily "formal." There not only can be, but must be, a variety of manifestations of what I here call form, but each is an instance of the "same thing." The form of something is the real manifesting itself in the world. For religious premoderns, the sacred is the real manifest in the symbolic order of things—it is the form not just of individual things but of things as a whole—and religion gives us that form/order.

It is important to note that rational ordering and symbolic ordering are not necessarily at odds with one another. Within a symbolic order, rational discourse is one of the forms in which the real is manifest. Therefore, it is not opposed to symbolic ordering but a possible part of any symbolic order. In contrast, in a rational ordering, symbolic discourse cannot be made an instance of reason, except as a parasitic form of reference, as ambiguous or "poetic" speech.[25] As a result, though within a symbolic ordering there is no necessary opposition between the rational and the symbolic, that opposition may be necessary to a rational order.[26]

Living as we do in an age when modernism is the common sense for perhaps most human beings (at least those under the sway of progress and its Euro-American manifestation), when we are asked to talk or think about religion, we usually do so as if religion were one of several regions of life. On this view, there are many regions of my life: work, politics, family, morality, academics, economics, leisure, and so on. Religion is one of these regions of our lives, and some people's lives may have no such region. Though we engage in activities that involve the various regions of our lives, we assume that each is, strictly speaking, separate from the others, though possibly overlapping; in themselves, each region is on an equal footing with the others, and each region is differentiated in value from any other only by my valuing of it, in other words by my interests, desires, or needs.[27]

In contrast, for the premodern, religion is *not* one of several possible regions of life. Instead, it is the field within which any other regions or aspects are marked out and related to each other. Religion is that which makes regions possible and which gives the world as a whole unity, order, and meaning in and through symbols. To use Platonic language, religion reveals the "form" of the world. On this view, we can still speak of regions of human endeavor and interest, but ultimately those regions, such as economics or morality or politics, get their meaning in themselves and in their relations to each other, as well as their relative weight and importance from religion rather than from our valuing.

If we understand religion this way, then I think we must conclude that the religious and the critics of religion implicitly agreed to give up the Bible as a sacred text when they agreed to take it as a referential text like any other referential text rather than as a symbolically ordering one. For to understand the Bible by means of a referential theory is to take it as a manifestation of one region of human experience among others. It is to take it as something on a conceptual and ontological par with others of its regions, rather than as something incomparable because it is a revelation of what gives meaning to any possible region of life. For moderns, religion is a region of life; for premoderns, it is the form of life, the way in which life is enacted. The eighteenth- and nineteenth-century interest in reading the Bible with the methods that one would use to read any other book was, implicitly, a recognition that the Bible was no longer *the* text about human existence but one of many texts, each referring to or describing more or less accurately a different dimension or region of human reality.

The disagreement between Catholicism and the Reformation over the nature of symbols is one locus of this difference between symbolic ordering and reference. The doctrine of transubstantiation is the most obvious instance of this difference in the understanding of symbols. Because those outside the Roman Catholic tradition do not accept that doctrine, they also often reject the idea that symbols are incarnations rather than mere references. However, one need not accept transubstantiation, at least not as it is usually understood, to accept that symbols are incarnations. As the word *transubstantiation* implies, the problem with the doctrine for those who are not Roman Catholics is that it requires one to believe that the substance of the Eucharist has become, essentially and substantially, the actual flesh and blood of Jesus Christ. Such an understanding of the Eucharist is the consequence, on the one hand, of believing that symbols are incarnations, and, on the other, of having an Aristotelian/Thomistic metaphysics of substance and, therefore, a commensurate explanation of what it means for a symbol to be an incarnation.[28]

However, one could believe that symbols are incarnations without accepting an Aristotelian metaphysics of substance and the explanations of incarnation that follow from it. The tight connection between the two ideas is only a historical one. Those who accepted the first of these ideas but not the second would not hold to the doctrine of transubstantiation in the dogmatic sense. Even Catholics have other alternatives for understanding the doctrine of transubstantiation—non-Thomistic, Augustinian ones, for example. Jean-Luc Marion explains the Eucharist neither as a mere "perceptible medium for a wholly intellectual or representational process,"[29] nor as "an imposture of an idolatry" by which "the community would seek to place 'God' at its disposition like a thing,"[30] but as an incarnation of the eucharistic gift,[31] as a temporalizing memorial, a physical memorial that orders the present and, in doing so, grants the future: "The Eucharist anticipates what we will be, will see, will love: *figura nostra,* the figure of what we will be, but above all ourselves, facing the gift that we cannot yet welcome, so, in the strict sense, that we cannot yet figure it."[32] Thus, Marion argues that the bread and wine (or water for Latter-day Saints) are incarnations of Christ without arguing that they become, in substance, his body and blood; he argues for transubstantiation without arguing for that which most of us associate with transubstantiation and which non-Catholics find religiously and philosophically objectionable. Marion does so with an understanding similar to that which we see in Eliade and others: symbols are incarnate orderings of our world.

One way to understand Marion's point better is to consider that early Christians also did not take the Eucharist as a mere reminder but as a corporate (in other words, an embodied, incarnate) *act,* part of or a focal point of a way of life. For early Christians, the Eucharist is something the Church *does* and *becomes* rather than merely something by which one signifies and recalls. To *remember* the sacrifice of Jesus is to take part in a community and the life of that community. It is to incarnate the divine community—the body of Christ (e.g., 1 Cor. 12:27; Eph. 4:12)—and to become incarnate in it, not merely to *recall* a past event. (If the sacrament were merely a matter of recall, one could effectively perform the sacramental ritual by passing out slips of paper on which was written, "Remember Christ and your relation to him"—or even with an e-mail message to that effect or a note in one's tackle box.) For early Christians and, presumably, for contemporary ones, to partake in the elements of the Eucharist is to be and become something—to be made something ("incarnated" in the divine community, Zion) in and through ritual—not merely to recall a past event.[33] Of course, one cannot become what one must by merely recalling that past event at some times, but the point stands that the ritual's function cannot be understood only in terms of recollection. Marion's point about how the Eucharist temporalizes—incarnates—is similar.

In contrast, the Reformation understanding of symbols breaks the *incarnans* of the symbol, the material of the symbol, from the *incarnatum,* that which is manifest in the symbol. In doing so, it makes the relation of symbol and what it manifests a matter of reference.[34] Rejecting the Reformation, Catholicism continues to insist that the *incarnans* and the *incarnatum* cannot be separated: the *incarnans* is more than something that helps us think about the *incarnatum*. Certainly one need not be a Catholic to think that this

29

insistence has something valuable to say. The issue is not one of Catholics versus Protestants, especially for those like ourselves who are neither. The point is that contrary to the modernist understanding, religions do not take symbols merely to be referential; they understand them as something more (even when their theologies deny that they do, as in much Protestantism). Contemporary philosophical arguments about reference and meaning point in the direction of a need for something more. The anthropology of religions suggests that we must understand that religion requires more than referentially valid beliefs. The Catholic tradition has called this something more *incarnation,* a term that I adopt as informative, though I will supplement that term with another: enactment. To be incarnate is to *be,* materially, a manifestation of, an instance of, what is supposedly only referred to. On this way of thinking, the symbol *is* what it incarnates (or what "in-forms" it, if we use Platonic language) rather than merely a representation of or reference to it. To use the language of Aristotle, to be incarnate is to en-act (the literal meaning of *actual* is "enacted") that to which we might think the thing refers.

In the Catholic tradition, the Eucharist and a crucifix are both sacred and symbolic objects because they are each a material enactment—an incarnation—of Christ as Savior rather than only a reminder of Him. The Catholic doctrine of transubstantiation, as officially explained, assumes that in the case of the Eucharist, the incarnation of Christ in the sacramental symbols means that the bread and wine of the sacrament become the actual, physical flesh and blood of Christ. That is what incarnation must mean if one holds to a classical understanding of substance. I argue that the assumption of classical substances is philosophically as well as theologically unnecessary. Thus, the dogma of transubstantiation, as justified Thomistically, is a logical and historical error: we can understand symbols, including the sacrament, as incarnations without the traditional doctrine of transubstantiality—as Catholics also assume in the case of other symbols, such as the crucifix, which are incarnations, but not transubstantiations in the traditional sense. Based on this possibility, I will argue further that we can understand scripture as an incarnation or enactment of history rather than a representation of it.

However, though the Catholic tradition gives us some purchase on understanding what it means to speak of scripture as incarnation, it is insufficient. We must go further, for though the medieval Catholic tradition shows how to understand the sacrament and other rituals as well as ritual objects as incarnations, it fails to attend fully to scripture. The Reformation reverses this problem, giving attention to scripture but rejecting the understanding of ritual and sacrament as incarnation. And this is true even though the Reformation and Christian humanism also speak of the Bible as an incarnation of Christ, as Erasmus does in speaking of the text as the body of Christ.[35] In spite of what might appear to be incarnational language in Reformation works, we can see the shift from enacted incarnation to representation in the seventeenth-century debates over theater (a debate between written text—representation—and enactment). As Richard Helgerson says, "Where print fixes the author and frees the reader, performance does the reverse. It frees the performer and fixes—transfixes—the audience. Performance allows the self a Protean adaptability, but skillfully managed, it overwhelms its audience, rendering it captive to impressions that defy interpretation. For over a millennium the Western community of Christian believers was held in at least a semblance of unity, despite theological difference and hierarchical schism, by the power of ritual performance, only to disintegrate into countless mutually hostile churches when the printed word replaced performed ritual as the primary source of authority."[36] One could make many points from this observation, from points about the importance of the temple to an explanation of why priesthood authority, something enacted rather than spoken or written down, loses its importance in Reformation belief. However, for our purposes, the point is that the rise of Protestantism involved a shift from scripture as incarnation (enacted presentation) to scripture as written re-presentation.

Having rejected the enactment of incarnation, the Reformation finds itself in trouble when it tries to preserve the sacred character of scripture, even though it insists on that. By the eighteenth century, the Reformation relied on referential theories of meaning, with the consequence that scripture, too, lost its sacred character. Writing cannot do the work that the Reformation places on its back; it always falls short of re-presenting its object.[37] Though individual Protestants and Protestant churches may think of scripture otherwise, *in principle* it ceases to be sacred.[38] For the Reformation, scripture refers to what is sacred, but it is not itself a manifestation of what is sacred. This is because the Reformation gives up the possibility of understanding symbols as incarnations and replaces the incarnational understanding of symbols with the modern theory of reference that comes to the fore.

Thus, the key to the alternative understanding of history that I think saves us from the dilemma of academic history on the one hand, and ahistory on the other, is to understand the scriptures as incarnational: *the scriptures are literal history, but their history is incarnational rather than representational.* But the question of what it means to speak of incarnation remains.

To better understand what it means to say that a symbol (and, therefore, also a religious text) is an incarnation, consider an example from the contemporary Belgian philosopher, Paul Moyaert. When Moyaert's father died, he inherited his father's cup. The cup, which he uses for his coffee every morning, has a surplus value. It cannot be reduced to instrumental values. For example, it cannot be reduced to an instrument for helping Moyaert recall his father. If it were, such a perspective would make the cup, as symbol, only a means for having a particular mental attitude, such as contemplative recollection or psychological reverence for his father. That kind of understanding of the cup will not do. Among other things, it robs the cup of its *symbolic* value by making it possible that anything, even something that Moyaert chose arbitrarily, could serve the same purpose. If a symbol were only something for creating a mental attitude, then Moyaert could choose a pebble from the street in front of his own house to remind him of his father, but it is no coincidence that symbols do not come into being in such an arbitrary fashion. They are not mere keepsakes (and even the keepsake is rarely, if ever, arbitrary or merely subjective).

The cup is not just a tool for recollecting; the surplus value of the cup comes from the fact that Moyaert's father touched it. Thus, its character as a symbol is a matter of contiguity rather than representation or instrumentality. However, when Moyaert uses the cup, it isn't that by doing so he touches his father *in absentia*. The cup isn't a substitute for his father—another reason that it isn't essentially a reminder. Though the cup can remind him, often Moyaert uses it without explicitly recalling his father. Instead, the cup is a symbol of Moyaert's father because it does something for Moyaert *in spite of himself:* even when he isn't thinking of his father, the cup demands Moyaert's reverence. It connects Moyaert to his father even when Moyaert isn't conscious of his father. In a small way, the cup gives a symbolic order to Moyaert's world, an order that relates him to his father and to the rest of the world, an order that cannot be reduced to his intentions to recall his father. *It is as if the cup remembers Moyaert's father for Moyaert.*[39]

Thus, not only does the cup not refer to or even represent Moyaert's father, it does not take his place. In a very real sense, it takes *Moyaert's* place rather than his father's. In that sense, Moyaert is willing to grant something like but not identical to consciousness—within the symbolic order—to his father's cup. This approaches what we see described in anthropological encounters with so-called "primitive" religions: symbols are objects that do something in spite of our intentions. They do something that we otherwise could attribute only to human beings. In this sense, religion is magical—though we must avoid equating magic with naïve or bad science.[40] The cup is an incarnation rather than a reference; it gives a symbolic order to Moyaert's world rather than a rational one, and the cup gives order by embodying that order in the live world that it orders.

It is important to emphasize that this result—that symbols operate in a "magical" way—is because the reverence that characterizes life in a symbolic ordering is not a matter of consciousness. Of course conscious reverence for the sacred is possible. However, one could not have the mental attitude of reverence without already being in a symbolic ordering, an ordering that gives one the possibility of reverence, at least partly by giving objects that demand reverence. The symbolic order gives objects as objects of reverence, so to be within the symbolic order is to *be* reverent, to attend to the sacred, whether or not one is explicitly conscious of and attentive to that order. For to be within a symbolic ordering is to be ordered by, to have the world ordered by, that symbolic ordering. The objects and possibilities of the world, especially but not only ritual objects and possibilities, are related to each other in and through the fact that they manifest the ordering of the symbolic; the symbolic ordering gives them their place and their relations in the world, and it makes possible our understanding. And in ritual acts, one's own body, as well as the objects to which one attends, are loci for such incarnations of the symbolic. Symbolic relations do not come from mental acts and attitudes; they make acts and attitudes, such as conscious reverence, possible.

One way to state my thesis is to say that scripture is incarnation and religion is sacred ordering. Thus, difficulties occur when, with the onset of modernism, scripture becomes, like any other book, something that is understood merely referentially, and religion ceases to be thought of as *the* ordering power of the world and becomes one sphere of interest among many, a sphere that must be ordered by something else. For modernism, that "something else" is reason, though for Christian premoderns, it is the incarnate Divine—and this difference in the ordering "principle" produces the chasm (and the common antipathy) between the two.

We see a symptom of this loss of symbolic ordering in Descartes's *Discourse on Method of Rightly Conducting the Reason and Seeking Truth in the Sciences* (published in 1637). In the *Discourse,* Descartes tells us that he needs something by which to adjudicate between the various plausible opinions he learned in the schools. Finding nothing, he takes up the method of geometry, namely formal reason. In addition, Descartes obviously confines religion to the region of morals. He not only speaks of the moral truths of his country and Catholicism (truths that he accepts as provisional),[41] he also mentions the truths of faith.[42] Nevertheless, Descartes does no more than mention the truths of faith. Rather than being that which orders the regions of our lives, for Descartes, religion is one region of human life among other possible regions, a region that can be ignored or set to the side as one goes about laying a foundation for understanding the world and its various regions.[43] Descartes finds himself in a chaos in which nothing can be known or trusted. Prior to the Reformation, the Church had given the world its order, but that order has failed for Descartes. Thus, something other than religion must order life as a whole, including religion. For Descartes, religion has ceased to give order to the world and has become one of its regions. His project in the *Discourse* (and in the *Meditations on First Philosophy*) is to allow reason to order life by giving us the method for conducting/ordering reason, in other words by showing us that reason can order itself.[44]

That Descartes believes we *need* a method for ordering reason is evidence that the symbolic ordering no longer has force. Descartes confuses our means for dealing with the various regions of existence, namely reason, for the ordering authority of the world. He makes it clear that he has settled on a method for conducting reason and finding truth because he has no way of choosing between the various opinions of his predecessors.[45] Thus, finding nothing that orders reason, Descartes must give a rational method for ordering it. Yet the necessity of grounding reason in itself would never have occurred to an ancient Greek or a medieval Christian, Jew, or Muslim because, whatever the many differences between them, for each, the exercise of reason occurs *within* an ordering that is prior to and fundamental to reason. Whether *physis* or Divine creation, reason has a ground that is, on a modern view, nonrational.[46] Even those thinkers such as the Averroists, for whom the truths of reason and the truths of faith are ultimately commensurable, do not assume that something is true because it is rational. Instead, something is rational because it is true. For such premodern thinkers, reason's being is granted by the symbolic ordering, even if the rational order and the symbolic order are ultimately identical. Thus, for those in the centuries before modernism, there *had* been means for adjudicating between various plausible opinions. For Christians, the Church provided those means, and order came to the world through them. Descartes's inability to adjudicate between differing opinions and his subsequent search for a method shows us that by Descartes's time a radical shift has already taken place, a shift away from an understanding that finds the use of reason within what is given by a symbolic ordering. Prior to modernism, the world had been given order by the Divine, and reason was a tool for dealing with and in that order, though not itself the source of order. However, the loss of the Divine as an anchor left reason and the world without moorings and, so, required something like the four-part rational method that Descartes prescribes.[47]

This loss of the Divine as ground shows up in the difference between modern and premodern understandings of certainty. Prior to modernism, Christian certainty was the certainty of salvation, a certainty *given* by the life of faith. Thus, though Christians had certainty, that certainty did not include a complete apprehension of the rational (in other words, of the mind of God). With modernism the ground shifts: since certainty is no longer given, it must be achieved; one must have a method for gaining certainty. Since, as we see in Descartes, the method is itself a rational method, the rational is thought of as self-revealing. Based on the biblical teaching that humans are made in God's image (Gen. 1:26), human reason is rethought and at least implicitly modeled on the mind of God, a mind that has become, strictly speaking, capable of only purely theoretic understanding. As a result, modernism assumes that the use of the proper method, a self-grounding method, will lead one to the complete capture, the complete apprehension, of the rational (which, though no longer identical to the mind of God, continues to be thought in the same terms: for example, as self-revealing, atemporal, and fundamentally theoretic). This shift changes the meaning of everything—the rational, certainty, method, knowledge—in such a way that the premodern understanding becomes inaccessible to thought, incomprehensible and at best naïve and primitive.[48]

One way to see the difference between a modern and a premodern understanding of religion is to focus on the question of signs. In LDS scripture, the Lord says to Adam: "Behold, all things have their likeness, and all things are created and made to bear record of me, both things which are temporal, and things which are spiritual; things which are in the heavens above, and things which are on the earth, and things which are in the earth, and things which are under the earth, both above and beneath: all things bear record of me" (Moses 6:63). We often read this passage and similar ones as if they speak of signs referentially. However, there are problems with that view. The understanding that this citation exemplifies was a common one among ancient thinkers, including Augustine, so consider his reflection on signs and on the claim in question. In one obvious reading, Augustine is said to argue that signs are essentially referential. The referential character of signs seems difficult to avoid in *On Christian Doctrine* 1.2 and 2, where Augustine seems to give a standard, modern theory of signs, a referential theory. However, it is important to notice that in Augustine's discussion God is not a creature, so we cannot refer to Him.[49] Nevertheless, all things, particularly corporeal things, point to God.[50] It follows that all things point to God, but none refer to Him. In addition, Augustine explicitly compares the Incarnation with speech,[51] but the Incarnation cannot be understood as a merely referential event. Thus, though *every thing* (every creature) is a sign, the final object of signs, which makes all other signs possible as signs, is no thing (because no creature) and cannot be referred to. The consequence is that for Augustine (and I think also for the scriptural passage in question), we cannot understand signs merely referentially; referential theories of signs are only partial theories. Something more is needed, namely God.

Notice also that, according to traditional Christian doctrine, after the Fall human beings are unable to see God directly, a thought often expressed for Latter-day Saints in the idea that we cannot see God "with natural eyes" (Moses 1:11; D&C 58:3; 2 Cor. 12:1–4). From this comes the traditional Christian view that language, veiling and obscuring as it may be in some sense, is not only a consequence of the Fall, it is also a blessing. Language gives human beings our only access to the Divine, which otherwise would blind us. If, as modernism suggests, the words that refer to God and divine things were mere signs, tools for thinking *about* or referring *to* something else, then for them to function as signs we would also have to have direct access to the referent, to God, which is impossible. Merely referential signs require that what they refer to be available to the person who understands them.

Consider a simple sign: my driver's license. My license has a name, a number, and a picture. They each refer to me and together they represent me. To understand this reference and representation— for any one of them or all of them as a group to function as a sign—a person taking my license as a sign must have access not only to these signs but also to that to which they refer. In principle, a person must be able to encounter me independent of those signs. He or she must be able to see, hear, or touch me independent of my license. Without that, the license cannot refer to me because the merely referential sign is a substitute for the thing signified; the license is a substitute for my person. Imagine a case in which someone says, "This license has a referent, but the picture isn't the picture of the person it refers to, the number isn't that person's number, and the name on it isn't the referent's name." No one would take the person's claim seriously. As mere references, signs function only if that to which they refer is also independently accessible to those who read them.

If we understand symbols as a kind of referential sign, then we understand signs of God as substitutes for Him, and, therefore, we assume implicitly that we have direct access to Him. However, signs of God do not work that way, for if they refer, they do so across a chasm with nothing available on the other side. Of course, religious people will deny that nothing is available on the other side, but that *makes* my point rather than contradicts it. The religious can see and listen to and be commanded by something to which the religious symbol refers, not because it refers in the same way that an ordinary sign does (in other words to something public, something that anyone can see or hear independent of the sign), but because, being enlightened by the Divine rather than fundamentally by reason, they see the "other side" *in* and *through* the symbol.[52]

Embodying the Divine

Though there are several positions among premodern thinkers regarding signs, I think we can characterize them as generally taking the words of scripture not to be merely referential signs of a divine reality (though they may have what we could call a referential component). Instead of referring to the divine as do ordinary signs, the words of scripture are an embodiment of the divine, an incarnation; they embody the divine order of that to which, on a modern view, they seem only to refer.[53] Thus, according to Carol Harrison, in spite of the homonymy, instead of translating Augustine's word *signum* as "sign," we should understand it to mean *sacramentum,* itself a translation of *mystērion:* what is secret or hidden.[54] And we must remember that the *mystērion* is not just temporarily hidden. It is hidden in principle; in other words, it is invisible to human or "natural" eyes; we see it only by revelation.

On such thinking, the visible—the elements and objects of the created world, the history of the world, our lives together—bears (incarnates, enacts) rather than refers to spiritual reality. It bears and enacts it as depth and richness—as mystery in the strict, positive sense of that word, "a secret"—just as the human body bears and enacts the depth and richness and mystery of the person. For a Muslim, a Jew, or a Christian, the full history of the world is necessarily a history understood under the order of divine creation. Thus, strictly speaking, the actual, literal history of the world is invisible *except* as the symbolic ordering of creation embodies and reveals it. Any other history is an abstraction from that literal history. For the religions of the Bible and Qur'an, scripture is an important incarnation of the divine ordering (as are ordinance, authority, tradition, and so on). Scripture embodies what would otherwise be invisible to us, what is in itself unrepresentable because it exceeds reference. Scripture embodies and bodies forth the divine ordering of the world and its events. For premoderns, that embodiment is history, literal history, not the accurate reference to and description of events that have no order or meaning other than the chronology of time and the relations of reason.[55]

For Christians, the Incarnation of Christ is the perfect instance of the conjunction of *factum* and *sacramentum:* Christ is neither a representation of divine reality nor a reference to it. He is not something given to help us recall Divinity.[56] He *is* that divine reality perceptible to human beings. As such, He is also the perfect analogy for scripture: "In the case of scripture, the visible, created, temporal order cannot simply be shunned as an ambiguous, misleading imitation of a spiritual truth which is better grasped by the mind. Rather, . . . Scripture is the 'incarnate' form of the Christian revelation."[57] Similarly, New Testament statements about the Church being the body of Christ suggest that one encounters Christ *in* the Church. The Church is an incarnation of Christ, not a simple signifier of or reference to Him—an incarnation in the sense I have discussed earlier, namely something that materially manifests or enacts a symbolic ordering.

Though this language of incarnation, as in speaking of the Church as the incarnation of Christ, is scriptural (e.g., 1 Cor. 12:27, Eph. 4:12), it strikes Latter-day Saints as odd. It is sufficiently odd for a Latter-day Saint audience that we assume it to be metaphorical or a matter of simile. We want to say, "The Church is *like* the body of Christ," though that is not a particularly informative clause. The problem is that given standard English usage, we think of incarnation as an event in which something that is without a body becomes manifest in something embodied. Therefore, we speak of that event as "the incarnation of x, y, or z," where the variables stand for the unembodied thing in question. Since Christ is embodied, it is not clear how He could become incarnate in the Church. In fact, according to our standard usage, to say that He does suggests that He is not already incarnate himself.[58]

However, consider that Joseph Smith says, "There is no such thing as immaterial matter. All spirit is matter."[59] According to his teachings, my body is not the incarnation of something nonbodily, for the spirit is also incarnate. In fact, in reference to bodies, there are no nonincarnate things.[60] This suggests that we cannot understand incarnation as something unembodied becoming embodied. What, then, can we mean by *incarnation?*

Our common usage and the history of thought about incarnation make it difficult for us to think of incarnation in terms consonant with the Prophet's teaching. His teaching defies that usage and history. Nevertheless, I do not think we are faced with an insurmountable difficulty. We must think carefully about embodiment. We must ask what it means to say that we "have" a body, given that we cannot mean that something unembodied possesses or inhabits something embodied and we do not explain that usage when we speak of one kind of body (a spirit body) possessing another (a physical body).[61] Though this is not as simple as it first might seem (thinking otherwise than our usual prejudgments and understandings is often difficult, even when we know they are wrong), there are philosophers, such as Maurice Merleau-Ponty, who may help us begin to do this thinking. Put broadly, Merleau-Ponty argues that to be embodied is to inhabit (to "enact," if you will) a world in a particular way:[62] "We must . . . avoid saying that our body is *in* space, or *in* time. It *inhabits* space and time"[63] "To be a body, is to be tied to a certain world."[64] Taking off from Merleau-Ponty's insight, perhaps we can say that the body is one's attitude (in the literal sense—"fittedness; disposition; posture"—rather than in mentalistic terms). The body is the position one takes in the world, where *position* refers not only to a spatio-temporal position that we can fix by specifying a set of coordinates, but also to one's temporal relations to other things, persons, and so on—one's orientation. We have a body like we have an idea or a fear, not as a possession, but as the way in which I project myself in living and in relating to others and other things.[65] Consciousness is part of my bodily attitude, but not the sum of it.

Given this thinking about incarnation, we can expand it to think about incarnation in general: to speak of something as an incarnation is *not* to say that something else, something nonmaterial, has come to be material in it. It is to say that a particular attitude, a particular way of being situated in and among the things there are, comes to be manifest or enacted in it. Of course, to be situated in the world in a particular way is always, necessarily, also to be situated with regard to *what* there is. There is no pure, unembodied enactment or presentation. In a strictly scientific attitude (an attitude that scientists need not take except when they are explicitly doing science, an attitude that is not the same as their mental attitude or personal beliefs) there is no relation to God. The scientific region, the region in which one investigates bodies using the assumptions, methods, and background of science, is necessarily godless.[66] Scientific objects, themselves "impoverished" or abstracted objects, incarnate the work and understanding of that region. Other objects incarnate other regions and orderings.[67] Thus, to say that the Church is an incarnation of Christ is to say that in the Church one finds oneself situated and oriented in the world in a way given by Christ toward things revealed by Christ as they are revealed by Him—a world that Christ has enacted and that enacts its relation to Him as Creator. Similarly, to say that scripture or an ordinance is an incarnation is to say that in the material existence of these things—as scripture and ordinance rather than as abstracted to merely so-called objective qualities—we are given an orientation in the world: relations to things, meanings and values of things, the existence and nonexistence of things.

As incarnations in a symbolic ordering, symbols are opaque beings rather than signs with multiple reference. The use of the word *incarnation* to describe the being of entities that give symbolic order is not accidental, for signs are like the living, enacting body, as Augustine explicitly says: "How did He come except that 'the Word was made flesh, and dwelt among us?' It is as when we speak."[68] The opacity of the living human body, the density and richness that, in principle, cannot be made transparent, means that no single, final description of a human being is possible. This opacity need not be something arcane or complex. Seeing it and understanding it does not require great erudition, on the one hand, or mumbo-jumbo, on the other. For example, the opacity of living persons, an opacity consequent on their embodiment, both physical and spiritual, is an ordinary, everyday experience: a person cannot be reduced to one "meaning" or perspective, though a person has meaning and one has perspectives on any person.[69] One could argue that nonhuman objects, both animate and inanimate, are similarly dense. The incarnational character of scripture makes it also dense and opaque—embodied—but the opacity of scripture is different from the unclarity of a poorly formed assertion.

Assertions that can have more than one meaning are unclear because they are faulty as assertions. They are ambiguous at best. However, it follows that all language ought to be clear in the same way that assertions are clear only if all language is best understood as assertional and referential. If scripture is not to be understood, fundamentally, by means of a referential theory of meaning, then one cannot criticize it as if it were a set of referential assertions. Scriptural opacity and depth are different from ambiguity. One cannot reduce the density of scripture to multiplicity of reference as do most of the critics of the Bible and most of its defenders.

Both poetry and scripture attend to what exceeds language and attention; both are matters of reverence for what exceeds and explains us. There is not enough space here to decide how they are related. It is enough to notice that they at least overlap, and that overlap helps us see how religious language differs from merely referential language. In the languages of both poetry and religion, I intend what is beyond my understanding, though often by means of something that does not, especially at first glance, itself transcend my gaze. I intend what transcends my intention. Thus, in both poetry and religion one speaks, but *not* to make everything transparent and easily accessible. In fact, among other things, in both one *denies,* by one's way of speaking, by the language itself and its "content" (as if the two could be separated), the transparency of what one intends and one's ability to master it or fully intend it. Religious and poetic languages show us that meaning is not reducible to reference, for they mean without being fully able to refer, without *trying* to refer. They mean by incarnating that which they mean rather than merely referring to it.

The languages of poetry and religion incarnate things that one is mastered by rather than master of. In those languages, what I mean—what my words and thoughts supposedly intend—outstrips what I understand, outstrips what *I* mean. The object of my intention exceeds my intention, of any possible intention (see note 69). However, what exceeds my meaning is not another meaning, not something to be said "in other words." The abundance of meaning does not suggest that, given sufficient time, I will be able to say everything, that the abundance will disappear.[70] Thus, what I intend in poetry or religion is never an object in the strict sense of that term ("something placed or thrown before me, clear to my sight and examination"), making the word *intention* itself problematic, though it will do for now.[71] Because of this abundance or excess, the languages of prophecy and poetry do not dissimulate an adequacy and clarity of understanding that belie the truth of what they say. They are not clear and distinct languages, the languages that Descartes proposes for modernism, *because* they remain true to that of which they speak. For prophecy and poetry, as Walter Benjamin says, "Truth is not 'an unveiling that destroys the secret,' but the revelation that does it justice."[72]

It may seem that this discussion of the abundance of scriptural language implies that scripture is necessarily obscure, but that does not follow. The alternative to understanding the opacity of scripture as multiple reference is not to understand it as obscure; scriptural language is neither essentially obscure nor essentially meaningless. Just as opacity and the abundance that opacity makes possible are not the same as unclarity, they are not the same as obscurity. Isaiah is not more of a prophet than Nephi because he is more difficult to read; the abundance, depth, and richness of incarnation should not be confused with obscurity.[73] Any religious person has had the experience of discovering new meaning in texts that she has read before, often many times. That is a phenomenon of abundance, of the excess of meaning—of the incarnation of scripture—not a phenomenon of ambiguity or obscurity. Religious ordinances are a perfect example of the kind of abundance that we find in religion and scripture. In religious rituals, in other words in symbolic ordering enacted in ritual objects and on my body, my words and actions intend more than I, as an individual human being, can possibly intend, though they can and often are themselves quite simple and straightforward.[74]

To take scripture as incarnational is neither to conflate historical understanding and accurate description nor to take scripture to be essentially referential. Neither is it to take scripture to be merely metaphorical or poetic (in the impoverished, everyday sense of that word). To see scripture as incarnational, as opaque and revelatory, is to see it as telling the *literal* truth, as giving the literal history of the world. As Frank Kermode says, speaking accurately of incarnational interpretations (though he does not recognize them as incarnational): "The spiritual sense so authorized [in other words, within the structure of the medieval Catholic Church, official as well as unofficial] was the true literal sense."[75] This identification of "spiritual sense" and "literal sense" is surprising to contemporary ears. After all, we take the literal truth to be the truth that most accurately describes or refers to what happened, independent of any symbolic ordering, and we take the "spiritual sense" to be something beyond the literal, to what we call "merely symbolic." Premoderns, however, do not disjoin the literal and the spiritual. For them, the word *literal* means something quite different. For them, it means, "what the letters, i.e., the words say," rather than, "what an objective report would say." "What x says" and "what x describes accurately" do not mean the same, even if the first is a description. Even a careless reading of medieval discussions of scriptural exegesis will show that the medievals' interest was not in deciding what the scriptures portray, but in what they say. They do not take the scriptures to be picturing something for us, but to be telling us the truth of the world, of its things, its events, and its people, a truth that cannot be told apart from its situation in a divine, symbolic ordering.

Of course, that is not to deny that the scriptures tell about events that actually happened. They are about real people and real events. What I propose is not a way to reduce the premodern understanding of history to a modern view, to one that denies the historicity of scripture by taking scripture to refer to a transcendent, nonhistorical reality by means of only *seemingly* historical stories. Premodern interpreters of the Bible understand the scriptures to be about actual events. For them, what the scriptures say includes portrayal of and talk about real things. However, premodern interpreters do not think it sufficient (or possible) to portray the real events of real history without letting us see them in the light of that which gives them their significance—their reality, the enactment of which they are part—as history, namely the symbolic order that they incarnate. Without that light, portrayals cannot be accurate. A bare description of the physical movements of certain persons at a certain time is not history (assuming that such bare descriptions are even possible). "Person A raised his left hand, turning it clockwise so that .03 milliliters of a liquid poured from a vial in that hand into a receptacle situated midway between A and B" does not mean the same as "Henry poured poison into Richard's cup." Only the latter could be a historical claim (and even the former is no bare description).

History is not possible without meaning and significance; perhaps not even mere chronicle is. The question is where that meaning and significance derive from. For premodern Bible interpreters, the divine order that events incarnate gives them their meaning. A literal history, therefore, necessarily incorporates and reveals that order. Any history that does not incorporate it is incomplete and, therefore, inaccurate.[76] It is inaccurate because it does not embody the divine order that makes it what it is. That means that premodern literal histories—the accurate portrayals of what happened, if one continues to insist on referential language—will differ significantly from literal histories told under the aspect of a different order, such as that of the rationalism of modernism.

As already noted, modernism, too, requires that meaning be "added" to otherwise bare events so that we can understand them. In modernism, too, something besides our accounts orders those accounts and stabilizes meaning. However, with the Enlightenment, modernism does not recognize a divine order as the source of order and stability. Modernist history intentionally and necessarily ignores any divine ordering of history, taking up, instead, the order of causation as understood scientifically. This is not a matter of perversity or anti-theism on the part of modern historians. There are sound, methodological reasons for such an assumption in academic history, as there are in the "hard" sciences.[77] Nevertheless, it follows that modernist historians cannot mean by the word *history* what premoderns mean, and modernist criticisms of premodern histories, such as the histories we find in scripture, will beg the question. In modernist history, reason rather than the Divine gives the ultimate order of things, so reason becomes the arbiter of any claims about divine order, rather than the reverse. Modernist history and scriptural history are incompatible.

In conclusion and summary: If we understand scripture by means of a referential theory of history, then we assume that there is an original event that we represent (re-present) in language; on that view, a historian repeats the original event by constructing a description that represents the event as fully and accurately as possible. However, such a theory of history is problematic, for to the degree that a historian can be successful there is, ironically, no real history, only the repetition of something that is always the same. One explanation for the unending necessity of writing histories that represent an original event might be that, though there is an original event that we describe in our histories and for which there is, in principle, one complete description, our language, methods, and so on are finite. Thus, we do not come to an end of giving the one, complete description. However, in addition to the problem already mentioned (namely that such a theory seems to deny history even as it describes it), we can ask these questions: How can one justify the claim that there is such an event and that there is one ideal description of that event without encountering the very difficulty one is trying to avoid? With what language does one understand and discuss the event that is in continual need of redescription? How is it available to the historian apart from the finite language that he or she uses to describe it? The only possible answer seems to be that historians are engaged not only in the accurate description of events, but that they are so engaged based on some kind of intuition (in the strict, philosophical sense) of something that is, in principle, not ultimately capturable in human expression.

Because of this difficulty, some conclude that even if we begin with the view that there is only one, ultimate description of an event, we are driven to conclude that there is nothing to history except what we say about it. Recognizing the problematic character of claims to intuitions of something ultimately ungraspable, they take what they think is the only remaining position: history is only a socially determined, infinitely redescribable matter, a matter of what we have to say about it and no more. Though that position and variations of it have become fashionable lately, it is a position fraught with problems, among them that to say something is a human construction, even that it is *necessarily* a human construction, is not to say that it is *only* a human construction. I think that the position also entails that the person coming to this conclusion is self-contradictory, arguing for radical historicism and invoking a principle that is not to be understood from a radical historicist position. In short, in spite of the current popularity of this response to the problem, I think it is less sound than the flawed, referential position against which it responds.

I too conclude that writing history involves an intuition of something more than what we can say. However, it is difficult to know what it means to *say* that. For example, I don't think the usual referential theories, which gloss over the problem, are adequate. I have attempted to give one answer, though not the only one, to that question: scriptural history is a matter of divine incarnation. And I am supposing that academic history is another kind of history, a kind that answers very differently the question of what more there is to history than what we can say, a way that is, therefore, strictly speaking, not comparable to scriptural history because it incarnates something very different and even incomparable.

On the view for which I argue, one can understand scriptural history using a premodern understanding of what makes history as a starting point. For premoderns, genuine, literal history is essentially symbolic, or in other words, incarnational. For moderns, it is essentially referential. With the rise of modernism, symbols came to be understood as references (even if complex ones), and, therefore, so did the Bible; scripture is a more or less accurate depiction of events that exist independent of other considerations. (And whether one takes them to be more or less accurate depends on one's religious disposition.) Premoderns, however, understand the Bible figurally or typologically, as incarnating a symbolic order and as giving an order to life through its symbolic work. To say that is *not* to say that people reading as premoderns understand the Bible to refer to another reality or to be merely fiction. In fact, exactly the opposite is true: for premoderns, history understood apart from revelation is a fiction, a necessary and convenient one for some purposes, perhaps, but nevertheless a fiction, for it doesn't give us the fullness of the events of history. Like moderns, those reading as premoderns understand that scripture orders human history by giving it a shape—a figure. However, they disagree with the moderns about what gives that shape. For premoderns, the revelation of scripture gives history meaning, without which there would be no real history, only chronology, if that.

For example, for medieval Christians the life of Christ as revealed in scripture is a figure or type that we can use to understand the scriptures as a whole and, therefore, history and our place in it. It isn't that Christ did not live or that the story of His life is merely "symbolic" of some other reality. Instead, truly to understand the life of Christ is to understand it as a life that *literally* (in other words, in the way that the texts say it) is a figure of our lives and history. Thus, to read the story of Israel's exodus from Egypt, forty years in the wilderness, and entry into the promised land as a figure of the granting of salvation, our continuing sinfulness, and the promise of possible blessedness as it shows us our relation to Christ, is not to impose an *additional* meaning onto the story of Israel. Contra some Jewish thinkers, neither is it to reduce the children of Israel to mere shadows, references to another reality. Instead, it is to see the biblical story of Israel as an incarnation of the symbolic order of which we, being religious, find ourselves to be part.

Those who read the Bible as an incarnation do not reduce its texts to what is "only symbolic," for the literal/symbolic disjunction is not a disjunction for them. For premoderns, reading the story of Moses and Israel typologically, figurally, anagogically, or allegorically is not what one does *instead of* or *in addition to* reading literally. Such readings are part and parcel of a literal reading. Premodern understanding does not reduce the biblical story to a reference to or representation of something else, though it also does not deny that there may be an important representative element in scripture. Instead, premoderns believe that to understand the story of Israel is *essentially* to understand history—actual history, the real events of the world—as incarnation, a continuing incarnation, as types and shadows, to use the language of the Book of Mormon (for example, Mosiah 3:15). It is to understand history as having an order and the events of history as related to each other within that ordering (an ordering that does not exist independent of events, and that cannot be reduced to those events as "bare" events). It is to understand history as part of a symbolic ordering, an ordering that is given not only in scripture, but also (perhaps most importantly) in ritual, ritual objects, and ritual language, as well as in the moments of history themselves. Thus, for premoderns, the biblical narrative is literal history—the literal truth, the truth "by the letter," that is told in the letters and words of the text as revealing and embodying the order given by God. The literal truth is the truth constituted in and through the text as incarnation, not the supposed truth supposedly only referred to by those letters and words.

In spite of appearances or what we might say when we are asked to talk about scriptural history without having reflected sufficiently on our experience with it, I think that most Latter-day Saints read scripture as an incarnation of a symbolic ordering.[78] We may often do so confusedly and inconsistently, but we do. That is *why* we feel compelled to defend the historicity of the scriptures, whether we do so naïvely or with a full range of scholarly, theoretical, and interpretational tools at our disposal. This is especially true for adherents, such as we are, of religions in which symbols and symbolic acts figure prominently. The informality of LDS sacrament meetings may make us think otherwise, but the Church's all-encompassing social structure and the importance of temple liturgy show that Latter-day Saints' lives, like the lives of other religious people and perhaps more than many, continue to be ordered symbolically.

For the most part, we have lost or forgotten the vocabulary and concepts for talking about our participation in a symbolic order and our reading of scripture as part of that participation. As a result, when called on to talk about scripture or to teach lessons from it or to speak reflectively about it, we resort to language and methods that ignore the symbolically ordered character of our lives and that deny the incarnate character of scripture by making it merely referential. The fact that we mix implicit attention to scripture as symbolic ordering with an insistence on simple reference often confuses our reading. Nevertheless, it remains possible not only to continue to read scripture as incarnational rather than merely referential, but to do so more explicitly than we have done.

James E. Faulconer is professor of philosophy, Brigham Young University.

Notes

1. I owe many people thanks for their critical responses to this paper, though they need not take responsibility for what I say here: Noel Reynolds, Michael Arts, Grant Boswell, Paul Hoskisson, Brandie Siegfried, Daniel Graham, Mark Wrathall, and many others. In addition, I am grateful to Brigham Young University, which granted me a leave during which I wrote the first drafts, and to the Catholic University of

Leuven (Louvain), Belgium, whose faculty, especially Paul Moyaert and Rudi Visker, offered philosophical insight and genuine friendship as well as criticism, helping me to remember why I studied philosophy and became a professor in the first place.

2. Philosophically, modernism is a way of thinking about the world that dominated from roughly 1500 to about 1800, though it continues as an important force into the present. In that regard it is important to note that for philosophy, *modern* and *contemporary* are not synonyms. However, though modernism was the dominant way of thinking from 1500 to 1800 and though that period has given its name to modernism, what we call modernist thought is not confined to that historical period. There were modernist thinkers and elements prior to modernism and, obviously, there continue to be modernist thinkers. See Steven Daniel, "Paramodern Strategies of Philosophical Historiography," *Epoché: A Journal for the History of Philosophy* 1, no. 1 (fall 1993): 41–63.

3. For example, see Thomas Sheehan, *The First Coming: How the Kingdom of God Became Christianity* (New York: Random House, 1986).

4. During the last several years there has been a sometimes rancorous discussion among Latter-day Saint scholars about how to understand history. I think the rancor of that discussion has died down—thank goodness—so I hope that I can take up this related question without becoming embroiled in that earlier debate. What follows is *not* a criticism of academic history or historians or their methods. To offer another understanding of what the word *history* can mean is not to suggest that there is something wrong with other meanings of the word. We make a mistake when we use a notion of history inappropriate to the context at hand, not when we use a different notion of history. That mistake, a kind of equivocation, is what I believe often happens in the debates between those who defend scriptural historicity and those who attack it, as well as between those who deal with that historicity by means of differing understandings of history. For an important though, I believe, generally misunderstood discussion of several possibilities for history, see Friedrich Nietzsche, "On the Uses and Disadvantages of History for Life," in *Untimely Meditations,* trans. R. J. Hollingdale (Cambridge: Cambridge University Press, 1983), 57–123.

5. One problem with this view, a problem that I cannot explore here, is that on such a view there can be nothing new in the world. What-is is always and only what has already been; everything was given "in the beginning," and nothing else can be. Though, under the influence of Greek philosophy, this understanding has been a feature of much traditional Christianity—perhaps most explicitly in Calvinism—it is a view that is out of character with Christianity, in which the hope for what is to come, what Bloch calls "the Not-Yet-Conscious," plays a crucial role. The not-yet is a notion without which it is difficult to understand how such things as repentance and exaltation can have meaning, but if everything already has been given, then there is that which we can describe as genuinely not-yet. Of course the same criticism can be applied to those who think of religious truth as the expression of a Platonic realm of truth, a view more common among orthodox Latter-day Saints. See Ernst Bloch, *The Principle of Hope,* vol. 1, trans. Neville Plaice, Stephen Plaice, and Paul Knight (Cambridge, Mass.: MIT Press, 1986), 114–78.

6. Though I am not using the word *myth* in its everyday sense—a false or fanciful story—I do use it here to denote an account that is not historically true. I recognize that the common scholarly meaning of the word *myth* does not include that it is not historically true, but I am not using the word in that sense. However, if one were to use the word in that scholarly sense, then one could take my argument to say, among other things, that scripture *is* myth, but the myth of scripture and its factual history are not mutually exclusive.

7. Cf. Jean-François Lyotard, *The Postmodern Explained: Correspondence 1982–1985,* trans. and ed. Julian Pefanis and Morgan Thomas (Minneapolis: University of Minnesota Press, 1992), 31–32.

8. Literary criticism also owes much to those debates. Most of the positions taken in literary criticism are descendants of the positions taken in the eighteenth- and early nineteenth-century debates about the Bible, and even those positions that are not directly descended from those debates two hundred years ago often rely on parts of those arguments and positions. One need only read Frei's overview of the debates about biblical meaning to see that much of the contemporary row over texts and meaning amounts to little more than a rehash of those earlier discussions. See Hans Frei, *The Eclipse of Biblical Narrative: A Study in Eighteenth and Nineteenth Century Hermeneutics* (New Haven: Yale University Press, 1974).

9. Among other reasons, the terms are problematic because the periodization of history is a questionable and peculiarly modern practice, because the definitions of the periods take modernism as their standard, and because those names of the periods do not name specific periods of history so much as ways of thinking. As I will use the terms here, *premodern* and *modern* are general terms. There were a variety of ways of understanding history prior to modernism, and there are a variety of ways of understanding it in modernism. However, there is, nevertheless, a divide between the two. Thus, in spite of the difficulties of doing so, I will use the word *premodern* to refer to an understanding of history perhaps best exemplified in medieval thinking, and I will use the word *modern* to refer to the "scientific" ways of understanding history that came to dominate with modernism.

10. Though I do not agree with his conclusions, Frei's seminal work on biblical meaning and the influence of the modern understanding of history on our understanding of biblical meaning serves as my starting point. See Frei, *The Eclipse of Biblical Narrative.*

11. However, whether we talk about real things in the real world in a *referential* way (i.e., as explained by a referential theory) remains a question. Strictly speaking, reference *per se* may be impossible, as thinkers such as Frege and Davidson argue. It does not follow that we cannot speak of the world, only that we do not do so in the way that referential theories of meaning assume that we do, namely by correlating our meaningful sentences with states of affairs in something like a one-to-one manner.

12. I will take up the issue of signs from a Derridean standpoint: every system of signs depends on something outside the system, so no system of signs can completely capture that to which it refers. Plus, there is always more to reality than any

interpretation of it, though we can give only interpretations. Nevertheless, I do not think the Derridean character of my argument is essential to it, as I will argue later. The points I take from Derrida could also be made using other contemporary philosophers, including Anglo-American ones. See Kevin Hart, *The Trespass of the Sign: Deconstruction, Theology, and Philosophy* (Cambridge: Cambridge University Press, 1989), for a readable, more detailed overview of Derrida's discussion of signs and for a treatment of the relevance of that discussion to religious understanding. For an excellent criticism of Derrida, see Françoise Dastur, "Heidegger and Derrida: On Play and Difference," *Epoché: A Journal for the History of Philosophy* 3, nos. 1, 2 (spring and fall, 1995): 1–23, though her criticism does not undo this point about signs and referentiality. Eco has made a similar argument. See Umberto Eco, *A Theory of Semiotics* (Bloomington, Ind.: Indiana University Press, 1976).

13. This means also that reference is inherently unstable, not only in its inability to be explained by any theory of reference but also over time. As the context of an event changes over time (and the event has temporal as well as momentary context) so too does the event, as anyone who genuinely believes in repentance must believe. The present can change the past or there is no difference between repentance and simple regret.

This idea of backward causation sounds nonsensical to most people (though how to explain repentance as anything other than a change of mind rather than a purification remains a mystery unless we invoke backward causation). However, consider an example that I think can serve as an analogy: rhythm. The moments of a rhythm cannot be discreet as are the moments in a time line. If they were, they would not be moments of a rhythm. Rhythmic moments require ("contain" already) their before and their after to be at all. One hit on the head of a drum is not part of any rhythm; each beat in a rhythm is what it is only in its relation to each of the other beats, only as it fits into the rhythm as a whole. Consequently, as one varies a rhythm at any particular beat, the meaning of each *previous* beat changes. Since beats are defined in their relation to each other, the change in the relation between the various beats has changed the beat in the past into something new, something other than what it was. The past beat no longer exists as it did. At the time the drum head was struck initially, the beat was one thing; however, with subsequent strikes that past event is something other than what it was. If events are what they are in relation to each other, then the analogy suggests that their meaning could change over time.

14. Explaining Derrida's position, Caputo says: "Derrida does not deny but delimits reference; what he denies is reference-without-difference. Without *différance* [Derrida's technical term for what happens in acts of reference: the sign differs from its object and defers complete identification, never completely corresponding to its object]. *Différance* does not lock us up inside anything. On the contrary, *différance* is a doorway, a threshold (*limen*), a door through which everything outgoing (reference, messages sent, etc.) and incoming (messages received, perceptions, etc.) must pass. A threshold supposes both an inside and an outside. . . . On this accounting, proper names refer *in actu exercitu,* in the exercised act, in actual use, in the concrete happening or the factual event. . . . It is a wonder, a little difficult to account for, but it happens. . . . [It is] something that philosophy is forced to swallow while being unable to digest." (See John D. Caputo, *Against Ethics: Contributions to a Poetics*

of Obligation with Constant Reference to Deconstruction [Bloomington, Ind.: Indiana University Press, 1993], 76).

As I said, the misunderstanding that is attributed to Derrida is the claim that there is nothing external to language—it is common, so common that it has become the "common sense" of those who criticize Derrida. Nevertheless, it is mistaken, as a careful reading of Derrida—in the context of his background in Husserl and Heidegger—will show. Out of ignorance some continue to make and repeat this mistake because it has become so common. Others, such as Huston Smith, seem to do so more willfully. See Huston Smith, "The Religious Significance of Postmodernism: A Rejoinder," *Faith and Philosophy* 12, no. 3 (July 1995): 409–22.

15. Catherine Pickstock, *After Writing: On the Liturgical Consummation of Philosophy* (Oxford: Blackwell, 1998), 19.

16. This explains why so many who read the works of thinkers Derrida, Lyotard, and Levinas cannot see anything in them *but* nihilism; since such thinkers reject modernism's understanding of fixity, those readers assume that the thinkers in question must argue for no fixity at all.

17. See Nietzsche, *Untimely Mediations.*

18. Those who assume that the absence of a risk-free, universal viewpoint results in thorough-going relativism share with the Enlightenment the assumption that meaning is either constituted as the Enlightenment says it is or that there is no meaning. With most contemporary philosophers, I deny that assumption. As a consequence, vicious relativism doesn't necessarily follow from my denial of an Archimedean leverage point for understanding and interpretation.

19. For example, echoing what other contemporary philosophers have also said, Derrida says: "There is no morality without faith, faith in the other. There is no social experience without bearing witness, without attestation, the recognition of a dimension of trust and faith. This is not a religious point; it is the general structure of experience," (Jacques Derrida, conversation with author, Paris, France, 1 March 1996). The first of the *Lectures on Faith* made a similar point more than one hundred years ago, and it presumably echoes what the Prophet Joseph Smith believed. Joseph Smith might reply to Derrida: "True, it is the general structure of experience, but that is a religious point, for religion gives the general structure to experience." See *Lectures on Faith,* comp. N. B. Lundwall (Salt Lake City: Deseret Book, 1985).

20. Such a view is consequent on the traditional Christian understanding of God; as an unembodied being, God is omnipresent. For such an omnipresent being, knowledge is aperspectival, i.e., universal. Thus, as the Renaissance and Enlightenment argument goes, since we are made in God's image, to the degree possible, our knowledge also should be aperspectival and universal. However, one can believe in God's knowledge, understanding, and omniscience without assuming that they are to be understood in these universal, aperspectival terms. Much of David Paulsen's work is dedicated to showing the alternative.

21. For background in understanding my discussion of symbolic ordering, one should read sections 31 and 32 in Martin Heidegger, *Being and Time,* trans. John

Macquarrie and Edward Robinson (New York: Harper and Row, 1962), and perhaps the material leading up to those sections. There he discusses understanding and the necessity of preunderstanding to understanding and interpretation. (By *understanding* Heidegger means something like "implicit understanding," and by *interpretation* he means the explication of understanding.) The correlate discussion of prejudice in Hans-Georg Gadamer, *Truth and Method,* rev. by Joel Weinsheimer and Donald G. Marshall, 2d ed. rev. (New York: Continuum, 1993), 265–300, and the discussion of prefiguration (also called *mimesis*) in Paul Ricoeur, *Time and Narrative,* trans. Kathleen McLaughlin and David Pelloever, vol. 1 (Chicago: University of Chicago Press, 1984), 1–64, might be helpful. Both Gadamer and Ricoeur rely heavily on Heidegger's work. Guignon's book may also be helpful. See Charles Guignon, *Heidegger and the Problem of Knowledge* (Indianapolis: Hackett, 1983).

Briefly put, what we think of as understanding requires preunderstanding; preunderstanding gives us our possibilities for understanding. As we have understood since Plato, our understanding of the world cannot begin from zero, *ex nihilo.* Something, some way in which the world gives itself to us prior to reflection, makes understanding possible. But the world does not give itself as the bare presence of mere things. It always—*always already*—gives itself to us in shape and relations, in a figure. The world gives itself to us, prereflectively, as configured. Thus, a fundamental preunderstanding is the configuration of the world (the *kosmos*) within which one finds oneself oriented in the world: an ordering gives the possibilities for understanding by configuring—reconfiguring—the world. Various things can serve to order—language and mathematics, for example. A symbolic ordering is a preunderstanding in which symbols and symbol systems (as opposed to sign systems) are fundamental, though not exclusive, to the configuration in which one is oriented.

22. This reduction of religion to sets of beliefs is also consequent on the traditional understanding of God and the way that understanding led to the Enlightenment. On a voluntaristic Christian view, God's will is coextensive with his knowledge, which is ideal and is at least a representation of the world. Thus, humans' image of God or human knowledge, i.e., representation of the ideal, like God's knowledge, is prior to or fundamental to human action and life. This explains why Western thought consistently values theory over praxis. On a voluntarist view, religious beliefs are representations to ourselves of the religious aspect of the ideal world. As such, they make it possible for us to act in religious ways. Therefore, beliefs are fundamental to religion. We generally take recognition of and adherence to a particular set of beliefs to be identical with being an adherent of that religion. Note that it is possible to understand a good deal of modernism as an outgrowth of voluntarism in theology. For an argument to this effect, see Klaus Held, "Civic Prudence in Machiavelli: Toward the Paradigm Transformation in Philosophy in the Transition to Modernity," *The Ancients and the Moderns,* ed. Reginald Lilly (Bloomington, Ind.: Indiana University Press, 1996), 115–29. To take religion to be a matter of symbolic ordering is to reject this understanding of the connection between religion and belief. Of course, I do not necessarily reject everything about voluntarism, only those features that make belief and representation fundamental to action in the way that voluntarism does.

23. I am hesitant to define what I mean by *sacred*. I fear a kind of definitional blasphemy, but I can say that it has to do with what is excessive, in other words, abundant, and determinative. The sacred "transcends" the world of our experience and our ability to explain (though it transcends without having to be, itself, in or of another quasi-Platonic realm) and it "explains" the world (by grounding that world, though—again—it is not a ground outside or beyond the world). Those curious about how to think such transcendence and ground might find Heidegger's *Principle of Reason* interesting. Though it is not about the sacred, it does deal with transcendence without making transcendence other-worldly. See Martin Heidegger, *The Principle of Reason,* trans. Reginald Lilly (Bloomington, Ind.: Indiana University Press, 1991).

24. I use the language of form and content here for heuristic reasons. As we usually understand that language, it requires another world to which this world refers, i.e., something like a theory of representation. However, one need not be a Platonist or a representationalist to find the language of form meaningful and helpful. For the ancients, *form is that in which the real shows itself, presents itself.* That is the point, and the point need not be understood in representational terms as Aristotle well shows. Put otherwise: the language of form and content can be helpful, though the danger is that we will understand that language via a theory of representation or something like it. The work of Heidegger, for example, is amenable to this way of thinking. I believe that Wittgenstein's work is similarly amenable to form and content language, though of course neither Heidegger nor Wittgenstein would use the word *form* in its Platonic sense because of the metaphysical, representational baggage that the word carries with it; Heidegger speaks of horizons, Wittgenstein of forms of life. In what follows, I will discuss how form can be that in which the real shows itself without assuming that there is another world to which the form must be correlate.

25. Searle's work is an interesting and relevant example of the attempt to take the language of symbolic ordering as parasitic. See John R. Searle, *Speech Acts: An Essay in the Philosophy of Language* (Cambridge: Cambridge University Press, 1969).

26. Ironically, however, the exclusion of symbolic ordering from the rational is self-defeating since rational language cannot avoid the intrusion of the symbolic via such features of language as metaphor; we no longer understand words such as *inference* and *therefore* from out of the metaphors that inform them, but if all metaphorical language were removed, even the language of logic, like all language, would cease to function.

27. Some may expand on this, not placing the value in the individual, but in the group. However, the basic structure remains the same: the distinction between regions is determined subjectively or intersubjectively.

28. This is not to say that the dogma of transubstantiation begins with Aquinas. Rather, he formulates philosophically the justification for a dogma that has been generally argued for (though not always required to be believed) since at least the tenth century and that was made dogmatic only with the Fourth Lateran Council (1215). The Thomistic interpretation of Aristotle's doctrine of substance takes substance to be that which exists in itself or that which remains what it is, though it might have differing qualities at different moments. For more on substance, see

Aristotle, *Categories* 2a.10–19; *Metaphysics* 1017b.10–27. The second of these characterizations of substance makes possible the doctrine of transubstantiation as understood in the dogma of the Catholic Church: the bread takes on the substance of Christ's body, though in doing so it has different qualities than it does in the person of Jesus Christ. However, one caveat: Pickstock takes a position very much like that of Marion, arguing cogently and more fully than he that the Thomistic interpretation is not what makes that doctrine implausible. Rather, the implausibility results from the metaphysics of Duns Scotus and the consequent spatialization of ontology. Before Scotus, the sacrament of the Eucharist was understood as the embodied, temporal link of the past to the present and to the future. As such, it connected the meaning of the past event of the Atonement to the coming event of the Apocalypse through the present. Therefore, the Eucharist was the embodied presenting of the Atonement, an act. (See Pickstock, *After Writing,* 160–65.)

In contrast, under Scotus's influence, the Eucharist later "instantiated a transposition from a *temporal* distribution (which linked sacramentally the past and present to the eschatological future), to a *spatial* one, according to which the sacramental 'action' became less a nonidentical repetition continuous with the 'original' event and more a simple, positive, authoritative 'miracle' in the present" (160), the presence of a thing. On this reading, "that which exists in itself" is dynamic rather than static, more like an event than a thing. See Martin Heidegger, *Aristotle's Metaphysics θ, 1–3: On the Essence and Actuality of Force,* trans. Walter Brogan and Peter Warnek (Bloomington, Ind.: Indiana University Press, 1995), for a discussion of this way of understanding Aristotle and, thus, also Aquinas. Thus, Pickstock reads Aquinas's pre-Scotistic explanation of the Eucharist and transubstantiation as escaping my criticism, above, though her understanding of Aquinas's explanation fits well with my understanding of how ordinances, symbols, and texts work in the premodern world.

Whatever one might think is the most coherent explanation of the doctrine of transubstantiation, my point is that medieval Christians rejected the modernist assumption that the most important sign in Christianity, the Eucharistic wafer, is a material thing that merely directs our attention to something immaterial and invisible. Their understanding of the Eucharist implicitly rejects any simple version of reference, and that rejection can be generalized to their understanding of symbols and to the meaning of texts, as I argue we must do to understand the literal character of scripture.

29. Jean-Luc Marion, *God without Being,* trans. Thomas A. Carlson (Chicago: University of Chicago Press, 1991), 166–67.

30. Ibid., 164.

31. Ibid., 171–72.

32. Ibid., 174.

33. Dom Gregory Dix, *The Shape of the Liturgy* (London: Adam and Charles Black, 1945), 29 ff. and 78 ff.

34. Thus, one takes a Reformation view when one understands scripture as a more or less successful attempt to describe events accurately *and* when one takes it to be essentially ahistorical and referential to something transcendent.

35. Quoted in Richard Helgerson, "Milton Reads the King's Book: Print, Perform-ance, and the Making of a Bourgeois Idol," *Criticism* 29, no. 1 (1987): 4.

36. Ibid., 6.

37. Writing falls short when it assumes that the relation between the written word is simple reference rather than enactment, for it will always fail to reach that which it supposedly represents because, as only reference, it removes itself from the *act* in which genuine reference occurs. Reference is an act, not a relation.

38. Ironically, I take it that the nineteenth- and twentieth-century conservative Christian interpretations of *sola scritura* are the consequence of the fact that scripture has lost its sacred character—an insistence on its sacred character when the rational underpinnings for thinking it sacred have disappeared.

39. Paul Moyaert, Lecture, Catholic University of Leuven, 8 January 1996. It is not central to the thesis of this paper, but I should note that I distinguish memory from recall: recall is a psychological event; memory is what we share and participate in. As such, it gives us direction (intention) beyond our subjective intentions, often intentions we do not know. It also creates expectations of us that are beyond our will. Though the cup remembers for Moyaert, it may not always or ever recall for him.

40. For an interesting discussion of symbolic ordering and its power—in the context of witchcraft rather than magic—see Jeanne Favret-Saada, *Deadly Words,* trans. Catherine Cullen (Cambridge: Cambridge University Press, 1980). The introduction to her work also shows why symbolic ordering cannot be reduced to primitive science.

41. René Descartes, *Discourse on Method,* 3.1.

42. Ibid., 3.6.

43. Interestingly, Descartes reduces the religious region to the moral, a reduction that begins at about his time and grows more prevalent until, today, the identity of religion and morality is common sense—in spite of Nietzsche's pointed and accurate attacks on such religion. Such common sense robs religion of its vitality.

44. As Levinas shows in *Totality and Infinity: An Essay on Exteriority,* trans. Alphonso Lingis (Pittsburgh: Duquesne University Press, 1969), 48 ff., Descartes's attempt relies on the necessity of something beyond the rational. Nevertheless, Descartes seems not to have understood the degree to which the necessity of recourse to the Infinite undercuts his methodological claims. Even if he did understand that, it is certainly the case that those following him did not. See René Descartes, *Meditations on First Philosophy,* 1, 3.

45. Descartes, *Discourse on Method,* 2.4.

46. Of course, if one does not have the narrower definition of reason that modernism adopts, then it becomes possible to identify the ground of reason (in the modern sense of *reason*) with reason itself, as ancients and medievals usually do.

47. Descartes, *Discourse on Method,* 2.7–10.

48. In spite of the way that, for heuristic reasons, I have described the change from premodernism to modernism and in spite of the way that modern thinkers often portrayed and understood themselves, modernism was no sudden and absolute rupture with its past. Such things as Greek *episteme* combined with the Christian idea of an external nature over which humans rule, the certainty of salvation, ascetic "methods" for achieving salvation, and voluntarism are important antecedents of modernism. Nevertheless, with modernism's explicit rejection of its roots and its move to the subject (individual consciousness) as fundamental, a very new understanding of things and the world entered into European history. For more on the antecedents of modernism, see Louis K. Dupré, *Passage to Modernity: An Essay in the Hermeneutics of Nature and Culture* (New Haven: Yale University Press, 1993).

49. Augustine, *On Christian Doctrine,* 1.5.

50. Ibid., 1.6.

51. Ibid., 1.13.

52. The difference between what Augustine and Aquinas mean by *enlightenment* and what the moderns mean is another way to mark the difference between the medieval and the modern. The former has to do with the gift of seeing the sacred in the temporal, seeing the sacred order of the temporal, the latter has to do with using reason critically. For the former, see Augustine, *The Literal Meaning of Genesis.* For the latter, see Kant, "What is Enlightenment?" in *Kant Selections,* ed. Lewis White Beck (New York: Macmillan, 1988), 462–67.

53. The incarnationist view of scripture is not confined to Christianity. Speaking of the medieval Jewish mystical understanding of Torah, Fishbane says, "On this view the Bible . . . is ontologically unique principally because it is nothing less than a dimension of divinity itself." See Michael Fishbane, *The Garments of Torah: Essays in Biblical Hermeneutics* (Bloomington, Ind.: Indiana University Press, 1989), 35.

54. Carol Harrison, *Beauty and Revelation in the Thought of Saint Augustine* (Oxford: Clarendon, 1992), 85–86, 203–4.

55. Suppose, however, that one cannot accept the argument that symbols are best understood incarnationally, that one still feels that symbols must be understood as references, as a kind of sign. Even then, it is impossible for us to refer adequately and accurately to the history of the world. Human understanding may hold some few points of that history together, but it cannot hold them together as a whole, especially not as an ordered whole. For human understanding, the *kosmos* becomes, at best, a blur of amorphous shapes in an ancient mirror (see 1 Cor. 13:12). If the *kosmos* can be comprehended, only God can do so. Therefore, even if scripture were referential rather than incarnational, for a believer only the divine revelation of history—in other words, scripture—could be an accurate reference to and representation of that history

as a whole, something that scientific history neither attempts nor wishes to give. The events of history can be understood only as they fit into the whole of which they are a part. Thus, even the particular events of a divine history could not be understood except from within the perspective of a divine revelation, the perspective purportedly offered by scripture and a perspective purposefully and necessarily unavailable within the parameters of modern historiography.

56. For Latter-day Saints the comparison is even closer: the Son is an incarnation of the Father without being the same being as the Father.

57. Harrison, *Thought of Saint Augustine,* 82.

58. Alternatively, it suggests something that we find too mysterious, something like the standard interpretation of the doctrine of transubstantiation.

59. Joseph Smith, *Teachings of the Prophet Joseph Smith,* comp. Joseph Fielding Smith (Salt Lake City: Deseret Book, 1938), 301–2.

60. This is how I read the Prophet's seemingly tautologous statement that there is no immaterial matter.

61. Talk of spirit bodies possessing physical bodies doesn't explain what it means to have a body since according to LDS doctrine, spirits, too, *have* material bodies.

62. One reason that I find Merleau-Ponty's discussion helpful is that it echoes Paul's way of talking about what it means to be a Christian. See, for example, Romans 7 and 8, where it is clear that the change that occurs in a Christian is not a change of characteristics or obedience but a change of being (compare 7:22–23 with 8:8–9). For Paul, the division is not between inner and outer, or mind/spirit and body, but between living by the Spirit and living according to one's will, i.e., living according to the world. For Paul, to be a Christian is to inhabit the world in a particular way, not to subscribe to a particular set of beliefs (though beliefs will follow from the fact that one inhabits the world as a Christian—see note 22). See also 1 Cor. 1:26–29, especially verse 28, where Paul speaks of the Saints as "non-being," suggesting that the difference between Christians and non-Christians is a matter of their *being.*

63. Maurice Merleau-Ponty, *Phenomenology of Perception,* trans. Colin Smith (New York: Routledge & Kegan Paul, 1962), 139.

64. Ibid., 148.

65. Ibid., 174 n. 1.

66. This is *not* to criticize scientists for that attitude or to suggest that God ought to be part of science. A great many other important things also do not exist in a world inhabited scientifically, things such as morality and value or, of less consequence, good taste in food or clothing. That absence is the consequence of the specialized incarnation required of science and is only a problem if scientists (or more often those who idolize science because they know too little of it) forget that such a specialized incarnation is not the only one, the best one, or the final one. See Martin Heidegger, "The Age of the World Picture" and "Science and Reflection," in *The Question*

Concerning Technology and Other Essays, trans. William Lovitt (New York: Harper Colophon, 1977), 115–82.

67. Moyaert's discussion of symbols is a discussion of symbols as incarnations.

68. Augustine, *On Christian Doctrine,* 1.13.

69. I have in mind here Edmund Husserl's concept of *Abschattungen,* "profiles." We know an object only in its profiles, but it is always excessive of those profiles as well as of any imaginative combination of profiles. It is important to recall that a combination of profiles is *always* the result of an act of imagination; the objectivity of an object is the work of imagination rather than perception.

70. The Enlightenment had this overcoming of all abundance and excess as its goal. In Derridean terms, it aimed at the identity of text and world. However, the excess of meaning is a function of the embodiment of the world and ourselves and it makes continued speaking and relation possible. Thus, the implicit goal of the Enlightenment was the destruction of the body by the reduction of everything to certainty—absolute irrelation and silence, absolute death.

71. Both Levinas's and Marion's discussions of intention are instructive. See Levinas, *Totality and Infinity,* 23, 27–29, 49, 122–30, 204–9, 257–61, 294–95; Marion, *God without Being,* 18–23).

72. Walter Benjamin, *The Origin of German Tragic Drama,* trans. John Osborne (New York: Verso, 1977), 31, translation revised. See also the text that Benjamin may have in mind, namely Nietzsche's preface to the second edition of *The Gay Science,* section 4, where Nietzsche compares the will to see everything to Egyptian boys who desecrate temples: "We no longer believe that truth remains truth when the veils are withdrawn; we have lived too much to believe this. Today we consider it a matter of decency not to wish to see everything naked, or to be present at everything, or to understand and 'know' everything." See Friedrich Nietzsche, *The Gay Science,* trans. Walter Kaufmann (New York: Random House, 1974), 38.

Perhaps this is a way of explaining the Savior's remark in Matt. 13:13: "Therefore speak I to them in parables: because they seeing see not; and hearing they hear not, neither do they understand." That idea is an important part of the Christian tradition, though it is often a scandal to believers as well as nonbelievers. The traditional explanation for parables and parabolic language is: "The motives for symbolism are secrecy and revelation, as accommodated to the abilities of the interpreters. God used symbols so that 'the most sacred things are not easily handled by the profane but are revealed instead to the real lovers of holiness' (1105C, 283)." See Paul Rorem, *Pseudo Dionysius: A Commentary on the Texts and an Introduction to Their Influence* (Oxford: Oxford University Press, 1993), 25. My argument suggests that perhaps, instead, parables are to be explained as the only possible responses to those who demand that the language of religion be "clear and distinct." Parables demand that their hearers deal with them as something containing a secret, but a secret that, it turns out, cannot simply be removed. Of course, the two explanations are not mutually exclusive.

Note also that the view I propose contests Kermode's explanation of the secrecy of parables and, therefore, of what it means to understand a narrative. See Frank

Kermode, *The Genesis of Secrecy: On the Interpretation of Narratives* (Cambridge, Mass.: Harvard University Press, 1979).

73. Of course, these remarks do not imply that we ought to avoid clear and distinct language. Our preference for such language is not merely contingent. Taking the identity of intention and expression to be an ultimate good for writing is an outgrowth of our Cartesian goal of mastery over everything with no remainder, the transparency of the world. However, the identity of intention and expression is sometimes a good—when that identity *is* possible, then our language ought to embody it. If our language does not, it fails. It is inadequate. Nevertheless, languages other than the language of clarity are also possible, even necessary. For one thing, if they are not possible, then it is not clear how to avoid making the desire for knowledge a desire, ultimately, for annihilation—see note 70.

74. The Latter-day Saint and Catholic recognition of the need for ordinances and for authority in ordinances is a recognition of the inadequacy of individual intentions when it comes to understanding or invoking the Divine. In general, Protestantism disagrees on this point, but its disagreement runs the risk of reducing religion to the thoughts and feelings of the individual, to only a psychological attitude. See my "A New Way of Looking at Scripture," *Sunstone* 18 (August 1995): 78–84 (an unfortunate title, not of my choosing) for a sketch of an argument for the necessity of authority. See also Marion, *God without Being,* 153 ff., from which I have adapted that argument.

75. Kermode, *The Genesis of Secrecy,* 19. However, Kermode misunderstands the relation of the Roman Catholic Church to medieval scripture interpretation, accepting without question the modernist view of the matter. He applies the distinction between what the texts are about and what they mean, and he criticizes biblical texts for their failure to describe events accurately. As a result, he does not seem to understand the incarnational character of premodern interpretation or its communal character. He also misunderstands Heidegger's discussion of interpretation.

76. We must remember, however, that we decide accuracy relative to the region or order within which a description occurs and to the purposes for which it is given. A scientific description would be inaccurate in a scriptural text; a scriptural description would be inaccurate in a scientific text. In either case could one rectify the inaccuracy of the description by saying more, by giving more detail, by looking more closely, by correcting one's "mistakes"? No, for the inaccuracy is a function of the relation between the description, the place in and purpose for which it is given, and the order which gives it meaning rather than a function of the descriptive skill of the person offering the description.

77. For a discussion of some of these reasons, see Heidegger, "The Age of the World Picture."

78. Many non-LDS Christians probably also continue to read symbolically, especially those often thought of as literalists or conservatives.

Historical Plausibility: The Historicity of the Book of Abraham as a Case Study

3

John Gee and Stephen D. Ricks

In attempting to prove the historicity of any document or event, historians should use primary sources. For the historian of the ancient world, however, these sources are often both rare and obscure. By comparing a text with other texts and archaeological material from the same time and place, a historian can propose the historical plausibility of a document when its authenticity is not certain. In order to establish the Book of Abraham as a historically authentic ancient document, one must consider many elements, including: setting; the presence and nature of Egyptian influence in Abraham's place and time, including governmental, social, and religious institutions; and the presence of comparable personal and place names in the ancient Near East of Abraham's day. Yet even under the best of circumstances, historical plausibility establishes probability, not proof.

Historical sources come in several basic varieties: primary and secondary, contemporary and later, textual and archaeological. Primary sources are first-hand accounts, while secondary sources are not. Thus primary sources include diaries, letters, and legal documents, while secondary sources include histories, textbooks, and encyclopedias. Contemporary sources are written at the time of the events or soon thereafter, while later sources are sometimes written much later. Textual sources contain texts, some sort of writing (hopefully comprehensible), while archaeological sources include all sorts of material objects with or without writing. Under ideal conditions, the historian uses contemporary primary sources.

For the historian of the ancient world, however, conditions are much less than ideal. First, the historian's resources are limited to whatever has survived. Second, "without secondary materials, we would often be left only with isolated and unrelated facts presented by individual primary sources, which would in themselves offer little hope of erecting an all-important chronological framework."[1]

The historian of antiquity has to make do with what is available. How does he or she determine whether a later secondary source is accurate? For example, most of the history of ancient Israel is based on the books of Samuel and Kings in the Bible. Yet those books were compiled at a much later time—after all, they mention events in the "seven and thirtieth year of the captivity of Jehoiachin king of Judah" (2 Kgs. 25:27).[2]

Historical plausibility offers a possible solution to this sort of problem. We will illustrate both the problem and the solution with the Book of Abraham and several other ancient documents. We want to avoid the sort of special pleading that is often applied to scriptural texts—that because the texts are scriptural, they are not allowed the latitude normally granted other texts.[3] One of the ironies of historical plausibility is that "for the purpose of the exercise, we shall suppose that, like the Babylonian and Egyptian works, the Pentateuch [or whatever work we are interested in testing, such as the Book of Abraham] has no religious relevance to us."[4]

The problem centers around which of two mutually exclusive methodological assumptions one chooses, given here in the words of (1) a preeminent Mesopotamian historian (J. A. Brinkman) and (2) a largely ignored Egyptologist (Gun Björkman):

> 1. Where no sound evidence exists to the contrary, an isolated document, according to its capacity, is to be accepted as historically accurate until proven otherwise. Without this principle, there would be no hope of writing political history for ancient Babylonia.[5]

> 2. Undoubtedly many scholars still adhere to the opinion that the statements of a source can be regarded as reliable as long as the opposite has not been proved. It must be emphasized, however, that . . . the burden of proof does not rest on the skeptical scholar but on the scholar who accepts the statements of his source as credible evidence.[6]

Because these are assumptions, they are made before one even begins studying the source, and they color the entire study.

While there is no indication that a consensus exists on this issue (or any other issue) among historians,[7] there are indications that the first is the sounder view. One indication is that those who actually write Egyptian history have not only generally ignored the second view but have *deliberately* ignored it.[8] As Friedrich Blass correctly observed over a century ago, "Once you assume that a document is a fake, no arguments and no evidence to the end of time can ever vindicate it, even if it is absolutely genuine."[9] Tests for forgery are all negative tests; they are not and cannot be set up to show that a document is genuine, only that it is a forgery.[10] "Finality can probably never be reached. We have to be satisfied with an accumulation of indication, large or small."[11] Accordingly, most historians of the ancient world (even Björkman) assume their documents to be genuine unless given sufficient reason otherwise. Björkman was concerned to show that there was no support for the historical situation described in the *Instruction for Merykare* among contemporary documents. He failed, however, both to demonstrate that anything in the *Instruction for Merykare* was at odds with his control documents and to apply those strict assumptions to his control documents. Thus those who actually write Egyptian history still use the *Instruction for Merykare* even though the historical situation it describes is not supported by any other Egyptian document.[12] Likewise, those who write Mesopotamian history discuss the Sumerian King List as follows: "If the King List speaks of the hegemony of foreign powers like Mari, or Awan and Hamazi somewhere to the east, we cannot dismiss this as mere legend, but have to give it the benefit of the doubt even if there are no contemporary records of such a domination."[13] Scientists do not jettison their theories because there are some problems. The philosopher and historian of science Thomas Kuhn asks us to note "what scientists never do when confronted by even severe and prolonged anomalies. Though they may begin to lose *faith* and then to consider alternatives, they do not renounce the paradigm that has led them into crisis. They do not, that is, treat anomalies as counter-instances,"[14] though this is exactly what the critics of the Book of Mormon or the Book of Abraham would have us do. In practice, then, a historical document is accepted as historically accurate until proven other-wise.

Historical Plausibility

What allows us to accept a document as historically accurate according to its capacity is its historical *plausibility*. Historical plau-sibility relies on the aggregate of information to provide a consistent picture of events and processes. It assumes that historical conditions at a given time and place are consistent and that change over both time and place varies consistently. That is, documents and artifacts produced at a given time and place have a certain commonality that may vary as both time and place change. For example, handwriting in Greek business documents changes slightly over a hundred-year time span, but the changes over a two- or three-hundred-year period are much more marked;[15] because documents produced at the same time share a commonality of handwriting style, this commonality is what allows for documents to be dated paleographically. Similar commonality is what allows for the identification of pottery found in archaeological excavations and surveys and for the dating of occupa-tion of a particular site based in the pottery identifications made.

Documents also follow certain patterns in layout, language, script, paleography, vocabulary, genre, specificity, onomastics, and cultural referents (including governmental, social, and religious institutions and practices). To the extent that a document matches others in these areas, it is historically plausible. Since this is normally the case, historical plausibility is rarely an issue, even though the majority of documents show at least one and sometimes several peculiarities.[16] Thus "a single example would be insufficient; a series of indisputable anachronisms alone could carry weight in assessing the age of a composition."[17] When a document presents a number of inconsisten-cies or anachronisms, or its historicity is in jeopardy, historical plausibility becomes an issue.

Historical plausibility relies on the comparison of a text with other texts and with archaeological material from the same time and place. When this information is absent because the work in that area is either undone, incomplete,[18] or unavailable for whatever reason, it is customary to look to neighboring locations at the same time (particularly those regions known to have been in cultural contact) or the same location at earlier or later periods (assuming continuity). This introduces an element of uncertainty into the control of the evidence, as continuity between time and place cannot necessarily be assumed.[19] An uncautious search for parallel material can often degenerate into a wild grab for anything, no matter how remote.[20] A historical parallel that is remote in both time and place might indicate historical possibility, but it does not establish historical plausibility.

Historical plausibility is not a universally accepted method—indeed the elements which comprise historical plausibilty are not themselves agreed upon—as the following example illustrates. One of the most brilliant compositions of the Middle Kingdom, the story of Sinuhe takes the form of a tomb biography.[21] But unlike other tomb biographies, it has never been found on any tomb; instead it has been found in numerous later copies on papyrus or on ostraca. Sinuhe provides a good test case because it is less susceptible to the special pleading from both sides that plagues discussions of the historicity of scripture.[22] Is Sinuhe a historical source? The great American archaeologist William F. Albright considered it to be "a 'substantially true account of life in its *milieu*' on the grounds (1) that its 'local color [is] extremely plausible,' (2) it describes a 'state of social organization' which 'agrees exactly with our present archaeological and documentary evidence,' (3) 'the Amorite personal names contained in the story are satisfactory for that period and region,' and (4) 'Finally, there is nothing unreasonable in the story itself.'"[23] In other words, Albright considered Sinuhe historical on the basis of historical plausibility. More recently, K. A. Kitchen has outlined the following indicators of historicity in Sinuhe: (1) He has a name and definite titles. The narrative takes notice of (2) contemporary rulers, (3) other individuals abroad, and (4) topography, in and outside of Egypt.[24] All of this compares well with Egyptian autobiographies but contrasts with Egyptian fiction, which contains an absolute minimum of specifics, which looks back into the distant historical past, and where fantasy predominates: "Unlike the fictional works, there is no 'once upon a time' element, no anonymity about main characters, no vagueness about locations, and no fantasies or magic marvels."[25]

The debate over the historicity of Sinuhe, however, rages on, even though all agree that Sinuhe accurately reflects its historical and cultural milieu.[26] If there is no consensus on the historicity of this text, we can hardly hope that the critics would accept the historical authenticity of a scriptural text such as the Book of Abraham even if all the evidence we currently have were to point to its authenticity. This does not mean that historical plausibility is not a useful tool in ascertaining historicity, but it does mean that plausibility and proof of authenticity are two different things.

Historical plausibility is useful when trying to determine the ancient nature of a text. The demotic tales of Setna Khamwas,[27] for example, accurately reflect their ancient Egyptian milieu. The first two stories of the cycle are, in fact, some of the most revealing documents about the way Egyptians thought. They have thus been used to illustrate many facets of Egyptian culture. Many examples of marriage contracts ($s\underline{h}$ n $s'n\underline{h}$) have been preserved from ancient Egypt,[28] but Setna I illustrates how they were used.[29] Likewise, though archaeological examples of game boards are attested, and the Book of the Dead makes reference to playing on them,[30] Setna I is the only text that actually gives an account of the game.[31] Yet Setna is not a historical text but a historical romance: in it Setna Khamwas breaks into the tomb of the long-dead Naneferkaptah, who is said to be the son of Pharaoh Merneptah, and carries on conversations with him. But the historical Khamwas was the older brother of the then future Pharaoh Merneptah. With the Setna tales, no one doubts either that Khamwas was a historical personage or that the Setna tales reflect their cultural milieu, but no one grants the Setna tales historicity. Though the cultural situation is correct, the historical situation fails. Thus historical plausibility is useful in determining whether a document is ancient but not necessarily whether it is historical.

Showing that the document is ancient is a sufficient condition for establishing the historical accuracy of the Book of Mormon or the Book of Abraham. Since both the Book of Mormon and the Book of Abraham are often rejected as being neither ancient nor authentic simply by virtue of the story of their translation, explaining how they can possibly be historically plausible becomes more difficult than the alternative. The author of the Setna stories lived in a continuation of the same culture as Khamwas and spoke a descendant of the same language. But Joseph Smith lived in a different culture separated in time, space, and language from the books he translated. Thus this same test of historical plausibility can and should also be applied to our study of the Book of Abraham. Because the Book of Abraham is available to us only in translation, considerations of layout, language, script, paleography, and vocabulary play a much lesser role.[32] Still, considerations of genre, specificity, onomastics, and cultural referents (including religious, social, and governmental institutions) can be used.

Key to the discussion of the Book of Abraham as a historically authentic ancient document is its likely setting (whether in northern or southern Mesopotamia), the presence and nature of Egyptian influence in that part of the world in the late third to early second millennia B.C. (the likely time period for Abraham's activities), and the presence of comparable personal and place names in the Book of Abraham and in the ancient Near East at that time.

The Setting of the Book of Abraham

Before situating Abraham in place, let us situate him in time. There are two ways to do this. One could examine the Book of Abraham and try to determine when to place it historically by the various historical allusions under the dubious assumption that we have enough information about enough time periods and places to do so. "If, however, there are insufficient elements of established date with which to compare, the argumentation may easily lead to nothing but a vicious circle."[33] Therefore we will take a conventional dating approach. This means that we will accept the standard chronologies and the dates given (with the understanding that there may be errors) and work from there. Abraham seems most likely to have lived in the 2000s to 1800s B.C.[34] This time period corresponds to the archaeological time period generally thought to provide "the most suitable background for the patriarchal sagas in the Book of Genesis," the Middle Bronze Age II (ca. 2000–1550 B.C.).[35] Middle Bronze Age II is also seen as corresponding to the Twelfth through Seventeenth Dynasties in Egypt[36] (the Middle Kingdom, 2040–1640 B.C.)[37] and the Isin-Larsa and Old Babylonian Periods in Mesopotamia (2017–1595 B.C.).[38] This gives us some written sources in Mesopotamia and Egypt, but few written sources for Syria–Palestine, where Abraham lived most of his life.[39]

Let us now move on to geographical concerns: Was the setting of Ur in the Book of Abraham northern or southern Mesopotamia? In the early years of biblical research, historians situated Ur of the Chaldees (and in several passages in the Book of Abraham, "Ur, of Chaldea") in northern Mesopotamia, in the region close to Haran. There it remained "until the name of Sumerian Ur began to turn up in the cuneiform inscriptions deciphered during the latter half of the nineteenth century."[40] From that time the balance of scholarly opinion shifted to Sumerian Ur, until today it has become nearly unanimous.[41] The standard argument is that the southern or Sumerian Ur, located at Tell el-Muqayyar, was Ur of the Chaldees because (1) the ancient name of the site was Úri(m), (2) the Chaldeans could be the Kaldu, (3) Sir Leonard Wooley found a golden figure of a goat eating a tree at Tell el-Muqayyar, (4) and both Úri(m) and Haran were centers of moon god cults.[42] Of these, the first two are the major arguments; the latter two are ancillary arguments and do not convince in and of themselves.

But what of northern Mesopotamia as the site of Ur? Let us consider the following facts about a northern location:

1. Does the itinerary make sense? The outspoken scholar of the ancient world, Cyrus Gordon, argues: "Ur of the Chaldees in Genesis has to be north or east (probably northeast) of Haran for Terah's itinerary to make sense. By the same token, the 'Chaldees' of Abraham's Ur have nothing to do with Babylonia."[43] Robert Martin-Achard, who considers both options, concludes that it was not at all beyond the realm of possibility for the family of Abraham to have settled in the environs of southern Ur and then to have gone to Canaan by way of northern Ur and Haran.[44] Actually, in the light of the Book of Abraham, a location of Ur west of Haran would make the most sense, because the easiest way to avoid the problems with Egypt described in Abraham 1 would be to flee to the other side of the Euphrates until political conditions changed.[45]

2. The phonetic argument that Tell el-Muqayyar must be Ur of the Chaldees is not convincing. The reading of the signs that designate the ancient site, ŠEŠ-UNUG/AB^{ki}MA, are usually read as Úri^{ki}-ma (with the -ma *Auslaut* attached) which we have read as Úri(m).[46] There are also in the vicinity of the Syrian site of Ebla towns attested by the names of Úr, Ù-ra-an, Ù-ra-mu, Ù-ra-ú, Ù-rí-mu, Ù-rí-um,

U̇-ru$_{12}$, U$_9$-ru$_{12}$, all of which are at least phonetically as close to Ur as Úri(m).[47] These are only those attested in the political control of Ebla. A tablet from level VII at Alalakh (Old Babylonian period) mentions a place called ^{uru}Ú-re-e^{ki} [48] (to which Úri(m) is phonetically equivalent), and this same place is apparently also attested at both level IV at Alalakh (Late Bronze Age)[49] and at Ugarit (Ras Shamra);[50] another ^{uru}Ú-ra in Hittite domains is attested at both Alalakh and Ugarit.[51] The mere use of the qualifier "of the Chaldees" implies that more than one Ur existed anciently.

3. At the root of the problem is the term "Chaldees" or "Chaldeans." A historical survey of the development of our English term might clarify the issues involved. The *English* term derives originally from the Akkadian term *Kaldū*. The origins of the Kaldu are obscure, coming in a period from which we have only a few scant sources.[52] But onomastic evidence indicates that they were of West Semitic stock from Upper Mesopotamia or Syria but became rapidly assimilated into Babylonian culture.[53] The Assyrian king Ashurnasirpal II (878 B.C.) mentions a defeat of the Kaldu immediately after the battle of Sūru in the land of Suḫi.[54] By the time of Shalmaneser III (858–824 B.C.), the Kaldu are described as three tribes (the Jakini, the Amukāni, and the Adini) living in Babylonia. Despite their being neighbors, "the Assyrians do not seem to have been well acquainted with these people."[55] The Kaldu also appear in the campaigns of Shamshi-Adad V (814–812 B.C.) as allies of Marduk-balassu-iqbi.[56] By 769 B.C. Eriba-Marduk had followed Marduk-apla-usur, the first known Chaldean to occupy the throne of Babylon.[57] On his fourth campaign (700 B.C.), the Assyrian king Sennacherib campaigned against Shuzub, "the Chaldean who dwells in the midst of the marsh" in southernmost Mesopotamia.[58] The Chaldean hegemony of Babylon continued to the conquest of Babylon by Cyrus the Persian in 539 B.C.[59] The Persians referred to geographical units more than ethnic groups and thus do not mention the Chaldeans, only the Babylonians (*Bābiruviy*) in their inscriptions.[60] The Greek general Xenophon, on his return from serving as a mercenary on the campaign of Cyrus the Minor (400 B.C.), mentions the Chaldeans (*Chaldaioi*) in connection with the *Kardouchoi* (Kurds)[61] as a warlike people blocking the way to Armenia,[62] and as at war with their neighbors, the Armenians.[63] Thus they had moved again.

The widespread notoriety of the Babylonians as seers and healers spread throughout the Greco-Roman world.[64] Thus the Romans used the term *Chaldaeus* as a synonym for "soothsayer, astrologer, numerologist, charlatan."[65] Thence the term passed into English. The English term used to translate the Hebrew term *kasdîm* (Gen. 11:28) is "Chaldees." The Jews, in exile in Babylon, associated the ethnic group, the Kaldu or Kaldayyu, who ruled Babylon and spoke Aramaic when Judah was taken captive to Babylonia, with the Kasdim of Abraham's day.[66] Thence three things have been associated with the term: the place where the Kaldu then lived[67] (Babylonia), the language they then spoke (Aramaic; see Dan. 1:4), and the religion they then practiced (a false one from the Jewish and Roman view).[68] Until the modern decipherment of cuneiform (and thus in Joseph Smith's day), the English terms centering around "Chaldean" were used to designate "Mesopotamian" (in the larger sense of the word), the language we now term "Aramaic" and its dialects (such as Syriac), and "superstitious."[69] Since the decipherment of cuneiform,[70] the term "Chaldean" has tended to become more restricted to a specific ancient ethnic group, the Kaldu.[71] The question thus revolves around whether or not the Jews during the Babylonian exile were correct in associating the Kasdim of Abraham's day with the Kaldu of their own day, both of which would have been translated into English in Joseph Smith's day as "Chaldeans." In the final analysis, we are seeking the location of the Kasdim of Abraham's day, whether or not they were identical to the Kaldu. These considerations point to a northern location for Ur.

Historical Plausibility

Among the tests for the historical plausibility of the Book of Abraham, genre, specificity, onomastics, and cultural referents (including governmental, social, and religious institutions) are significant to consider when dealing with Egyptian influence in northern Mesopotamia and Syria during Abraham's lifetime.

Genre

The Book of Abraham is a first-person narrative, representing an autobiography. As part of this autobiography, the author narrates

events that happened to him (Abraham 1–2), visions that he received
(Abraham 3), and "a knowledge of the beginning of the creation . . .
as [it was] made known unto the fathers" (Abr. 1:31; 4–5). Autobiographical texts are common in Egypt during the Middle Kingdom (as
they are from the Fourth Dynasty until Persian times). Though the
story of Sinuhe is the most notable and the most extensive, others are
well known.[72] The Book of Abraham does not follow the form of a
traditional Egyptian autobiography (though there is no particular
reason it should).[73] Autobiographical texts are also known from the
Old Babylonian period in Mesopotamia.[74] Examples of texts from
Middle Bronze Age Syria–Palestine are as previously noted rare, but
autobiographical texts are also known from Alalakh in the Late
Bronze Age.[75] Gudea cylinder A is perhaps the most famous Mesopotamian text discussing a vision, but this is pre-Sargonic and thus dates
too early;[76] nevertheless there is an Old Babylonian text where god
talks with man.[77] If no Egyptian account of a vision is recognized
from the Middle Kingdom, Egyptian rituals from the Middle Kingdom discussing how to cause visions are known.[78] Cosmological
material is used in historical texts known from Sargonic period texts
from Mesopotamia.[79] From the Old Babylonian period also comes a
well-known, lengthy cosmological text that dovetails into (purportedly) historical events.[80] Cosmology is also extensively used in
religious texts both of Middle Kingdom Egypt and of Old Babylonian
Mesopotamia.[81]

Specificity

In the Book of Abraham, unlike in ancient fictional works, but
as in Sinuhe, "there is no 'once upon a time' element, no anonymity
about main characters, no vagueness about locations, and no fantasies
or magic marvels."[82] Specific geographical locations on the way to
Egypt are named: Potiphar's Hill (Abr. 1:10, 20), the plain of Olishem
(1:10), the land of Ur of Chaldea (1:20; 2:4, 15), Haran (2:4–6, 15),
Jershon (2:17–18), Shechem (2:18), Bethel (2:20), and Hai (2:20). All
of these places are outside of Egypt, and if no Egyptian place names
are mentioned that can be checked with Egyptian documents, it is
because Abraham never arrives in Egypt in the published Book of
Abraham.[83]

Onomastics

There must be a plausible use of personal names, that is, names of men, gods, and places that fit the area and period of time. Some of these names suggest a linguistic and cultural melting pot,[84] but it is better to concentrate on those names that are attested in the proper time and place.[85] That there are few written documents from the region at the time of Abraham means that we must usually cast our net wider to include examples from other periods and areas.[86]

Many of the names in the Book of Abraham are Hebrew, transcribed in the transliteration system that Joseph Smith used, which, though standard for the early nineteenth century, is not used today. Both Kokob (Abr. 3:13) and Kokaubeam (3:13, 16) derive from Hebrew *kōkāb*, "star" (e.g., Num. 24:17), *kōkābim*, "stars" (e.g., Gen. 1:16; compare Akkadian *kakkabu*, "star,"[87] Ugaritic *kbkb*, "star,"[88] Syriac *kawkab*, "star,"[89] Arabic *kaukab*, "star,"[90] Ethiopic *kokab*, "star").[91] Shaumahyeem (Facsimile 1:12) is indeed Hebrew *šāmayim*, "heaven(s)" and is related to the Hebrew word Shaumau (Facsimile 1:12, modern transcription *šāmāh*), "to be high." Raukeey-ang (Facsimile 1:12) is the transcription for Hebrew *rāqia'*, "firma-ment." Gnolaum (Abr. 3:18) is Joseph Smith's transcription of the Hebrew word *'olām*, "eternal." Though these are Hebrew, the prob-lem with trying to use them in the strictest sense as evidence of being attested in the proper time and place is that we have no Hebrew inscriptions contemporary with Abraham. They are attested for the proper place at a later time and in a cognate language (Akkadian) at the same time, but in another place. Although we do not have any evidence from the correct time and place that Hebrew was used, we also have no evidence that Hebrew was not used at that time and place; we simply have no evidence to say one way or the other.

The name Kolob (Abr. 3:3–4, 9, 16; 5:13) is perhaps the most famous name to come from the Book of Abraham. The transliteration system that Joseph Smith used for Hebrew used the letter *k* for two different Hebrew letters: *k* and *q*.[92] Thus the name Kolob fits well with two Semitic roots. Either it could be from **qlb* (Arabic *qalb*, "heart")[93] or **klb* (Akkadian *kalbu*, "dog,"[94] Ugaritic *klb*, "dog,"[95] Hebrew *keleb*, "dog," [e.g., Ex. 11:7], Syriac *kelb, kalbā'*, "dog,"[96] Arabic *kalb*, "dog,"[97] Ethiopic *kalb*, "dog").[98] Both are used for stars or constellations, the former in Arabic for Regulus;[99] the latter, in Akkadian, represents "the constellation Hercules,"[100] while in Syriac it represents the star Sirius;[101] in Arabic it represents the constellation Canus Major, especially the main star Sirius.[102] The root *qlb* seems less likely because it is not attested until much later Arabic and not in earlier languages.

The Book of Abraham gives the word "Rahleenos" as what the Chaldeans called "hieroglyphics." This word is problematic, not only because of our ignorance of who the Chaldeans were or what language they spoke in Abraham's day as discussed above, or our general ignorance of the languages known to have been spoken in the region at that time (e.g., Hurrian),[103] but also because we have very few ancient languages where we do know the word for "hieroglyphs."[104] Here again, we do not have enough information to make a general comment.

The gods mentioned in the Book of Abraham are also worth discussing.[105] Elkenah (Abr. 1:6–7, 13, 17, 20, 29) has been explained as ᵈIl-gi-na[106] but seems best explained by Hebrew *'ēl qānāh / 'ēl qōneh (šāmayim wā 'āreṣ)*, "God created / God creator of heaven and earth" (Gen. 14:19, 22; cf. Phoenician *qn' 'rṣ* , "creator of the earth," Hittite *Elkunirša*). Libnah (Abr. 1:6, 13, 17) has been explained as ᵈLa-ban[107] but may be related to Hebrew *lebānāh,* "moon" (e.g., Isa. 24:23; from the root *lābān,* "white" [e.g., Gen. 30:35]). The name of Mahmackrah (Abr. 1:6, 13, 17)[108] might be related to Hebrew *mimkār,* "merchandise" (e.g., Lev. 25:14). Korash (Abr. 1:6, 13, 17)[109] is attested as a name in New Kingdom Egypt *(K3rs).*[110] Though a similar Hurrian name *Ku-ra-az-zi* is attested from the Middle Bronze Age II level at Alalakh,[111] it does not seem close enough phonetically to justify connecting. Again, any proposed connections fail to match contemporary evidence from the correct location, at least as much due to the absence of contemporary evidence from the region. The standard set is so high and our current knowledge of the region at that time so small that any correspondence would be surprising.

The name Olishem in the phrase "the plain of Olishem" (Abr. 1:10) has received much comment, though generally in footnotes.[112] A Rim-Sin (2254–2218 B.C.) inscription mentions a town *Ú-li-ši-im*ki or *Ú-li-šé-em*ki [113] in connection with Ebla:[114] "He (Nergal) bestowed upon him [Naram-Sin] the Amanus too, the Cedar Mountain, and the

Upper Sea, and, by the weapon of Dagan, exalter of his kingship, Naram-Sin, the mighty, defeated Armanum and Ebla. Then, from the hither face of the Euphrates, he smote the river(-bank) as far as Ulisum, as well as the people whom Dagan had for the first time bestowed upon him, and they bear for him the burden of Ilaba his god. The Amanus too, the Cedar Mountain, he conquered completely."[115] The name also perhaps appears either as *Irissym*[116] or *3wšamm*[117] in Twelfth-Dynasty execration texts (ca. 1991–1783 B.C.) from Egypt. If this is the same place, its presence in the contemporary execration texts is an indication that it lay in the Egyptian sphere of influence during the Middle Kingdom.

Because there is little material from the proper time and place,[118] a negative result in onomastic evidence says nothing. That any evidence at all appears is a positive indication.

Government

The inscription that describes Sixth-Dynasty Egyptian king Pepi I's (ca. 2289–2255 B.C.) campaign into Syria indicates that the Egyptian army included a full entourage of Egyptian priests and other religious functionaries, along with interpreters and various other royal bureaucrats.[119] Indeed, evidence of the campaigns of Pepi I into the Syro–Palestinian area can be seen in a vase with his cartouches found in the inner court of Palace G at Ebla,[120] where Egyptian artifacts are attested from the Fourth Dynasty[121] to as late as the Thirteenth-Dynasty pharaoh Hetepibre Hornedjheriotef "the Asiatic" (ca. 1760 B.C.), a ceremonial mace of whose was buried in the Tomb of the Capridi at Ebla.[122] Lacking descriptions from the Middle Kingdom of Egyptian incursions into Syria, we must assume that similar conditions applied. That this assumption is reasonable is indicated not only by the Egyptian officials who left their inscriptions with their titles in the Sinai,[123] and by the story of Sinuhe which discusses Egyptian emissaries in the area,[124] but also by the same sort of archaeological remains. The Book of Abraham provides us with a similar picture of an Egyptian presence in northern Syria, complete with priests and bureaucrats.

From other evidence, particularly from the site of Byblos, the Lebanese coastal city, we know that there were extensive relationships between Twelfth-Dynasty Egyptian pharaohs (1991–1783 B.C.) and northern Syria in the time in which Abraham lived.[125] The rulers of Byblos wrote their Semitic names and stele in hieroglyphs and used the Egyptian title of governor.[126] Asiatic campaigns are attested for some Twelfth-Dynasty reigns,[127] but for the most part the area of Canaan seems to have acquiesced to Egyptian influence.[128] The foundation deposit from the temple of Tod deposited under Sesostris I (1971–1926 B.C.) included not only Cretan vessels but also Mesopotamian cylinder seals.[129] The story of Sinuhe, also set during the reign of Sesostris I in the Twelfth Egyptian Dynasty, relates the account of an Egyptian government official who fled Egypt upon the assassination of Amenemhet I (1991–1962 B.C.), the Pharaoh whom he served.[130] The story relates in a very artful way his travels into northern Syria and gives us a very clear picture of cultural features of that time. Amenemhet III (1844–1797 B.C.) is attested both at Ugarit (Ras Shamra) and Aleppo.[131] Amenemhet IV (1799–1787 B.C.) is attested at Beirut.[132] Egyptian officials, members of the royal family, and other Middle Kingdom objects are attested (from south to north) at Tell Jemma, Tell el-Ajjul, Lachish, Gezer, Jericho, Shechem, Megiddo, Beth-shan, Beirut, Byblos, Baalbek, Qatna, Ras Shamra, Alalakh,[133] and Ebla.[134] Whether by trade or by conquest, the Egyptians if nothing else exerted clear influence. Egyptian officials include treasury officials,[135] governors,[136] and accompanying bureaucratic staff[137] in charge of sending levies of food, weapons, lead, copper, precious stones, oil, trees, vessels, wine, cattle, and slaves to Egypt.[138] "From these facts there emerges the impression of domination by the pharaohs, uneven and interrupted, no doubt, but on the whole vigorous. . . . In view of this progressive increase in our knowledge, we shall err less if we exaggerate than if we minimize the hold the Twelfth Dynasty had over Syria and Palestine."[139] Vague memories of this Middle Kingdom domination in Asia might survive in a Demotic account.[140] Yet the Book of Abraham requires not domination but merely influence.

We may thus see Abraham not as a burnous-hooded Bedou quietly moving through a shadowy oriental half-world but as a sophisticated man who lived and moved within a sophisticated, culturally rich, and religiously diverse and engaged land.[141] In the view of Cyrus Gordon, Abraham's "contacts and freedom of movement reflect a sophisticated milieu where an international order . . . made such a career and such enterprise possible."[142]

Social Organization

Plausible social organization is also demonstrable in the Book of Abraham by the references to geography and political organizations. Abraham refers to the "land of the Chaldeans" (Abr. 1:1) or "land of Chaldea" (1:29), the "land of Canaan" (2:4, 15, 16), the "land of Jershon" (2:17), and the "land of Egypt" (1:23). The land of Ur includes Potiphar's Hill (1:10, 20) and the plains of Olishem (1:10). Egypt is clearly depicted as a state, while the land of Chaldea is a smaller political entity, having some social order and controlling some towns. But the lands of Canaan and Jershon are not political units, nor does Haran control more than presumably its immediate surroundings. This matches the picture of the Egyptian state during the Middle Kingdom as well as what we know of the social organization of northern Syria[143] and the city states of the land of Canaan during the Middle Bronze Age II period.[144]

Abraham moves about in these lands taking "the souls that we had won in Haran" (Abr. 2:15), settling down or moving on as the need arises. This not only matches the picture of nomadism during the Old Babylonian period[145] but also matches the picture of societal institutions of the same time.[146] Abraham's journey into Egypt is during a general time when many "Asiatics" are attested in Egypt.[147]

Religion

As a final consideration for the historical plausibility of the Book of Abraham, let us consider the exportation of Egyptian religion into the Syro–Palestinian area. We begin with a modest detour to the facsimiles. This is another point at which the critics of the Book of Abraham have come up short. Incidentally, these critics have been looking at the facsimiles but have avoided dealing with the text itself with, according to Brother Nibley, "almost hysterical touchiness."[148]

Figure 9 of Facsimile 1 is described as the "idolatrous god of pharaoh" and is depicted as a crocodile. What are the connections between the crocodile god Sobek and the Egyptian king?

1. The hieroglyph of the crocodile was used not only in the name of the crocodile *msḥ* but also as determinative in words such as *skn* "to lust after," reflecting its voracious sexual appetite, and *'d,* "to be aggressive, angry."[149] Similarly, the mythical Ammut—fearsome devourer of the hearts of the wicked in the judgment of the after-life—was presented as a composite creature: "her front is a crocodile, her rear is a hippopotamus, her middle is a lion."[150] But the crocodile that was elevated to the status of god the Egyptians called Sobek (in Greek times pronounced Souchos).[151] Its connection with royalty is shown by the crocodile being used to write the word *ity,* "sovereign."[152]

2. "Sobek assimilates the god of the king into himself ('S[obek] nimmt also den Königsgott in sich auf')," so that "hymns of praise to the king and his crowns can be addressed directly to Sobek,"[153] in which Sobek is "viewed as a manifestation of Horus, the god most closely identified with the kingship of Egypt."[154]

3. In Utterance 317 of the Pyramid Text, the king appears as Sobek: "Unas has come today from the overflowing flood; Unas is Sobk, green-plumed, wakeful, alert. . . . Unas arises as Sobk, son of Neith. . . . Unas is lord of seed who takes wives from their husbands, whenever Unas wishes, as his heart urges."[155] This rapacity is apparent not only in the actions of the pharaoh who steals Bata's wife in the Tale of the Two Brothers from Papyrus D'Orbiney,[156] and in the ironic punishment of the adulterer by delivering him to the crocodile in Papyrus Westcar,[157] but also in the Book of Abraham (Abr. 2:22–25).

4. Sobek was prominent in the Twelfth and Thirteenth Dynasties (1991–1640 B.C.). Among commoners, Sobek was the most popular theophoric name element in the Twelfth Dynasty,[158] and the most popular name compound in the Thirteenth Dynasty.[159] This popularity extended to the royalty as well: the last ruler of the Twelfth Dynasty was Queen Sobeknofru (1787–1783 B.C.).[160] Nine of the rulers of the Thirteenth Dynasty (1783–1640 B.C.) were named Sobekhotep.[161] Additionally, two rulers of the Seventeenth Dynasty were named Sobekemsaf.[162] By contrast, there is a comparative decline in Sobek worship in the New Kingdom, when the worship of Amen-Re (and a very brief period of Aten worship) prevailed. Sobek did not regain this sort of prominence until the Greco-Roman period.

5. Sobek is found throughout Egypt. Cylinder seals of the cults of Sobek in a variety of locations throughout Egypt are attested from the reign of Amenemhet III through the Thirteenth Dynasty.[163] Twelfth-Dynasty remains of his temples are found in both Kom Ombo[164] and Crocodilopolis (Medinet el-Fayyum).[165] Most noteworthy, however, there are images of Egyptian deities, among whom is Sobek, found in Middle Bronze Age II levels at Ebla in Syria, clear evidence of the export of the cult of Sobek to Syria at that time.[166]

Recently one critic argued that "the religious persecution described in the Book of Abraham is unattested in the ancient world before the reign of Antiochus IV Epiphanes"[167] (ca. 215–163 B.C.). However, the destruction of the Jewish temple at Elephantine by Egyptians in 410 B.C. was earlier.[168] Evidence from Abraham's day shows that the Egyptians did execute people for religious reasons. For example, a Thirteenth-Dynasty stele from the sacred precinct at Abydos, requires that "as for anyone who shall be found within these stelae, except for a priest about his duties, he shall be burnt."[169] Sesostris I decapitated and burned anyone involved in misconduct in the temple.[170] At Mergissa (outside Egypt but under Egyptian control) among the remains of a Twelfth-Dynasty Egyptian execration ritual was found the human sacrifice of a Nubian.[171] It is worth noting that this is Middle Kingdom evidence and not the New Kingdom evidence.

What Is at Stake?

What is at stake if the Book of Abraham is jettisoned as unhistorical? Most Latter-day Saints do not turn to the Book of Abraham for astronomical information, nor do they generally quote the facsimiles in sacrament meeting talks. Rather, they turn to the Book of Abraham because it contains the clearest statement on the preexistence (3:21–28), the most concise statement of the purpose of life (3:25),[172] and the most comprehensive and succinct version of the Abrahamic covenant (2:11).[173] Furthermore, Abraham's stirring quest (1:2) is scarcely matched anywhere.[174] These are truly pearls of great price that Latter-day Saints are loath to trade for the mess of pottage that the critics offer them in exchange. What motivated the pioneers to undertake all that labor and to face all those hazards was not dim hope or wishful thinking about legends but a burning witness about what was really, historically true, a testimony of the canon of scriptures of the Latter-day Saints and the Prophet who revealed them.

History as Science

History, in spite of what historians may like to think, is not a science,[175] "for in history . . . the facts at our disposal are often severely limited and cannot be repeated or implemented at our will."[176] Historians cannot go back to the lab to run the experiment again. Ancient historians are in an even worse situation: "Any author dealing with the history of the ancient Near East realizes all too well the ephemeral quality of his work. The sources he uses are noted for their paucity and obscurity."[177] In some cases, one additional source can completely destroy the standard histories of the period. Thus, for scientists, as well as historians who think of themselves as scientific, the ability to make correct predictions on new sets of data is generally taken as an indication of the theory's correctness.[178] Not only does the Book of Abraham correctly predict the worship of Sobek in Syria in the Middle Bronze Age II period,[179] but it does so in the face of arguments of the learned in 1912 that such a thing was impossible.[180] During the Middle Kingdom, "language, writing, religion, magic and decorative motifs had found their way from the banks of the Nile into the Levant," and though the precise nature of the "domination by the pharaohs" of the Middle Kingdom, "still eludes us; fifty years ago it was barely suspected."[181] This is a telling point in the Book of Abraham's favor.

This lengthy discussion of the Book of Abraham as an example in historical plausibility shows the strengths and weaknesses of the method. Historical plausibility has a more difficult time with unique documents and events because they do not fit into a standard pattern. Yet it is precisely unusual documents and events where one invokes historical plausibility as an argument. The more common the document, the less need to invoke historical plausibility because historical plausibility becomes obvious. This sets up a tension between having enough things that are typical for a historical time period that a document's historicity is manifest, and having enough uniqueness for it to be more than commonplace. Historical plausibility is most effective when there are materials for comparison from the same time and place; and as materials for comparison differ of necessity from farther in time and place, the farther in time and place the less certain the analysis. But even under the best of circumstances, historical plausibility demonstrates plausibility, it does not establish proof.

John Gee is assistant research professor of Egyptology, and Stephen D. Ricks is professor of Hebrew, Brigham Young University.

Chronological Table

ca. 2289–2255 B.C.	Pepi I
2254–2218 B.C.	Rim-Sin
2040–1640 B.C.	Middle Kingdom in Egypt
2025–1763 B.C.	Isin-Larsa Period in Babylon
ca. 2000–1550 B.C.	Middle Bronze Age II in Canaan
ca. 2000–1800 B.C.	Middle Bronze Age IIA in Canaan
1991–1783 B.C.	Twelfth Dynasty in Egypt
1991–1962 B.C.	Amenemhet I
1971–1926 B.C.	Sesostris I
1894–1595 B.C.	Old Babylonian Period in Babylon
1844–1797 B.C.	Amenemhet III
1799–1787 B.C.	Amenemhet IV
1792–1750 B.C.	Hammurapi
1787–1783 B.C.	Sobeknofru
1783–1640 B.C.	Thirteenth Dynasty in Egypt
ca. 1760? B.C.	Hetepibre Hornedjheriotef "the Asiatic"
ca. 1750–1650 B.C.	Middle Bronze Age IIB in Canaan
ca. 1650–1550 B.C.	Middle Bronze Age IIC in Canaan
1640–1550 B.C.	Seventeenth Dynasty in Egypt
1550–1070 B.C.	New Kingdom in Egypt
883–859 B.C.	Ashurnasirpal II
858–824 B.C.	Shalmaneser III
823–811 B.C.	Shamshi-Adad V
769 B.C.	Eriba-Marduk on throne in Babylon
704–681 B.C.	Sennacherib
700 B.C.	Fourth campaign of Sennacherib
539 B.C.	Cyrus conquers Babylon
410 B.C.	Destruction of the Jewish temple in Elephantine
400 B.C.	Cyrus the minor's campaign, Xenophon becomes general
215–163 B.C.	Antiochus IV Epiphanes
A.D. 1835	Purchase of the Joseph Smith Papyri
A.D. 1842	Book of Abraham published
A.D. 1844	Assassination of Joseph Smith
A.D. 1845	Layard begins excavations at Nineveh
A.D. 1846	Henry Rawlinson publishes the Behustan inscription

Notes

1. J. A. Brinkman, *A Political History of Post-Kassite Babylonia 1158–722 B.C.,* Analecta Orientalia 43 (Rome: Pontifical Biblical Institute, 1968), 26.

2. Outside of evidence in the Book of Mormon, the present form of biblical texts cannot be traced before the third century B.C. "Unless earlier manuscripts are found, we cannot establish the earlier history of the stories with any certainty; every account we may give will be hypothetical and speculative. It is important to recognize and accept this fact, and so to avoid claiming as certain conclusions what are only deductions built upon theories and assumptions." A. R. Millard, "Methods of Studying the Patriarchal Narratives as Ancient Texts," *Essays on the Patriarchal Narratives,* ed. A. R. Millard and D. J. Wiseman (Winona Lake, Ind.: Eisenbrauns, 1983), 35.

3. See Edwin Yamauchi, "The Current State of Old Testament Historiography," in *Faith, Tradition and History: Old Testament Historiography in Its Near Eastern Context,* ed. A. R. Millard, James K. Hoffmeier, and David W. Baker (Winona Lake, Ind.: Eisenbrauns, 1994), 27–28; Millard, "Methods of Studying," 41.

4. Millard, "Methods of Studying," 42.

5. Brinkman, *A Political History,* 25.

6. Gun Björkman, "Egyptology and Historical Method," *Orientalia Suecana* 13 (1964): 11.

7. For a detailed historical discussion of professional attitudes, see Peter Novick, *That Noble Dream: The "Objectivity Question" and the American Historical Profession* (Cambridge: Cambridge University Press, 1988), 415–629.

8. Björkman notes that Posener read his essay but ignored Björkman's conclusions about the historical value of the *Instruction for Merykare* in Georges Posener, "Syria and Palestine c. 2160–1780 B.C.," *The Cambridge Ancient History,* 3d ed., ed. I. E. S. Edwards, C. J. Gadd, and N. G. L. Hammond (Cambridge: Cambridge University Press, 1971), 1.2:533–35, as did William C. Hayes, "The Middle Kingdom in Egypt: Internal History from the Rise of the Heracleopolitans to the Death of Ammenemes III," *Cambridge Ancient History,* 1.2:466–67; William W. Hallo and William Kelly Simpson, *The Ancient Near East: A History* (New York: Harcourt Brace Jovanovich, 1971), 239–41; Nicolas Grimal, *A History of Ancient Egypt,* trans. Ian Shaw (Oxford: Blackwell, 1992), 139, 145; Donald B. Redford, *Egypt, Canaan, and Israel in Ancient Times* (Princeton: Princeton University Press, 1992), 46, 67–68. The only acceptance of Björkman's views is Barry J. Kemp, "Old Kingdom, Middle Kingdom and Second Intermediate Period c. 2686–1552 B.C.," in B. G. Trigger et al., *Ancient Egypt: A Social History* (Cambridge: Cambridge University Press, 1983), 113. Miriam Lichtheim, *Ancient Egyptian Literature* (Berkeley: University of California Press, 1973–80), 1:8–9, 97, believes that the work is pseudepigraphic but still dates to the period of Merykare.

9. As summarized in Hugh Nibley, *The Prophetic Book of Mormon*, The Collected Works of Hugh Nibley, Vol. 8: The Book of Mormon, ed. John W. Welch (Salt Lake City: Deseret Book and F.A.R.M.S., 1989), 56.

10. This negative nature of tests for forgery is covered both by Friedrich W. Blass, "Hermeneutik und Kritik," *Einleitende und Hilfsdisziplinen,* Handbuch der klassischen Altertums-wissenschaft 1 (Nördlingen: Beck, 1886), 268–72, and by George J. Throckmorton, "A Forensic Analysis of Twenty-One Hofmann Documents," in Linda Sillitoe and Allen D. Roberts, *Salamander: The Story of the Mormon Forgery Murders* (Salt Lake City: Signature, 1988), 533–36.

11. Björkman, "Egyptology and Historical Method," 16 n. 1.

12. See the analysis in Björkman, "Egyptology and Historical Method," 9–33. It should also be noted that nothing has been found against using the *Instruction for Merykare* as a historical source.

13. J. N. Postgate, *Early Mesopotamia: Society and Economy at the Dawn of History* (London: Routledge, 1994), 28.

14. Thomas S. Kuhn, *The Structure of Scientific Revolutions,* 2d ed. (Chicago: University of Chicago Press, 1970), 77 (emphasis added).

15. A convenient discussion is found in P. W. Pestman, *The New Papyrological Primer,* 2d ed. (Leiden: Brill, 1994), 59–63.

16. Scholarly publications of documents routinely have commentaries either to show that the supposed peculiarity is not one, or to explain the peculiarities mentioned. So the presence of some peculiarities in and of itself does not usually constitute sufficient reason to reject historical plausibility.

17. Millard, "Methods of Studying," 42.

18. See the cautions in Yamauchi, "Old Testament Historiography," 34–35.

19. See the cautions in Millard, "Methods of Studying," 39–40: "The impression left by many of the essays noting or commenting on them [parallels adduced to the patriarchal narratives] is of their haphazard occurrence. . . . The 'parallels' have not resulted from comprehensive studies of ancient adoption procedures (to continue the example), but from the finding of a tablet here and another there, each in some way reminiscent of the biblical incidents. Sometimes a single text has been the basis for comparison; sometimes a group from one locality; sometimes, as we have said already, scattered documents. . . . Such a selective employment of ancient documents seems to be unsatisfactory."

20. For cautions about the use of parallels in the story of Abraham, see Millard, "Methods of Studying," 39–40.

21. See K. A. Kitchen, "Sinuhe: Scholarly Method versus Trendy Fashion," *The Bulletin of the Australian Centre for Egyptology* 7 (1996): 55–63. The classic work on tomb biography texts is Jozef Janssen, *De traditioneele egyptische autobiografie vóór het nieuwe rijk* (Leiden: Brill, 1946).

22. For example, all of the criteria used against scriptural texts outlined in Yamauchi, "Old Testament Historiography," 25–29, can be levelled against Sinuhe but are usually not. Sinuhe too (1) is written later than the events it describes, (2) lacks independent external corroboration of the major figure's existence, (3) involves the intervention of deity, (4) is ideologically conditioned, (5) narrates the story of an individual rather than a nation, and (6) betrays literary traits.

23. William F. Albright, *Archaeology and the Religion of Israel* (Baltimore: Johns Hopkins University Press, 1942), 62, as cited in Hugh Nibley, *Lehi in the Desert, The World of the Jaredites, There Were Jaredites,* The Collected Works of Hugh Nibley, Vol. 5: The Book of Mormon, ed. John W. Welch, Darrell L. Matthews, and Stephen R. Callister (Salt Lake City: Deseret Book and F.A.R.M.S., 1988), 3. Nibley used Albright's criteria to establish a case for the historical plausibility of the Book of Mormon.

24. Kitchen, "Sinuhe: Scholarly Method versus Trendy Fashion," 57.

25. Ibid., 60.

26. In favor of the historicity of Sinuhe are Alan H. Gardiner, *Egypt of the Pharaohs: An Introduction* (Oxford: Oxford University Press, 1962), 130–31, 142 ("In this story we come closer to reality than perhaps in any other piece of ancient writing"); William Kelly Simpson, "The Story of Sinuhe," in *The Literature of Ancient Egypt: An Anthology of Stories, Instructions and Poetry,* new ed., ed. William Kelly Simpson (New Haven: Yale University Press, 1973), 57 ("more or less factual account"); Kitchen, "Sinuhe: Scholarly Method versus Trendy Fashion," 55–63. Opposed to the historicity of Sinuhe are Horst Klengel, *Syria 3000 to 300* B.C.: *A Handbook of Political History* (Berlin: Akadamie, 1992), 40–42 ("fictitious biography"); Kemp, "Old Kingdom," 79, 143 ("literary romance"); Edward F. Wente, *Letters from Ancient Egypt* (Atlanta: Scholars Press, 1990), 17 ("a pseudo-autobiographical work"). Noncommittal on historicity are Redford, *Egypt, Canaan, and Israel,* 83–87 ("Sinuhe, whether fictional or not," "corroborates the archaeological picture to perfection"); Grimal, *Ancient Egypt,* 161–63 ("tale"); Hallo and Simpson, *The Ancient Near East, 246* ("propaganda"); Lichtheim, *Ancient Egyptian Literature,* 1:211 ("It may be a true story").

27. The basic work is still F. Ll. Griffith, *Stories of the High Priests of Memphis* (Oxford: Clarendon, 1900); photographs of the P. Setna I (= P. Cairo 30646) may be found in Wilhelm Spiegelberg, *Die demotischen Denkmäler,* Catalogue général des antiquités égyptiennes du Musée du Caire (Strassburg: Fischbach, 1906), 2.2: Tafel XLIV–XLVII; English translations in Lichtheim, *Ancient Egyptian Literature,* 3:125–51.

28. Examples gathered in Erich Lüddeckens, *Ägyptische Eheverträge,* Ägyptologische Abhandlungen 1 (Wiesbaden: Harrassowitz, 1960); to which add Richard A. Parker, "A Demotic Marriage Document from Deir el Ballas," *Journal of the American Research Center in Egypt* 2 (1963): 113–16.

29. See the discussion in Janet H. Johnson, "'Annuity Contracts' and Marriage," in *For His Ka: Essays Offered in Memory of Klaus Baer,* ed. David P. Silverman,

Studies in Ancient Oriental Civilization 55 (Chicago: Oriental Institute, 1994), 113–32.

30. Book of the Dead 17 § P3, in Thomas G. Allen, *The Book of the Dead or Going Forth by Day: Ideas of the Ancient Egyptians Concerning the Hereafter as Expressed in Their Own Terms,* Studies in Ancient Oriental Civilization 37 (Chicago: University of Chicago Press, 1974), 27 (translated "chess"); Erik Hornung, *Das Totenbuch der Ägypter* (Zürich: Artemis, 1990), 59, illustration on 60. This New Kingdom text derives from the older Middle Kingdom Coffin Text 335.

31. See Peter A. Piccione, "The Gaming Episode in the *Tale of Setne Khamwas* as Religious Metaphor," in *For His Ka,* 197–204.

32. The layout and artistic style of the facsimiles match those of the date of the manuscripts that they come from (based on paleographic and onomastic considerations). This tells us only that the manuscripts (assuming that the Book of Abraham comes from a nonextant portion of P. Joseph Smith I+XI+X) come from the Greco–Roman period. For the problems of dating the Joseph Smith Papyri, see John Gee, "Abracadabra, Isaac and Jacob," *Review of Books on the Book of Mormon* 7, no. 1 (1995): 71 n. 272. But the date of a manuscript is not the date of the text, as most works of ancient literature (including historical texts) are attested in manuscripts only much later than they were written.

33. Björkman, "Egyptology and Historical Method," 10.

34. See Paul Y. Hoskisson, "Where Was Ur of the Chaldees?" in *The Pearl of Great Price: Revelations From God,* ed. H. Donl Peterson and Charles D. Tate Jr. (Provo, Utah: Religious Studies Center, 1989), 121, 132 n. 5. More recent editions of the LDS Bible Dictionary eliminate the dates for Abraham entirely, as does the Church's "Guía para el Estudio de las Escrituras," 43. For the generally accepted dates for Abraham, see John Bright, *A History of Israel,* 3d ed. (Philadelphia: Westminster, 1981), 77–87 (Middle Bronze Age); J. J. Bimson, "Archaeological Data and the Dating of the Patriarchs," *Essays on the Patriarchal Narratives,* 53–89 (transition between MBI and MBII); Amihai Mazar, *Archaeology of the Land of the Bible 10,000–586 B.C.E.* (New York: Doubleday, 1990), 224–26 (MBII).

35. Mazar, *Land of the Bible,* 224–26; cf. Bright, *A History of Israel,* 85–86. For archaeological datings and synchronisms we rely on Mazar. Slightly different synchronisms are proposed in Redford, *Egypt, Canaan, and Israel,* for reasons that we find unconvincing; they are nevertheless within a reasonable period of each other. Other radical redatings proposed are completely unconvincing.

36. Mazar, *Land of the Bible,* 193–96. The correlation is between the Twelfth Dynasty and MB IIA (ca. 2000–1800 B.C.), the Thirteenth Dynasty and MB IIB (ca. 1750–1650 B.C.), and the Second Intermediate Period and MB IIC (ca. 1650–1550 B.C.). Fifteenth Dynasty Egyptian scarabs have been found in MB IIC contexts at Tell el-Ajjul, Tell el-Far'ah, Jericho, Gezer, Lachish.

37. For convenience, in Egyptian dates, we use John Baines and Jaromír Málek, *Atlas of Ancient Egypt* (New York: Facts on File, 1980), 36–37. This is within a few years of Grimal, 389–95, and Hallo and Simpson, *The Ancient Near East,* 299–302. These

are also within about thirty years of William C. Hayes, "Egypt—To the End of the Twentieth Dynasty," *Cambridge Ancient History,* 1.1:173–93.

38. For Mesopotamian dates, we use J. A. Brinkman, "Mesopotamian Chronology of the Historical Period," in A. Leo Oppenheim, *Ancient Mesopotamia: Portrait of a Dead Civilization,* 2d ed. (Chicago: University of Chicago Press, 1977), 335–48; additionally, for dates from Classical sources, we rely on *The Oxford Classical Dictionary,* 2d ed., ed. N. G. L. Hammond and H. H. Scullard (Oxford: Clarendon, 1970).

39. The written sources are mostly imports from Mesopotamia and Egypt; there are, however, 148 tablets from level VII at Alalakh dating to the Old Babylonian period; see D. J. Wiseman, *The Alalakh Tablets* (London: The British Institute of Archaeology at Ankara No. 2, 1953); Wiseman, "Supplementary Copies of Alalakh Tablets," *Journal of Cuneiform Studies* 8 (1954): 1–30.

40. Cyrus H. Gordon, "Where Is Abraham's Ur?" *Biblical Archaeology Review* 3, no. 2 (June 1977): 20.

41. Summary of the evidence for the opinion as well as contrary evidence may be found in Hoskisson, "Where Was Ur of the Chaldees?" 119–36.

42. See Hoskisson, "Where Was Ur of the Chaldees?" 123–27.

43. Cyrus H. Gordon, "Abraham and the Merchants of Ura," *Journal of Near Eastern Studies* 17, no. 1 (1958): 30. We do not agree with all of Gordon's contentions (Ḫaldi, for instance, was actually one of the gods of the Urartians). Nor can we accept Gordon's dating of the patriarchal narratives to the Amarna period; our own dating is outlined above.

44. Robert Martin-Achard, *Actualité d'Abraham,* Bibliothèque Théologique (Neuchâtel: Delachaux et Niestlé, 1969), 13.

45. Hoskisson, "Where Was Ur of the Chaldees?" 128–29.

46. The evidence and scholarly consensus has been gathered in Hoskisson, "Where Was Ur of the Chaldees?" 134 n. 24.

47. Giovanni Pettinato, *Ebla: A New Look at History,* trans. C. Faith Richardson (Baltimore: Johns Hopkins University Press, 1991), 213. We have listed all the towns given by Pettinato that are at least as close phonetically as Úri[ki]-ma, even those like BÀD-EN (=u₉–ru₁₂) where a literal reading of the signs as Sumerian "wall of the lord" might make more sense (this is the most egregiously dubious example). Advocates of placing Ur of the Chaldees at Tell el-Muqayyar (=Úri[ki]-ma) need to seriously deal with the phonetic arguments presented in Hoskisson, 123–24, 134 nn. 24–25. The candidates here are at least as close phonetically as Tell el-Muqayyar, and some of them much better (e.g., Úr). We are in favor of tighter controls on the phonetics, but if Úri[ki]-ma is included on phonetic grounds, these other candidates should also be considered as equally plausible.

48. Alalakh Tablet 56 line 8, in Wiseman, *The Alalakh Tablets,* pl. XIV.

49. Wiseman, *Alalakh Tablets,* 157 lists this as occurring on two tablets, Alalakh Tablets 105 (contract of Warad-Kubi) and 162 (census list), but the published version of Alalakh Tablet 105, in Wiseman, "Supplementary Copies of Alalakh Tablets," 9, has no such town.

50. Spelled [ur]uU-ra-e; RS 17.335+379+381+235 (reign of Niqmepa), in Jean Nougayrol, *Le palais royal d'Ugarit IV: Textes accadiens des archives sud* (Paris: Imprimerie Nationale, 1956), 73, planche XLIV.

51. RS 17.130, (with duplicates 17.461 and 18.03, reign of Niqmepa) in ibid., 103–5; Gordon, "Abraham and the Merchants of Ura," 28–29.

52. Brinkman, *A Political History,* 3, notes that for this four-hundred-year period of history (1158–722 B.C.) there are only about two hundred sources of any type. Before 722 B.C., only eighteen Chaldeans are mentioned by name; ibid., 265.

53. Following the analysis of Brinkman, *A Political History,* 265–66. Of the eighteen Chaldeans mentioned by name, fourteen are Akkadian, "showing that the Chaldean tribes—or at least their leaders—had rapidly become assimilated to Babylonian ways. Four names (Zabdi-il, Abdi-il, Jadi'-ilu, and Adinu) seem to be West Semitic as is the tribal name Jakin."

54. "*šu-ri-bat* GIŠ.TUKUL.MEŠ-*a* KUR *kal-du ú-sa-ḫ i-ip*" (my weapon waxed great; I laid the land of the Chaldeans low). AKA 352 iii 24, in A. Kirk Grayson, *Assyrian Rulers of the Early First Millennium BC* I (1114–859 BC), The Royal Inscriptions of Mesopotamia: Assyrian Periods 2 (Toronto, 1991), 214. Brinkman, *A Political History,* 260; Brinkman, "Merodach-Baladan II," *Studies Presented to A. Leo Oppenheim* (Chicago: Oriental Institute, 1964), 8 n. 8.

55. Brinkman, "Merodach-Baladan II," 8; Brinkman, *A Political History,* 260. The total number of Kaldu tribes known is five; Brinkman, "Notes on Arameans and Chaldeans in Southern Babylonia in the Early Seventh Century B.C.," *Orientalia* n.s. 46 (1977): 305–9.

56. Brinkman, *A Political History,* 261–62.

57. Ibid., 262.

58. "lúKal-dà-a-a a-šib qé-reb ida-gam-me" Sennacherib Cylinder C III.52–57, conveniently in Rykle Borger, *Babylonisch-Assyrische Lesestücke,* 2d ed., Analecta Orientalia 54 (Rome: Pontifical Biblical Institute, 1979), 1:77, 2:330; for the historical setting of this campaign see Brinkman, "Merodach-Baladan II," 26–27.

59. Overview in Joan Oates, *Babylon,* rev. ed. (London: Thames and Hudson, 1986), 111–14, 126–35; see now Grant Frame, *Babylonia 689–627 B.C.: A Political History* (Istanbul: Nederlands Historisch-Archaeologisch Instituut, 1992), 36–43.

60. See Roland G. Kent, *Old Persian,* American Oriental Series 33, ed. James B. Pritchard (New Haven: American Oriental Society, 1953), 116–57, esp. 143 n. 53.

61. Xenophon, *Anabasis* V.5.17.

62. Xenophon, *Anabasis* IV.3.4.

63. Xenophon, *Cyropaedia* III.1.34.

64. The phrase *seers and healers* comes from Homer, *Odyssey* XVII.384, and forms the basis of Walter Burkert's illuminating study of the spread of Near Eastern (mainly Babylonian) culture throughout the Greek world; for our purposes, see Walter Burkert, *The Orientalizing Revolution: Near Eastern Influence on Greek Culture in the Early Archaic Age,* trans. Margaret E. Pinder and Walter Burkert (Cambridge, Mass.: Harvard University Press, 1992), 41–87.

65. Juvenal, *Satires* VI.552–81; cf. Horace, *Carmina* I.11: "*nec Babylonios temptaris numeros.*"

66. For the phonetic justification, see Hoskisson, "Where Was Ur of the Chaldees?" 125.

67. See the usage in Jer. 24:5; 25:12; 50:1, 8, 25, 45; 51:4, 24, 35, 54; Ezek. 1:3; 12:13; Dan. 9:1; cf. Marcus Jastrow, *A Dictionary of the Targumim, the Talmud Babli and Yerushalmi, and the Midrashic Literature* (New York: Traditional Press, n.d.), 1:675.

68. See the usage in Ezek. 23:14; Dan. 2:2–4; cf. R. Payne Smith, *A Compendious Syriac Dictionary* (Oxford: Clarendon, 1903), 215, s.v. *'akled, kaldāy, kaldāyuwtā'.*

69. *The Oxford English Dictionary,* s.v. "Chaldaic," "Chaldaical," "Chaldaism," "Chaldaize," "Chalday," "Chaldic," "Chaldean," "Chaldeanizing," "Chaldee," "Chaldeish," and "Chaldaeism."

70. The decipherment of cuneiform is laid out instructively in Johannes Friedrich, *Extinct Languages* (New York: Dorset, 1957), 29–86. The real decipherment of Akkadian did not begin until the publication of the Behustan inscription by Henry Rawlinson in 1846 and the excavations of Layard at Niniveh in 1845, both after the death of Joseph Smith so the current usage of the term is not the same as in Joseph Smith's day.

71. An overview of the process is in Hoskisson, "Where Was Ur of the Chaldees?" 121–23.

72. Kitchen, "Sinuhe: Scholarly Method versus Trendy Fashion," 56–59; Janssen, *De traditioneele egyptische autobiografie.*

73. Abraham comes from the Syro–Palestinian area, not Egypt, and there is no reason why his autobiography should follow Egyptian norms.

74. Benjamin R. Foster, *Before the Muses: An Anthology of Akkadian Literature* (Bethesda, Md.: CDL, 1993), 1:104–5, 109–12.

75. On the statue of Idrimi. Translation of the statue may be found in A. Leo Oppenheim, "Babylonian and Assyrian Historical Texts," in *Ancient Near Eastern Texts Relating to the Old Testament,* 3d ed., ed. James B. Pritchard (Princeton: Princeton University Press, 1969), 557–58.

76. E. Jan Wilson, *The Cylinders of Gudea: Transliteration, Translation and Index,* Alter Orient und Altes Testament 244 (Kevelaer: Butzon & Bercker and Neukirchen-Vluyn: Neukirchener, 1996), 18–127.

77. Atrahasis I–III, in Foster, *Before the Muses,* 1:169–72, 177–78. For fuller bibliography, see below, n. 80.

78. Coffin Texts 89, 98–101, 103–5, 107, in Adriaan de Buck, *The Egyptian Coffin Texts* (Chicago: University of Chicago Press, 1935–61), 2:55–59, 92–105, 109–15, 118–20.

79. See the comments in Foster, *Before the Muses,* 1:52.

80. This is the Atrahasis legend; see W. G. Lambert and A. R. Millard, *Babylonian Literary Texts,* Cuneiform Texts from Babylonian Tablets in the British Museum 46 (London: British Museum, 1965), pls. I–XXVII; W. G. Lambert and A. R. Millard, *Atra-ḫasīs: The Babylonian Story of the Flood* (Oxford: Clarendon, 1969); Foster, 1:158–201; Stephanie Dalley, *Myths from Mesopotamia: Creation, The Flood, Gilgamesh, and Others* (Oxford: Oxford University Press, 1989), 1–38.

81. For Egyptian examples, see Lichtheim, *Ancient Egyptian Literature,* 1:131–33; for Mesopotamian examples, see Foster, *Before the Muses,* 1:118–19, 130.

82. Kitchen, "Sinuhe: Scholarly Method versus Trendy Fashion," 60.

83. The Book of Abraham is incomplete and the full text as translated by Joseph Smith was not published; see H. Donl Peterson, *The Pearl of Great Price: A History and Commentary* (Salt Lake City: Deseret Book, 1987), 45; Peterson, "Book of Abraham: Translation and Publication of the Book of Abraham," in *Encyclopedia of Mormonism,* ed. Daniel H. Ludlow (New York: Macmillan, 1992), 1:134.

84. The Middle Bronze Age texts from Alalakh also suggest a cultural melting pot and come from a range of languages; see Wiseman, *The Alalakh Tablets,* 125–53.

85. Cf. Millard, "Methods of Studying," 40.

86. For our purposes, the relevant languages are Hebrew, Akkadian, Hurrian, Ugaritic, and Egyptian.

87. *The Chicago Assyrian Dictionary* (Chicago: Oriental Institute, 1956–), 8:45–49, s.v. *kakkabu.*

88. Cyrus H. Gordon, *Ugaritic Handbook,* Analecta Orientalia 25 (Rome: Pontifical Biblical Institute, 1947), 237.

89. Smith, *Syriac Dictionary,* 208.

90. Hans Wehr, *A Dictionary of Modern Written Arabic,* ed. J. Milton Cowan, 3d ed. (Ithaca, N.Y.: Spoken Language Services, 1976), 846.

91. Thomas O. Lambdin, *Introduction to Classical Ethiopic (Geʾez),* Harvard Semitic Studies 24 (Ann Arbor: Scholars Press, 1978), 410.

92. *Supplement to J. Seixas' Manual Hebrew Grammar, for the Kirtland, Ohio, Theological Institution* (New York: West & Trow, 1835), 1.

93. This form survives into modern Arabic, see Wehr, *Modern Written Arabic*, 784–85.

94. *Chicago Assyrian Dictionary*, 8:68–72, s.v. *kalbu*.

95. Gordon, *Ugaritic Handbook*, 3:238.

96. Smith, *Syriac Dictionary*, 215.

97. Wehr, *Modern Written Arabic*, 836.

98. Lambdin, *Classical Ethiopic*, 409.

99. Wehr, *Modern Written Arabic*, 784–85.

100. *Chicago Assyrian Dictionary*, 8:72, s.v. *kalbu* 2; cf. 8:71, s.v. *kalbu* 1f.

101. Smith, *Syriac Dictionary*, 215.

102. Wehr, *Modern Written Arabic*, 836.

103. It is worth noting that of the words listed in the two volumes of Emmanuel Laroche, *Glossaire de la langue Hourrite*, 2 vols. (= *Revue Hittite et Asianique* 34–35 [1976–77]) (Paris: Klincksieck, 1976–77), only about one fourth of them have any sort of definition attached to them, and many of those are loanwords from Akkadian.

104. From the Rosetta Stone, we know that the Egyptians called them the *mdw-nṯr*, literally the "god's speech"; see Raymond O. Faulkner, *A Concise Dictionary of Middle Egyptian* (Oxford: Griffith Institute, 1962), 122. The English word "hieroglyphs" is simply borrowed from Greek. What "hieroglyphs" might have been in a comparatively well-known language like Akkadian is unknown.

105. N.B. The phrase "god of X" is an epexegetical, "explanatory" genitive and usually means "god X."

106. John M. Lundquist, "Was Abraham at Ebla? A Cultural Background of the Book of Abraham (Abraham 1 and 2)," in *Studies in Scripture, Vol. 2: The Pearl of Great Price*, ed. Robert L. Millet and Kent P. Jackson (Salt Lake City: Randall, 1985), 232, citing Anton Deimel, *Pantheon Babylonicum oder Keilschriftkatalog der Babylonischen Götternamen* (Rome: Pontifical Biblical Institute, 1950), 48.

107. Lundquist, "Was Abraham at Ebla?" 232, citing Deimel, *Pantheon Babylonicum oder Keilschriftkatalog*, 10.

108. Lundquist, "Was Abraham at Ebla?" 232, explained this as ^{d}*Ma-mi-ḫi*-rat citing Deimel, *Pantheon Babylonicum oder Keilschriftkatalog*, 69. This, however, is a misreading of the *canal* name ^{d}*Ma-mi-šar-rat;* see Anton Deimel, *Pantheon Babylonicum: Nomina deorum e textibus cuneiformibus excerpta et ordine alphabetico* (Rome: Pontifical Biblical Institute, 1914), 172; Edmond Sollberger, *Ur Excavations Texts VIII: Royal Inscriptions Part II* (London: British Museum, 1965), 19; Dietz

Otto Edzard, "Mami-šarrat," _Reallexikon der Assyriologie_ (Berlin: de Gruyter, 1932–), 7:329.

109. Lundquist, "Was Abraham at Ebla?" 232, suggests $^d Kur$-ra-$\check{s}u$-ur_4-ur_4, citing Deimel, _Pantheon Babylonicum oder Keilschriftkatalog,_ 75. This, however, is glossed in AN $^d An$-num K 4339 iv 20 as $^d En$-uru-mu $\check{s}\acute{a}$ $^{uru} Kar$-$^d Nin$-$urta$ "Enurumu of Karninurta [a place near Nippur in Middle Babylonian times];" see _Cuneiform Texts from Babylonian Tablets, &c., in the British Museum,_ pt. 25 (London: British Museum, 1909), pl. 14; Khaled Nashef, _Répertoire Géographique des Textes Cunéiformes_ (Wiesbaden: Reichert, 1977–93), 5:159.

110. It belongs to an official under the reign of Amenhotep I (1525–1504 B.C.); for his tomb biography, see Kurt Sethe, _Urkunden der 18. Dynastie,_ Urkunden des ägyptischen Altertums 4 (Leipzig: Hinrichs, 1906), 45–49. For the use of Egyptian _s_ for Semitic _š_ in the New Kingdom, see James E. Hoch, _Semitic Words in Egyptian Texts of the New Kingdom and Third Intermediate Period_ (Princeton: Princeton University Press, 1994), 436.

111. Alalakh Tablet 254 line 10, in Wiseman, "Supplementary Copies of Alalakh Tablets," 18.

112. Lundquist, "Was Abraham at Ebla?" 234–35; Hoskisson, "Where Was Ur of the Chaldees?" 136 n. 44; John Gee, "A Tragedy of Errors," _Review of Books on the Book of Mormon_ 4 (1992): 115–16 n. 64; Gee, "Abracadabra, Isaac and Jacob," 27 n. 28. Stephen E. Thompson, "Egyptology and the Book of Abraham," _Dialogue_ 28, no. 1 (spring 1995): 157 n. 67, complains that it is attested too early, but his argument is vitiated by three points: (1) the Book of Abraham mentions only the "plain of Olishem" (Abr. 1:10), not an inhabited place; (2) continuity of place names in the area is not unknown, e.g., Aleppo; (3) there is Middle Kingdom Egyptian evidence for the name (presented below).

113. For the alternate readings of the signs for the time and place, see Wolfram von Soden, _Das akkadische Syllabar,_ Analecta Orientalia 27 (Rome: Pontifical Biblical Institute, 1948), 43, 73, and compare the use of the _šé_ sign in a slightly later inscription by the Hurrian ruler Arishen (or Atalshen—the reading has not quite been decided though it is probably Hurrian _ari-šen_ "grant a brother"), in François Thureau-Dangin, "Tablette de Samarra," _Revue d'Assyriologie et d'Archéologie Orientale_ 9, no. 1 (1912): 1–4 (note the spelling A-RI-šé-en); for the historical background see Gernot Wilhelm, _The Hurrians,_ trans. Jennifer Barnes (Warminster: Aris & Phillips, 1989), 9; for the linguistic elements of the name, see Laroche, _La langue Hourrite,_ 1:52, 2:225–26.

It has been proposed recently that the signs U and U$_4$ (UD) were pronounced as /o/ in the Old Babylonian period; Aage Westenholz, "The Phoneme /o/ in Akkadian," _Zeitschrift für Assyriologie und Voderasiatische Archäologie_ 81 (1991): 10–19. Later Hurrian usage (which also is not always consistent) of the sign U to indicate /o/ during the end of the Kassite period is also intriguing; Gernot Wilhelm, "Hurritische Lexikographie und Grammatik: Die hurritisch-hethitische Bilingue aus Boğazköy," _Orientalia_ 61, no. 2 (1992): 124–25. Westenholz also shows that Old Babylonian scribes were not consistent in this and that Ú was also used for /o/ as well. This confusion is confirmed in the consistent use of U₄ as a phonetic gloss for the sign Ú in Proto-Ea 230, in *MSL XIV,* ed. Miguel Civil (Rome: Pontifical Biblical Institute, 1979), 41. In Old Babylonian times the usage of Ú for /o/ is at least possible; that is, a foreign word using an /o/ can be written with a Ú. Given this background, one could go so far as to propose a Semitic etymology for Olishem: Olishem might have once been Āli-Šem "the city of Shem." The name undergoing the Canaanite shift would have produced Olishem and then, its etymology obscured, transcribed in the Rim-Sin inscription as a phonetic *Ú-li-šé-em.* This etymology is, however, completely hypothetical.

114. Narâm-Sin b 5.2.13 (= UET I 275.2.13), in Hans Hirsch, "Die Inschriften der Könige von Agade," *Archiv für Orientforschung* 20 (1963): 74; English translation in Foster, *Before the Muses,* 1:52–53; Pettinato, *Ebla: A New Look at History,* 33.

115. Translation by Foster, *Before the Muses,* 1:52.

116. Kurt Sethe, *Die Ächtung feindlicher Fürsten, Völker und Dinge auf altägyptischen Tongefässscherben des Mittleren Reiches,* Abhandlungen der Preussischen Akademie der Wissenschaften Philosophisch-historische Klasse 1926, no. 5 (Berlin: Akademie der Wissenschaften, 1926), 38, Tafel 12 b5, read perhaps *irissym* (restored through duplicates). Due to the damaged condition of the texts we cannot be certain. For the date of the texts, see Georges Posener, "Ächtungstexte," in *Lexikon der Ägyptologie,* ed. Wolfgang Helck and Eberhard Otto (Wiesbaden: Harrassowitz, 1975–89), 1:68.

117. Sethe, *Die Ächtung feindlicher Fürsten, Völker und Dinge,* 53, Tafel 18 e27–28. This is normally taken as a defective writing of **'Urušalimum;* ibid.; Hoch, *Semitic Words in Egyptian Texts,* 493.

118. The number of names attested at Level VII at Alalakh is very modest. Cities attested there seem generally to have been in the general vicinity of Alalakh. Countries or lands (as indicated by the KUR determinative [Sumerian for "land"] rather than the URU determinative [Sumerian for "city"]) are limited to Awirashe, Alalakh, Alashia (Cyprus), Ebla, Karkamis, Rianni, Ugarit, and the lands of the Amorite, Gutti(ians), and Hurri(ans). Surprisingly, there is no mention of Egypt, even though there are clear indications of Egyptian influence at Alalakh.

119. Inscription of Weni 13–32, in Kurt Sethe, *Urkunden des Alten Reichs,* 2d ed., Urkunden des ägyptischen Altertums 1 (Leipzig: Hinrichs, 1932), 101–5; Lichtheim, *Ancient Egyptian Literature,* 1:19–20; see also Redford, *Egypt, Canaan, and Israel,* 54–55, 64.

120. Gabriella Scandone Matthiae, "Vasi iscritti di Chefren e Pepi I nel Palazzo Reale G di Ebla," *Studi Eblaiti* 1 (1979): 33–43; Paolo Matthiae, *I tesori di Ebla,* 2d ed. (Rome: Editori Laterza, 1985), tav. 36; Paolo Matthiae, *Ebla: Alle origini della civiltà urbana,* Frances Pinnock, and Gabriella Scandone Matthiae, *Ebla: Alle origini della civiltà urbana* (Milan: Electa, 1995), 283, 307.

121. Gabriella Scandone Matthiae, "I vasi egiziani in pietra dal Palazzo Reale G," *Studi Eblaiti* 4 (1981): 99–127. The stone vessels from palace G date from the fourth

to the sixth dynasty. No contact here need be supposed during Egypt's First Intermediate Period.

122. Gabriella Scandone Matthiae, "Un oggetto faraonico della XIII dinastia dalla 'Tomba del signore dei Capridi'," *Studia Eblaiti* 1 (1979): 119–28; Paolo Matthiae, *I tesori di Ebla,* tav. 80; Matthiae, Pinnock, and Matthiae, *Ebla: Alle origini della civiltà urbana,* 464–65, 478; Pettinato, *Ebla: A New Look at History,* 28; Harvey Weiss, ed., *Ebla to Damascus: Art and Archaeology of Ancient Syria* (Washington, D.C.: Smithsonian Institution Traveling Exhibition Service, 1985), 239–40.

123. Discussed in Redford, *Egypt, Canaan, and Israel,* 80–81.

124. Sinuhe B 94–95, in Georg Möller, *Hieratische Lesestücke für den akademischen Gebrauch* (Leipzig: Hinrichs, 1927), 1:11; Lichtheim, *Ancient Eyptian Literature,* 1:227; Redford, *Egypt, Canaan, and Israel,* 81–82.

125. Sesostris I, Amenemhet III, and Amenemhet IV are attested at Byblos. See Posener, "Syria and Palestine," *Cambridge Ancient History,* 1.2:532, 545, 590.

126. Posener, "Syria and Palestine," 545.

127. Amenemhet I, Sesostris I, Sesostris III, and Amenemhet III all claim Asiatic campaigns. See Posener, "Syria and Palestine," 537–38; Redford, *Egypt, Canaan, and Israel,* 77.

128. Posener, "Syria and Palestine," 538–43.

129. Françoise Bisson de la Roque, *Le trésor de Tod* (Cairo: Institut Français d'Archéologie Orientale, 1950); Posener, "Syria and Palestine," 543–44; Grimal, *Ancient Egypt,* 165; Gardiner, *Egypt of the Pharaohs,* 132. Unfortunately, the cylinder-seals are not adequately published.

130. For the text, see Roland Koch, *Die Erzählung des Sinuhe* (Brussels: Fondation Égyptologique Reine Élisabeth, 1990); Lichtheim, *Ancient Eyptian Literature,* 1:222–35; for a discussion of the historical implications of the story, see Redford, *Egypt, Canaan, and Israel,* 83–87.

131. Posener, "Syria and Palestine," 545–46.

132. Ibid., 546.

133. Examples of the Egyptian influence at Alalakh come from Level VII (Middle Bronze II period) and include many Egyptian and Egyptianized sealings; see Dominique Collon, *The Seal Impressions from Tell Atchana/Alalakh,* Alter Orient und Altes Testament 27 (Kevelaer: Butzon & Bercker, and Neukirchen-Vluyn: Neukirchener, 1975), 74–83, 185–86, pls. XXVII–XXVIII. Only one of the Egyptianizing sealings comes from Level IV (Late Bronze Age).

134. K. A. Kitchen, "Byblos, Egypt, and Mari in the Early Second Millennium B.C.," *Orientalia* n.s. 36 (1967): 40; Posener, "Syria and Palestine," 546–47; Redford, *Egypt, Canaan, and Israel,* 37–43, 81, esp. n. 64; Gardiner, *Egypt of the Pharaohs,* 132–33; scarab catalogue in William A. Ward, *Egypt and the East Mediterranean World 2200–1900 B.C.: Studies in Egyptian Foreign Relations during the First*

Intermediate Period (Beirut: American University of Beirut, 1971), 137–39, but since MBII corresponds to the Twelfth Dynasty, his chronological arguments can be safely ignored.

135. Redford, *Egypt, Canaan, and Israel*, 77–78, 81.

136. Posener, "Syria and Palestine," 545; Redford, *Egypt, Canaan, and Israel*, 81.

137. Redford, *Egypt, Canaan, and Israel*, 81.

138. For the slaves, see Redford, *Egypt, Canaan, and Israel*, 78; the other booty come from Sami Farag, "Un inscription memphite de la XIIe dynastie," *Revue d'Égyptologie* 32 (1980): 75–82, pls. 3–5; Redford, *Egypt, Canaan, and Israel*, 79.

139. Posener, "Syria and Palestine," 549–50.

140. Michel Chauveau, "Montouhotep et les babyloniens," *Bulletin de l'Institut Français d'Archéologie Orientale* 91 (1991): 147–53. Tales of this sort are seen to have been the source of Manetho's history; Donald B. Redford, *Pharaonic King-Lists, Annals and Day-Books: A Contribution to the Study of the Egyptian Sense of History* (Mississauga: Benben, 1986), 318–21, 333–37.

141. Cf. D. J. Wiseman, "Abraham Reassessed," in *Essays on the Patriarchal Narratives*, 141–45.

142. Gordon, "Abraham and the Merchants of Ura," 30. This, of course, is true of time periods other than those advocated by Gordon.

143. Postgate, *Early Mesopotamia*, 46–49; Klengel, *Syria 3000 to 300* B.C., 42. The Middle Bronze Age IIA period is characterized by the absence of any state over the area of Syria. During the MB IIB–C periods, there was a series of small regional centers such as Yamhad, Qatna, Karkamish, Urshum, Ugarit, and Gubla/Byblos that dominated their local area but held no overarching political hegemony; ibid., 44–80.

144. Mazar, *Land of the Bible*, 176–78, 197–98.

145. See the following selections from a series of articles: Michael B. Rowton, "Urban Autonomy in a Nomadic Environment," *Journal of Near Eastern Studies* 32 (1973): 201–15; Michael B. Rowton, "Dimorphic Structure and the Problem of the 'APIRÛ-'IBRÎM," *Journal of Near Eastern Studies* 35, no. 1 (January 1976): 13–20; Michael B. Rowton, "Enclosed Nomadism," *Journal of the Economic and Social History of the Orient* 17 (1974): 1–30. It also matches the picture from Egypt during the Middle Kingdom, see Posener, "Syria and Palestine," 550–58.

146. Postgate, *Early Mesopotamia*, 106–8, 255; A. Leo Oppenheim, *Ancient Mesopotamia: Portrait of a Dead Civilization*, rev. ed., ed. Erica Reiner (Chicago: University of Chicago Press, 1977), 75–76; Oates, *Babylon*, 68–70.

147. William C. Hayes, *A Papyrus of the Late Middle Kingdom in the Brooklyn Museum*, Publications of the Department of Egyptian Art (New York: Brooklyn Museum, 1955), 92–103. See also P. Kahun I.1 10–11, in F. Ll. Griffith, *Hieratic Papyri from Kahun and Gurob* (London: Quaritch, 1898), 2, pl. XII.

148. Hugh Nibley, *The Message of the Joseph Smith Papyri: An Egyptian Endowment* (Salt Lake City: Deseret Book, 1975), 53.

149. Alan H. Gardiner, *Egyptian Grammar,* 3d ed. (Oxford: Griffith Institute, 1957), 475, sign-list I3.

150. From the vignette to Book of the Dead 30B, in the papyrus of Hunefer (BM EA9901, sheet 3), conveniently in Ian Shaw and Paul Nicholson, *The Dictionary of Ancient Egypt* (New York: Abrams, 1995), 30, but the photograph is reversed and the Book of the Dead spell is misidentified; see also Bengt Julius Peterson, "Der Totenfresser in den Darstellungen der Psychostasie des altägyptischen Totenbuches," *Orientalia Suecana* 10 (1961): 31–40, esp. 35.

151. A popular overview of the Egyptian view of the crocodile may be found in Dorothea Arnold, *The Metropolitan Museum of Art Bulletin: An Egyptian Bestiary* 52, no. 4 (spring 1995): 32.

152. Gardiner, *Egyptian Grammar,* 475, sign-list I3.

153. Hans Bonnet, *Reallexikon der ägyptischen Religionsgeschichte* (Berlin: de Gruyter, 1952), 756.

154. Lichtheim, *Ancient Egyptian Literature,* 1:201.

155. PT 317 §§507–10, in Kurt Sethe, *Die altaegyptischen Pyramidentexte* (Leipzig: Hinrichs, 1908–22), 1:260–61; Lichtheim, *Ancient Egyptian Literature,* 1:40 (capitalization normalized). Commentary and discussion of syncretization of Sobek with Min in Hartwig Altenmüller, *Die Texte zum Begräbnisritual in den Pyramiden des Alten Reiches,* Ägyptologische Abhandlungen 24 (Wiesbaden: Harrassowitz, 1972), 218–20.

156. P. D'Orbiney 9/9–12/7, in Alan H. Gardiner, *Late-Egyptian Stories,* Bibliotheca Aegyptiaca 1 (Brussels: Fondation Égyptologique Reine Élisabeth, 1932), 19–22; translation in Lichtheim, *Ancient Egyptian Literature,* 2:207–8.

157. P. Westcar 1/20–4/10, in Simpson, *The Literature of Ancient Egypt: An Anthology,* 16–18.

158. William Kelly Simpson, *Papyrus Reisner I* (Boston: Museum of Fine Arts, 1963), 89–90; cf. Simpson, *Papyrus Reisner II* (Boston: Museum of Fine Arts, 1965), 59, and Simpson, *Papyrus Reisner IV* (Boston: Museum of Fine Arts, 1986), 41–42. The Reisner papyri date to the reign of Sesostris I; see ibid., 7.

159. Hayes, *A Papyrus of the Late Middle Kingdom,* 23–24.

160. Jürgen von Beckerath, *Handbuch der ägyptischen Königsnamen,* Münchner Ägyptologische Studien 20, ed. Hans Wolfgang Müller (Munich: Deutscher Kunstverlag, 1984), 67, 159, 200.

161. Ibid., 67–73, 160, 201–11; Shaw and Nicholson, *Dictionary of Ancient Egypt,* 273, count eight rulers.

162. von Beckerath, *Königsnamen,* 81–82, 161, 220–22.

163. Gathered together in Jean Yoyotte, "Le Soukhos de la Maréotide et d'autres cultes régionaux du dieu-crocodile d'apres les cylindres du moyen empire," *Bulletin de l'Institut Français d'Archéologie Orientale* 56 (1957): 81–95; and Gérard Godron, "Deux objets du moyen empire mentionnant Sobek," *Bulletin de l'Institut Français d'Archéologie Orientale* 63 (1965): 197–200.

164. Dieter Arnold, *Die Tempel Ägyptens: Götterwohnungen, Baudenkmäler, Kultstätten* (Zürich: Artemis & Winkler, 1992), 97–98.

165. Dieter Arnold, *Die Tempel Ägyptens*, 186.

166. Matthiae, Pinnock, and Matthiae, *Ebla: Alle origini della civiltà urbana*, 458, 476 (image of Osiris with atef crown), 459, 477 (image of Sobek), 460, 477 (images of Hathor and Horus). All of these artifacts were found in area P, EdVII7i-ii-iii, in the Settentrionale palace L.4070, and are dated by the archaeologists to MBII (1750–1650 B.C.). The artwork is Middle Kingdom in style.

167. Thompson, "Egyptology and the Book of Abraham," 156–60; the quote is from 160 n. 77.

168. The incident is fairly famous and references to it may be found in Gardiner, *Egypt of the Pharaohs*, 371; Alan B. Lloyd, "The Late Period, 664–323 B.C.," in *Ancient Egypt: A Social History*, 317; translation of the relevant document may be found in H. L. Ginsberg, "Aramaic Letters," in *Ancient Near Eastern Texts relating to the Old Testament*, 491–92.

169. Cairo JE 35256 lines 5–6, in Anthony Leahy, "A Protective Measure at Abydos in the Thirteenth Dynasty," *Journal of Egyptian Archaeology* 75 (1989): 42–43; Wolfgang Helck, *Historisch-biographische Texte der 2. Zwischenzeit und neue Texte der 18. Dynastie* (Wiesbaden: Harrassowitz, 1975), 18–19; Frank T. Miosi, *A Reading Book of Second Intermediate Period Texts* (Mississauga: Benben, 1981), 1–3. The decree seems to have been effective until Roman times; Leahy, "A Protective Measure," 54. Other examples of punishment by burning are gathered by Anthony Leahy, "Death by Fire in Ancient Egypt," *Journal of the Economic and Social History of the Orient* 27 (1984): 199–206.

170. Christophe Barbotin and J.-J. Clère, "L'inscription de Sésostris Ier à Tôd," *Bulletin de l'Institut Français d'Archéologie Orientale* 91 (1991): 8–11 and fig. 3.

171. Robert K. Ritner, *The Mechanics of Ancient Egyptian Magical Practice*, Studies in Ancient Oriental Civilization 54 (Chicago: Oriental Institute, 1993), 153–54, 162–63; for the date of the find, see also Posener, "Ächtungstexte," 1:68.

172. See John Gee, "The Role of the Book of Abraham in the Restoration" (Provo, Utah: F.A.R.M.S., 1997).

173. *Gospel Principles* (Salt Lake City: The Church of Jesus Christ of Latter-day Saints, 1981), 89, 91, 263.

174. Other passages cited in basic works include Abr. 3:19 in *Gospel Principles*, 7; Abraham 4–5 in *Gospel Principles*, 27; Abr. 5:7 in *Gospel Principles*, 30.

175. The assumption of the mantle of science by historians and the impact of the theoretical work of Popper and Kuhn is chronicled in Novick, *That Noble Dream,* 31–37, 298–99, 392–96, 524–37, 568–70.

176. Karl R. Popper, *The Open Society and its Enemies,* 5th ed. (New York: Harper & Row, 1966), 2:265.

177. Brinkman, *A Political History,* 1–2.

178. Popper, *The Open Society,* 2:259–60.

179. This, of course, presumes that the scholars have been correct in dating Abraham to the Middle Bronze Age II period, and that Ur of the Chaldees is in northern Syria.

180. John Peters to Franklin S. Spalding, in Franklin S. Spalding, *Joseph Smith, Jr., As a Translator* (Salt Lake City: Arrow, 1912), 28: "Chaldeans and Egyptians are hopelessly mixed together, although as dissimilar and remote in language, religion and locality as are today American and Chinese." This opinion was seconded by Samuel A. B. Mercer, "Joseph Smith as an Interpreter and Translator of Egyptian," *Utah Survey* 1, no. 1 (September 1913): 33: "I challenge any intelligent person who knows Chaldean and Egyptian history to read the first chapter of said book without experiencing the same feeling. Chaldea and Egypt are hopelessly mixed. . . . No one can believe that Abraham made such a blunder in his geography."

181. Posener, "Syria and Palestine," 550, 549; note also the discussion in Redford, *Egypt, Canaan, and Israel,* 76–77.

The Need for Historicity: Why Banishing God from History Removes Historical Obligation

4

Paul Y. Hoskisson

Key historical events in the scriptures require historicity to give substance to our faith. Since the Enlightenment, however, some scholars have proclaimed that the scriptures lack historicity. In the face of these doubts, some have argued that historicity is not necessary for belief. Latter-day Saints should be wary of the misleading arguments of critics and of simplistic solutions to those arguments.

A small group of critics maintain, contrary to Latter-day Saint belief, that it is not necessary to believe in the historicity of central events in the scriptures in order to have scriptural faith. In some extreme cases they also maintain that clinging to the historicity of certain events impedes understanding and development of scriptural faith. For example, one such critic, Thomas L. Thompson, explains that only when people come to understand "that the Bible does not speak about an historical Abraham, then a recognition of this leads us one step further towards an understanding of biblical faith. . . . In fact, we can say that the faith of Israel is not an historical faith, in the sense of a faith based on historical event."[1] Thompson concludes that if we insist on believing in a faith grounded in history, then we "have set up an exceedingly serious barrier to any acceptance of the biblical tradition as constitutive of faith."[2] What he means is that if we insist, for example, that there was a historical Abraham who placed his son on the altar to sacrifice him, then we are making it impossible for people to develop true scriptural faith, at least as he defines faith.

Furthermore, according to Thompson, learning that there never was an Abraham should not bother anyone, because "to learn that what we have believed is not what we should have believed is not to lose our faith."[3] In other words, just because we do not believe in a historical Abraham who entered into a covenant with God and received the promise of posterity, we should not despair. He contends that we should not have believed the scriptural story of Abraham in the first place! Now that we think we have discovered there never was an Abraham and have thereby been enlightened, as his reasoning goes, we would be free to make something entirely new and different out of the Abraham fiction. We could construct a new, spacious edifice without any historical foundation at all in this world, a wondrous building floating in the air.

As Latter-day Saints, we must reject this insidious view of scripture and scriptural faith. In fact, most Latter-day Saints intuit the strong bond that exists between our faith and historical events. Without reservation we acknowledge, as G. Ernest Wright stated for traditional Christianity, that in scriptural faith "everything depends upon whether the central events actually occurred."[4] As faithful members of The Church of Jesus Christ of Latter-day Saints, we declare that in our faith everything depends upon the historicity of what Elder Bruce R. McConkie called the three pillars of eternity—the Creation, the Fall, and the Atonement.[5]

In addition to the three pillars of eternity, I believe there are other key scriptural events that require historicity in order to give substance to our faith, including, among many others, the Flood; the near sacrifice of Isaac by Abraham; Moses' call to be a prophet; the reign of King David; Lehi's journey to the promised land; the resurrection and ascension of Jesus Christ; His visit to the more righteous remnant in the land of Bountiful; the First Vision of Joseph Smith; the return of Moroni; the miraculous translation of the Book of Mormon; and the restoration of the priesthood, the gospel, and the Church in these the latter days, just to name a few.[6] As Latter-day Saints we know, at least through intuition, that our faith rests on the historicity of these events. This essay will, however, focus on only a few of these events;

but the principles outlined will apply equally well to all the scriptural events we hold sacred.

Because I am aware of the scriptural admonition to reason together (D&C 66:7; and 68:1), I have sought to understand and articulate to myself why critics, such as Thomas L. Thompson, are wrong when they contend that historicity is not necessary to develop scriptural faith, and why Latter-day Saints and others are right in insisting that the historicity of certain central, scriptural events is necessary for there to be substance to our faith. The conclusions I have reached, and the reasons for these conclusions, form the basis for this personal essay. While I am solely responsible for the content, I am greatly indebted to friends, colleagues, and former teachers who have planted ideas, patiently listened to my questions, and given me unfettered feedback.[7]

Three Red Herrings

Before embarking on this journey of adding reason to faith, I need to warn about three red herrings. The first red herring would require that there be historical evidence for all events mentioned in scripture. As Latter-day Saints we believe that central scriptural events must be historical, but we do not require historical evidence in order to develop our faith. In most cases, historical evidence is not available at the present and in some cases may not have been available at the time the events occurred. For example, today we cannot find empirical evidence that Joseph Smith went into the woods on that spring day in 1820. Yet after his visit to the woods there would have been evidence that day and for some days to come of Joseph's presence. An astute observer could have verified Joseph's historical presence there. If Joseph had not been in the woods that day or any other spring day in 1820, and that fact could be verified, then great doubt would be cast on the rest of his story about the appearance of the Father and Son to him. Therefore, it is important that Joseph's presence in the woods that day could have been verified at or shortly after the time he went there, even if such evidence is no longer available.

However, even if we could establish empirically that Joseph went into and came out of the woods that day, we would not have proven the most important aspect of his story, namely, that he actually saw the Father and the Son while in the woods. That kind of historical knowledge, which lies outside the realm of empirical verification, comes only from personal revelation, which we as Latter-day Saints joyfully and dutifully seek. Therefore, as Latter-day Saints we do not necessarily seek for historical evidence that Joseph saw the Father and Son in the woods because historical evidence cannot confirm the historicity of the First Vision.[8] Latter-day Saints do not believe that all scripture must be historically verifiable, because the central event in Joseph Smith's early history is not the fact that he went into the woods (historically verifiable), but rather that the Father and Son spoke to him that day (not historically verifiable).

The second red herring proposes that if the historicity of a scriptural event is to stand, every detail of the scriptural record must be historical. Those who proffer this red herring, as A. H. Sayce described the case, insist that "a single error in detail, a single inconsistency, a single exaggeration, a single anachronism, [is] considered sufficient to overthrow the credit of a whole narrative. . . . It [is] expected that an ancient oriental annalist should express himself with the sobriety of a Western European and the precision of a modern man of science."[9] That is, if in the scriptural record of the event there is one tiny detail that is inaccurate or that cannot be historical, then any historicity of that scriptural pericope must be denied. This either/or proposition assumes that there can be no errors, major or minor, in the report of the Word of God, neither in its initial form nor in parallel versions, nor in any subsequent transmission. If there is a mistake, as the assumption goes, then it cannot be historical.

The assumption that there can be no errors in scripture, even minor ones, is called the doctrine of inerrancy. This doctrine began to assert itself in certain areas of Europe where the Reformation took root. "By the beginning of the seventeenth century, the Bible was seen by some Protestants in northern Europe as a deposit of *inerrant information,* including information about scientific questions, which had been dictated by God. Rather than being a record of events in which God was revealed, scripture itself was viewed as infallible knowledge in propositional form verbally imparted by God."[10] The doctrine of inerrancy is a red herring because at first glance inerrancy sounds wonderful. However, Latter-day Saints in general, along with most Christians,[11] reject the doctrine of inerrancy. Indeed, Latter-day Saint scriptures inform us of the struggle that some prophets have had in expressing the thoughts they were impressed to write down. Both Nephi and Moroni, the first and last prophets to write for our Book of Mormon, expressed the fear that their writing was not as powerful as their speaking. As Moroni stated it, "Behold, thou hast not made us mighty in writing. . . . Thou hast also made our words powerful and great, even that we cannot write them; wherefore, when we write we behold our weakness, and stumble because of the placing of our words" (Ether 12:24–25; for Nephi's remarks see 2 Ne. 33:1).

In addition, our scriptures warn us that there may be faults in scripture, particularly by later redactors, but that God is not responsible for such faults (Morm. 8:17).[12] We also believe that while what we have received is sufficient for the moment, there are still many things that God would like to reveal to us (2 Ne. 2:5; 2 Cor. 12:9; 2 Ne. 25:28; Omni 1:11; D&C 17:8; D&C 42:67; D&C 102:23; see also Article of Faith 9). As Latter-day Saints, we have no need to assert the inerrancy or all-inclusive nature of scripture, and therefore we do not feel the need to defend every tittle, jot, word, or phrase.[13] That is why minor inconsistences, incomplete passages, or slight inaccuracies in the scriptural record of central events are not a problem for Latter-day Saints. We are not forced to choose between absolutely inerrant scripture and scripture we cannot trust at all. The doctrine of inerrancy is a red herring that Latter-day Saints can safely ignore.

The third red herring would require us to accept or reject in its totality the historicity of *all* scripture. This either/or choice is a false dichotomy because there are other options. For example, there are scripture passages which presumably lack historicity (they may or may not be historical) but which are nevertheless normative.[14] The parables of the New Testament fall into this category because they often draw their efficacy from real-life experiences but do not necessarily claim to report historical events. Yet most Christians believe the parables to be normative. Therefore, the question for Latter-day Saints is not whether all scripture is historical or not, because parts of scripture lack historicity. The question is, rather, which parts of scripture require historicity in order to add content to our faith. Though there may never be complete unanimity among Latter-day Saints concerning which central events of our scriptures require historicity in order to give substance to our faith, I have suggested above a few scriptural events that Latter-day Saints should accept as historical.

With the dismissal of these three red herrings, I can proceed to the first part of this essay, namely, why Latter-day Saints must reject the conclusion of some biblical critics that the historicity of scriptural events is not necessary to develop faith.

Why Revisionist Critics Are Wrong

It is my hypothesis that two successive factors combined to produce the necessary environment in which, for some critics, historicity became irrelevant to the content of faith. First, the traditional theological concept of God (which Latter-day Saints reject) declares that God is not in this world, i.e., that God is transcendent. Second, the transcendence of God allowed the removal of God from history when, during the Modern Period (of which Latter-day Saints should be skeptical), our Western culture began to grow dependent on rationalism. With God removed from the history in scripture, the historicity of scripture no longer had any relevance for faith.

The transcendence of God entered traditional Christian theology in the early days of the Church Fathers, having been introduced into Christianity from Hellenistic/Greek philosophical concepts. In fact, the Hellenization of the Early Church was a natural process that began at least as early as the death of the Apostles. "The voice of the apostles had scarcely fallen silent when the church faced the need to define the faith in terms that intelligent men could understand. . . . Men can reason, however, only with the knowledge and concepts they have. In the ancient world this meant Hellenic (Greek) philosophy and pagan authors. So Christianity was forced by the need of men and the mission of the church into the world of pagan thought."[15] Under these conditions, the scriptural "conception, for example, of the one God whose kingdom was a universal kingdom and endured throughout all ages, blended with, and passed into, the [Greek] philosophical conception of a Being who was beyond time and space."[16] Thus, in post-Apostolic (i.e., Hellenized) Christianity, God came to be thought of as neither part of this universe nor in this universe. He did not, does not, nor ever will act in mortal time and corporeal space.[17] Instead,

God became "[a] Mind, a form separate from all matter, that is to say, out of contact with it, and not involved with anything that is capable of being acted on."[18]

Between the Renaissance and the beginning of the Enlightenment, the transcendence of God took on new implications. "With Galileo began the development whereby God was to become merely the original creator of the interacting atoms in which resides all subsequent causality. Nature, once created, was considered to be independent and self-sufficient. . . . As attention focused on natural causes, God's role was gradually relegated to that of First Cause."[19] Thus the natural philosophers of the Enlightenment, as expressed by the English virtuosi, could say that "nature is a complete and functioning machine that is not itself striving toward any ends, and God is the original First Cause, not the Final Cause."[20] In this wise, "God became primarily the Designer of the world-machine [the watchmaker], though various attempts were made to find a place for God's continuing activity within a mechanical natural order."[21]

What began in the Modern Period as an attempt to provide rational explanations for Christianity would by the end of the Enlightenment prove to undermine Christianity. Philosophers of the Enlightenment "moved away from the Christ-centered orientation of the Middle Ages and Reformation. 'Rational religion' had been intended as a support for the essentials of Christianity, but by the next century it was to become a substitute for them. Reason, originally a supplement to revelation, began to replace it as the path to knowledge of God. The change did not come about initially by open conflict but by the reinterpretation of Christianity from within."[22] This inevitably led to the view that "the world was no longer seen as the purposeful drama of the Middle Ages or even as the continuing object of providential supervision, as for Newton, but as a set of interacting natural forces. . . . The secularization of knowledge in science, as in other fields, meant that theological ideas, whatever their role elsewhere, were to be excluded from the study of the world."[23]

The result was that God, beginning in the Enlightenment, was also expelled from nature. He had been physically banished from the world when transcendence was imposed on Him many centuries earlier. With the rise of rationalism He was also excluded as a cause or even as a factor when studying about this world. Hume even undermined the argument for God as the First Cause.[24] This Enlightenment wresting of the control of science, with all of its positive and negative consequences, led to the attempts to remove God from the scientific study of nature and also from the study of history.[25] In fact, "God's wisdom was displayed primarily in planning things so that no intervention would be needed. . . . The rule of law, not miraculous intervention, is the chief evidence of God's wisdom."[26]

With God removed from nature and from history, the question then could be raised, "How can God act in a law-abiding world?"[27] How can God, who himself must be law-abiding, interfere in a world that was "assumed to be a complete mechanical system of inflexible cause and effect, governed by exact and absolute laws, so that all future events are inexorably determined"[28] without the necessity of God's intervention? The answer for many Enlightenment philosophers was that God does not interfere in the world order. In fact, many of the leading intellectuals of the Enlightenment, during the height of deism, "saw natural theology used as a substitute for revelation. The sufficiency of reason was confidently affirmed and scripture was assigned a subordinate role."[29]

With God removed from science, banned from history and relegated to being the First Cause, at best, and no longer "the continuing ruler of nature,"[30] scholars were free to ignore God as an ongoing cause of anything that happened in the world, because "all things occur in accordance with inflexible laws of cause and effect,"[31] with or without God being the First Cause.

All that is left is to assume—in good Enlightenment style and with the German Christian theologian Ernst Troeltsch—that "historical events are related by a causal nexus, that is, in a chain of cause and effect"[32] that can be subjected to the stark light of Enlightenment inquiry, for good or for ill. The result is that "there are Gospel critics who reject, on principle, any reports of divine intervention in the affairs of the world, anything that God is reported to have brought about other than what would have happened had only natural, this-worldly influences been involved."[33] Notice how the presupposition prejudices the conclusion: if the Enlightenment allows us to remove God from history, then history can be studied the way the Enlightenment requires. For believers to think that this is progress, as our Enlightenment culture would have us believe, is analogous to C. S.

Lewis' cogent remark that "it is surely absurd to regard as specifically Christian in (Saint Augustine) the acceptance of a *terrain* which had in fact been chosen by the enemy."[34]

Removing God from all history has led to one of the more important maxims of modern biblical criticism. As expressed by Troeltsch, this maxim states, "In the study of history we can arrive only at probability, not certainty."[35] The obvious result of this premise is that anyone who builds faith on the historicity of scriptural events can only be building on probability. Such faith, built on probability, can only be tenuous at best and, as Thomas Thompson would say, a destructive faith at worst. We are supposed to exclaim, "Who would ever want to build religious faith on probability, that is, the historicity of scripture?" Faith ought to be built on something more solid than probability! "We need to find a more sure foundation than historicity!" As Latter-day Saints we want our faith to be built on certainty (see Alma 32), but not solely on the certainties allowed by the Enlightenment. We would reject Troeltsch's premise and the rest of his syllogism, which is based on the Enlightenment extrapolation of the ideas of the transcendence of God. Latter-day Saints believe that we can arrive at certainty, but not necessarily through studying history and nature (i.e., science) the way the Enlightenment would require us to do it.

Coupled with the relegation of scripture to a secondary position, "the secularization of knowledge in science, as in other fields, meant that theological ideas, whatever their role elsewhere, were to be excluded from the study of the world."[36] When these ideas began to spread to what we today call the humanities, historical criticism was born. To begin with, the ideas of historical criticism were applied to the study of the classics, with the result that scholars had to "either accept the legends [of the early history of Greece and Rome] as a whole, like the historians of previous centuries, or reject them as a whole. And historical criticism had little difficulty in deciding which it was its duty to do."[37] They rejected them outright because, as they reasoned, "small errors of details were sufficient to cast doubt on the credibility of a historical narrative."[38]

With God no longer involved in history and with scripture assigned a subordinate role, it was only a matter of time before the same principles of historical criticism would be applied to the Bible.

After all, "the Scriptures of the Old Testament . . . are historical documents which must be examined according to the same method and upon the same principles as other documents which claim to be historical."[39] Why should the scriptures be an exception to the rule allowing reason and enlightenment to flood the world with truth? "Inevitably, therefore, the scientific criticism of the Old Testament followed upon the scientific criticism of the Greek and Roman historians, and if its tendency was destructive in the case of the one, it was only because it had already been destructive in the case of the other. . . . Abraham only followed Agamemnôn; and if the reputed ancestor of the Hebrew race was resolved into a myth, it was because 'the king of men' had already submitted to the same fate."[40]

The New Testament fared no better than the Old Testament. After Abraham became a myth, it was not long before the miraculous birth of Christ and His no-less-miraculous resurrection were also declared ahistorical. In fact, any biblical story that defied natural explanation, as delimited by the Enlightenment, was denied historical status.

In addition, some critics near the end of the Enlightenment sought to divest Jesus "of the supernatural nimbus with which it was so easy to surround Him, and with which He had in fact been surrounded. They were eager to picture Him as truly and purely human, to strip from Him the robes of splendour with which He had been apparelled, and clothe Him once more with the coarse garments in which He had walked in Galilee."[41] They sought to prove Jesus a man and not the Christ; and in this wise "Jesus and the Enlightenment worldview made peace." [42]

The Enlightenment certainly brought about some laudable changes.[43] However, those who accept the battlefield chosen by the Enlightenment as the only possible terrain to discuss religion have often concluded that there must be another way of reading scripture if they are to maintain faith in the historical remains of a Christian religion that has been emptied of divine historicity. Perhaps one of the most influential new ways of reading scripture was proffered by David Strauss, a German scholar writing in the middle of the nineteenth century.[44] In partial reaction to the Romantic movement, which itself was a reaction to the Enlightenment, he sought to provide Christianity with a better footing than the wobbly foundation of fragments remaining from the assault of the Enlightenment. "The great problem which Strauss attacked was, to what extent the New Testament narrative could fairly be said to be historical. This led him 'to reject the miraculous element in it,'"[45] just as the Enlightenment before him had done. Obviously Strauss had accepted the principles of rationalism when he wrote, "We can indicate a point at which in every instance [the] possibility [of a miracle] ceases, because here every historical analogy deserts us, every conceivability, according to the laws of nature, is at an end. If we begin with the most extreme case, so by a mere expression of blessing, Jesus can never have enormously increased the means of nourishment, never changed water into wine, nor can he in defiance of the laws of gravity have walked upon water without sinking into it; he cannot have recalled any of the dead to life."[46]

In other words, those parts of the New Testament that cannot be explained by the norms of rationalism established by tenets of the Enlightenment cannot be seen as historically true. Therefore, said Strauss, "Were we in a position to demonstrate historically, and with complete accuracy, all the possibilities upon which the introduction of Christianity might be dependent . . . the result would be that the view which regards the rise of Christianity as a miracle would be found to be erroneous."[47] Strauss did not mean that there had not been a historical Jesus or a historical movement sparked by followers of a historical Jesus. Rather, he simply denied the miraculous elements in the history of Christ while trying to maintain a belief in the man Jesus. In this Strauss was true to the injunction of Hegel, who said, "The critic's real object . . . ought to be 'to keep the faith unadulterated, and at the same time to keep science in harmony with it.'"[48] In other words, there is nothing supernatural in Jesus' life. It is only important that the followers of Christ practice a type of docetism in that they believe as if there were divine intervention in the life of Jesus.[49]

In the place of a belief in the historicity of scripture, Strauss posited the concept of myth, which grew out of his study of Hegel, particularly Hegel's "distinction between image or representation (*Vorstellung*) and concept (*Begriff*)."[50] As far as the New Testament was concerned, Strauss believed that the myth (i.e., story or *Vorstellung*) "represented a deficient mode" which the seeker of truth must "stride past" in order to reach the concepts being taught by scripture.[51]

In other words, the myth or story, which may or may not be historical, is the means to arrive at some idea or concept. Thus the story could be devoid of all historicity and yet contain an idea or a teaching point that the reader was supposed to imbibe.[52] In fact, the story could even be a hindrance to understanding the concept if the reader paused to take its historicity seriously.

Since Strauss first wrote of this mythical concept of reading scripture, many scholars have seized upon it as a way to reconcile Christian faith with Enlightenment rationalism. The result is that "the majority of divine deeds in the biblical history of the Hebrew people become what we choose to call symbols, rather than plain old historical facts."[53] As mentioned by the critic at the beginning of this essay, the story of Abraham becomes just a story, devoid of history. In fact, "the point" of one of the current methods of biblical criticism "seems to be that we should be so engrossed with the story, . . . that interrupting historical questions are out of place. Whether the story is based on anything that actually happened is irrelevant."[54] For those who accept the mythological (ahistorical) reading of scripture because God is not in our history, nor has He ever been in our history, neither does He now nor did He ever act in the history of this world, historicity becomes irrelevant at best and a hindrance to faith at worst. Nevertheless, as this imperious view continues, the Bible does contain stories (mythology, divine fiction, or whatever word the current vogue requires) to teach us how to be nice.

With the narrative passages of the Bible now resolved into myth (miraculous or logically impossible) and history (possibly historical), the next logical step was to eliminate the need to buttress the mythological pericopes with Enlightenment-style apologetics. As the Protestant theologian Rudolf Bultmann has argued, modern man cannot return to miracles or spiritual answers. For Bultmann, modern man "is *convinced that the mythological view* [by that he means accepting the miraculous passages of the New Testament even though they are devoid of historicity] *of the world is obsolete,*" because "all of our thinking is irrevocably formed by science"[55] (i.e., Enlightenment strictures). That is, because today we have accepted Enlightenment science as the only possible terrain, we cannot accept as historical the stories contained in scripture. "A blind acceptance of the New Testament mythology [i.e., the historicity of miraculous events] would be simply arbitrariness."[56]

Nevertheless, Bultmann followed the lead of Strauss when he contended that the mythological Christ depicted in the New Testament may not be identical with the Jesus of history. This bifurcation of Jesus Christ into myth (Christ) and history (Jesus), which had generally been accepted by the critics, led to attempts by apologists to shore up the historicity of Christ. Such apologies were and are misplaced, according to Bultmann. "The task of the historian," as Bultmann is summarized, "is thus not to prove that God can be proved to the satisfaction of modernity, *but rather to prove that God cannot be proved.* . . . Any attempt to buttress this decision [to believe] through external means, whether by idea, dogma, or historical science, is illegitimate, since it is motivated by unbelief. The 'quest for the historical Jesus' had been nothing but a century-old attempt to give the believer a reason for believing."[57] For those who follow this line of reasoning, the result is that any attempt to demonstrate the historicity of the miraculous passages of scripture only demonstrates a lack of faith on the part of the apologist and is not a valid avenue of inquiry. We are not supposed to believe that Jesus is the Christ, and any attempts to reconcile the two are misplaced.

Not all Christian scholars capitulated to all aspects of Enlightenment theology. The Swiss theologian Karl Barth "levelled biting criticism against the humanism of current biblical interpretation, and demanded an approach to the text bent to its subject matter. Instead of beginning with the human, with human speech or human thought about God, one had to begin with God, with God's speech and God's thought about human existence."[58] Yet even for the critics of the critics, "it did not mean turning away from modernity [Humanism and Enlightenment world view] and its demands, but a new and more critical encounter with its significance for the life of faith."[59] The critics of the critics could not simply give up the terrain chosen by the Enlightenment but rather sought to eliminate what they perceived as inconsistencies by creating salients somewhere else on the same battlefield.

At this point, we have come full circle, arriving at the point where this essay began, and which Latter-day Saints reject, namely, that for some critics of the scriptures historicity is not important for the content of scriptural faith because they have drained their faith of all historicity. Thus, their faith needs to be rescued by looking for ahistorical grounds for their faith.

On the basis of the teachings of the Restoration, Latter-day Saints need not become entangled in the rush to rescue a needlessly eviscerated faith. We reject both the transcendence of God and the removal of God from nature and history. We therefore reject their proffered emancipation of a scriptural faith that does not need to be rescued. We do not believe that God created the world out of nothing. As the Prophet Joseph Smith explained, "God had materials to organize the world out of chaos—chaotic matter."[60] God took chaotic matter and made a world out of it. He continues to act upon this world hourly, if not more frequently, though He may or may not exist in the time and space of this world. God is not transcendent but is rather, for lack of a better word, immanent.[61] He has acted in the history of this world, He does now act in its history, and He will yet act in the history of this world in a marvelous way.

Why Latter-day Saints Believe in Historicity

As Latter-day Saints we can safely reject traditional Christian concepts of God and the theological deductions of the Enlightenment. We can therefore ignore the conclusions of some higher critics. Yet even some Latter-day Saints, while believing that the Restoration produced "a great church . . . [which] enabled its members to reconcile religion with science and higher learning, . . . [and whose] principal concern was with the here and now,"[62] seem nevertheless to have accepted the conclusions of the Enlightenment. For example, one LDS historian has stated, "Because of my introduction to the concept of symbolism [a subset of the myth school] as a means of expressing religious truth, I was never overly concerned with the question of the historicity of the First Vision or of the many reported epiphanies in Mormon, Christian, and Hebrew history."[63] Because a few committed, active Latter-day Saints naively espouse such views, it is not enough to reject Enlightenment reasoning. We must also give reason for rejecting the conclusions which are based on those deductions (which I have done above) and for insisting upon the necessity of historicity for Latter-day Saint scriptural faith (which follows).

If God expects us in the time and space of this world to submit to ordinances and other physical requirements, then the scriptural passages which exemplify and instruct us concerning those actions must be historical. Surely, the premier example in scripture for such action is the precedent Jesus Christ set by His own baptism, as recorded in the New Testament. The Book of Mormon, in commenting on His baptism, clearly explains how Christ's example applies to all people. Because Christ submitted to the priesthood ordinance of baptism during his life on earth, all of God's children must also be baptized:

> And now, if the Lamb of God, he being holy, should have need to be baptized by water, to fulfil all righteousness, O then, how much more need have we, being unholy, to be baptized, yea, even by water! And now, I would ask of you, my beloved brethren, wherein the Lamb of God did fulfil all righteousness in being baptized by water? Know ye not that he was holy? But notwithstanding he being holy, he showeth unto the children of men that, according to the flesh he humbleth himself before the Father, and witnesseth unto the Father that he would be obedient unto him in keeping his commandments. Wherefore, after he was baptized with water the Holy Ghost descended upon him in the form of a dove. And again, it showeth unto the children of men the straitness of the path, and the narrowness of the gate, by which they should enter, he having set the example before them (2 Ne. 31:5–9).

If there is no historicity in the account of Christ's baptism, if He were not baptized in the waters of the Jordan River, then neither can we be required to be baptized in water in this life. If, on the other hand, Christ Himself was baptized, then we cannot escape its necessity and must also be baptized. Only when the historicity of this central, scriptural account is asserted does the doctrine that we must be baptized "by immersion for the remission of sins" become a belief with content that can be required of all people (Article of Faith 4). If the historicity is deemed irrelevant or nonexistent, then the baptism of Christ becomes not a necessary act to which we must submit, but rather, at best, a nice story which illustrates how we also might want to demonstrate our contrition or humility if we so desire. As John 14:12 clearly implies,[64] we too are supposed to perform the acts of Christ, in which case, the historicity of Christ's acts indeed becomes a necessity.

If Latter-day Saints believe that the scriptures are about *becoming,* as well as about *doing,* then historicity is also necessary because the historicity of scripture determines the depth and breadth of our becoming. No better illustration of this exists than the story of Abraham and the sacrifice of Isaac. Abraham was asked to sacrifice his son, a horrific act by any worldly standard. For Abraham it was doubly horrendous for two reasons. First, he himself had nearly been sacrificed. Second, he had been promised posterity without number, Isaac apparently being the fulfilment of that promise. Indeed, Abraham had very good reasons for doubting the necessity for the sacrifice.

Yet Abraham had faith that "whatever God requires is right, no matter what it is, although we may not see the reason thereof till long after the events transpire."[65] With that faith, "Abraham, when he was tried, offered up Isaac: and he that had received the promises offered up his only begotten son" (Heb. 11:17). It was Abraham's trial of faith to be asked to sacrifice his only heir; and he passed the test. He demonstrated by his actions the person he had become—obedient, faithful, and trustworthy. As James states the case, "Was not Abraham our father justified by works, when he had offered Isaac his son upon the altar? Seest thou how faith wrought with his works, and by works was faith made perfect?" (James 2:21–22). To state this in terms of this discussion on historicity, Abraham proved his faith by his works in this world. It is not enough to simply have abstract faith, because "faith, if it hath not works [in time and space], is dead" (James 2:17).

Without the historicity which Abraham's example provides, we have little reason to believe that the depth and breadth of our becoming must be on the same scale. Yet this is exactly what must happen in our life. As the Prophet Joseph Smith said to his contemporaries, "God hath said that He would have a tried people, that He would purge them as gold, . . . and we think also, it will be a trial of our faith equal to that of Abraham."[66] Years later, President John Taylor would quote Joseph Smith as saying, "It is quite as necessary for you to be tried as it was for Abraham and other men of God, and (said he) God will feel after you, and He will take hold of you and wrench your very heart strings, and if you cannot stand it you will not be fit for an inheritance in the Celestial Kingdom of God."[67] Therefore, Abraham, in developing strong faith, becomes the example we should follow if we expect to receive the promises made to Abraham.

If, however, there is no historicity to the sacrifice of Isaac, but it is simply a nice story (divine fiction at best, at worst it would have been a cruel, malicious joke), which illustrates the fact that we all must develop some kind of abstract faith, then we cannot be required to demonstrate our faith by our actions in this world. But if we desire to follow in Abraham's footsteps and receive the promises given to him, which the Restoration teaches are available to all those who are faithful (see D&C 132:49–50[68]), then we too must have our trials of faith. We too must demonstrate here and now, as Abraham did in his day, that we are willing to become what the Lord wants us to become by doing whatever the Lord requires of us. It is the historicity of Abraham's sacrifice that compels us to develop the same depth and breadth of faith that he did, though the trials we are called upon to pass through may be different than were Abraham's.

In addition to the becoming and the doing as reasons for the necessity of historicity in scripture, there is a third reason. Perhaps no event in God's recorded word is more important than the resurrection of Christ. He arose from the dead, and therefore all people, regardless of what they have done or have become, will also rise from the dead. "For as in Adam all die, even so in Christ shall all be made alive" (1 Cor. 15:22). Every individual ever born will resurrect; there is no choice; no one can escape the resurrection.

If Christ be not raised from the dead, then we as Christians would have no basis for our hope of a resurrection. And if there is no resurrection, then why should we believe and have faith in the other trappings of the gospel? As Paul says, it is not worth it in this mortal life to be a Christian if Christ were not resurrected. "Now if Christ be preached that he rose from the dead, how say some among you that there is no resurrection of the dead? But if there be no resurrection of the dead, then is Christ not risen: And if Christ be not risen, then is our preaching vain, and your faith is also vain. Yea, and we are found false witnesses of God; because we have testified of God that he raised up Christ: whom he raised not up, if so be that the dead rise not. For if the dead rise not, then is not Christ raised: And if Christ be not raised, your faith is vain; ye are yet in your sins. Then they also which are fallen asleep in Christ are perished. If in this life only we have hope in Christ, we are of all men most miserable" (1 Cor. 15:12–20). Christ resurrected, and the historicity of that event means that we will resurrect. The historical reality of the resurrection of Jesus also gives meaning and content to the rest of our Christian faith.

Conclusion

Without the historicity of the central events, scripture becomes little more than a manual for ethical living, illustrated with quaint, sometimes strange, and often implausible stories, stories that have no more value than any other form of literature. As a noted historian has attempted to explain, "One can find philosophical and religious truths in a Shakespearean tragedy even though the characters and events are wholly fictional."[69] If "questions of historicity and authorship should not be raised so that the moral message can reach [us] unimpeded,"[70] then we are free to teach Isaiah no differently than we would teach Shakespeare or Lorca or Pushkin or Kayam. The New Testament "myth" of Christ's resurrection would be the literary equivalent of the rescue of the goddess from the underworld in the "Descent of Ishtar."[71]

If Christ were not baptized, then our baptism would be no more efficacious than any other ritualistic act. Indeed, all ordinances would be irrelevant. If Abraham did not prove who he had become by his willingness to offer Isaac, then our faith need neither plumb that depth nor span that breadth. We could expect no trying of our faith. If there be no historicity to the resurrection of Jesus, then we could have no hope of a resurrection for us. Certainly there is no more fundamental element to Christian faith than the resurrection for us. Without Christ's historical resurrection there can be no Christian faith. And that is the point. The scriptures are not just about truth, religious or otherwise. The scriptures are also about doing what God requires, becoming what God desires, and looking "forward with an eye of faith" (Alma 5:15) to that glorious day when we will be brought into God's presence and exclaim, "Holy, holy are thy judgments, O Lord God Almighty" (2 Ne. 9:46). The historicity of the central events of scripture is absolutely necessary for there to be content in our doctrine, substance to our faith, and reason for our hope.

Paul Y. Hoskisson is associate professor of ancient scripture, Brigham Young University.

Notes

1. Thomas L. Thompson, *The Historicity of the Patriarchal Narratives* (Berlin: de Gruyter, 1974), 328–29. See also his newest book, *The Mythic Past: Biblical Archaeology and the Myth of Israel* (New York: Basic Books, 1999). I have not yet had access to this book.

2. Thompson, *Patriarchal Narratives,* 327–28.

3. Ibid., 328.

4. G. Ernest Wright, *God Who Acts, Biblical Theology as Recital* (London: SCM Press, 1956), 126.

5. Bruce R. McConkie, *A New Witness for the Articles of Faith* (Salt Lake City: Deseret Book, 1985), 81.

6. See note 4 in "Introduction" to this volume for J. Reuben Clark's short list of scriptural events that Latter-day Saints must believe actually happened.

7. I want to thank particularly C. Terry Warner, who, in the beginning of my struggle to understand what until then I had only intuited, helped me realize again that the presuppositions we begin with prejudice (and therefore limit) the range of possible conclusions.

8. Ian G. Barbour, in his book *Religion and Science: Historical and Contemporary Issues* (San Francisco: HarperCollins, 1997), 142–43, stated the case well: "Christian ethics do not consist of applying principles in discrete moments of decision but in our ongoing patterns of response shaped by stories. Character and vision are embodied in stories rather than in concepts or principles. . . . If no Exodus took place, and if Christ did not go willingly to his death, the power of the stories would be undermined. . . . *Jesus of Nazareth* was a historical person. . . . But in calling him Christ and in testifying to his redemptive role we are making statements of faith that are not historically provable, though they are related to historical evidence" (emphasis in original).

9. A. H. Sayce, *The "Higher Criticism" and the Verdict of the Monuments* (London: Society for Promoting Christian Knowledge, 1894), 15.

10. Barbour, *Religion and Science,* 13, emphasis in original.

11. The cogent remarks of A. H. Sayce, written nearly one hundred years ago in *Monument Facts and Higher Critical Fancies* (New York: Revell, [1904]), 124–25, are still applicable: "There was a time when the Christian regarded his Bible as the orthodox Hindu regards his Veda, as a single indivisible and mechanically-inspired book, dictated throughout by the Deity, and from which all human elements are jealously excluded. But heathen theories of inspiration ought to have no place in the Christian consciousness. Christ was perfect Man as well as perfect God, and in the sacred books of our faith we are similarly called upon to recognize a human element as well as a divine. The doctrine of verbal inerrancy is Hindu and not Christian, and

if we admit it we must, with the Hindu, follow it out to its logical conclusion, that the inerrant words cannot be translated into another tongue or even committed to writing. Nevertheless, between the recognition of the human element in the Old Testament, and the 'critical' contention that the Hebrew Scriptures are filled with myths and historical blunders, pious frauds and ante-dated documents, the distance is great."

12. Title page of the Book of Mormon, "If there are faults, they are the mistakes of men."

13. This is why authorized changes in the LDS scriptures do not, and should not, annoy Latter-day Saints who understand the revelatory nature of all scripture. Neither should Latter-day Saints be agitated by supposed or actual revisions in the LDS temple ceremony.

14. By normative I mean the passages provide the guides or norms by which we are required to order our lives. Thus, the story of the Good Samaritan, though perhaps lacking in historicity (but not in historical detail of the times), is normative in that in more recent tradition it has taught us whom we are to regard as our neighbor and what our behavior vis-a-vis our neighbor should be. Some critics use the derisive term "divine fiction" to describe normative stories that lack historicity.

15. Bruce L. Shelly, *Church History in Plain Language,* 2d ed. (Dallas: Word, 1995), 78.

16. Edwin Hatch, *The Influence of Greek Ideas on Christianity* (New York: Harper & Row, 1957), 239.

17. *Oxford English Dictionary,* 2d ed., s.v. "transcendent," 5: "Originally often connoting the denial of Divine action or interference in mundane affairs."

18. Hatch, *The Influence of Greek Ideas,* 241, with n. 1, "The above is taken from the summary of Aetius in Plut. *de plac. Philos.* 1. 7, Euseb. *Praep. Evang.* 14. 16."

19. Barbour, *Religion and Science,* 15.

20. Ibid., 20.

21. Ibid., 21.

22. Ibid.

23. Ibid., 35.

24. See Barbour, *Religion and Science,* 42–43: "David Hume (1711–76) held that only the reliable human knowledge is based on *sense impressions.* . . . Hume was thus led to assert that a scientific theory or law is simply a convenient summary and correlation of individual observations. . . . [With regard to the idea of *causality* Hume says,] we cannot observe necessary connection or any kind of compulsion or power that one event has over another. We observe only repeated temporal succession among sense impressions. . . . Thus 'laws of nature' are not prescriptions of what has to happen, and scientific knowledge is never universal or certain. Laws are only

human expectations based on previous experience. If causality is only a habit of expectation, Hume argues, then *the argument for God as First Cause* is undermined."

25. See Fackenheim's remarks as summarized in Bernhard W. Anderson, *The Living Word of the Bible* (Philadelphia: Westminster, 1979), 57.

26. Barbour, *Religion and Science,* 22.

27. Ibid., 31.

28. Ibid., 35.

29. Ibid., 36.

30. Ibid., 8.

31. Ibid., 16.

32. Ernst Troeltsch, as summarized in Anderson, *The Living Word,* 54.

33. William P. Alston, "Biblical Criticism and the Resurrection," in *The Resurrection: An Interdisciplinary Symposium on the Resurrection of Jesus,* eds. Stephen T. Davis, Daniel Kendall, and Gerald O'Collins (Oxford: Oxford University Press, 1997), 182.

34. C. S. Lewis, "Historicism," in *God, History and Historians,* ed. C. T. McIntire (New York: Oxford University Press, 1977), 229, emphasis in original.

35. Ernst Troeltsch, in Anderson, *The Living Word,* 54.

36. Barbour, *Religion and Science,* 35.

37. Sayce, *The "Higher Criticism,"* 12–13.

38. Ibid., 22.

39. Ibid., 26.

40. Ibid., 17.

41. Albert Schweitzer, *The Quest of the Historical Jesus,* trans. W. Montgomery (London: SCM, 1996), 4–5.

42. Roy A. Harrisville and Walter Sundberg, *The Bible in Modern Culture: Theology and Historical-Critical Method from Spinoza to Käsemann* (Grand Rapids: Eerdmans, 1995), 204.

43. For example, the same conditions that brought about the Enlightenment also brought about the idea of the separation of church and state. This idea was certainly fostered by the Enlightenment. Without the separation of church and state, the Restoration would hardly seem possible.

44. For an assessment of Strauss's place in theological history and his impact on Christian theology, see Harrisville and Sundberg, *The Bible in Modern Culture,* 89–110. See also the succinct biography in Gerald Bray, *Biblical Interpretation, Past and Present* (Downers Grove, Illinois: InterVarsity, 1996), 330.

45. Translator's Preface in David F. Strauss, *The Life of Jesus*, trans. J. L. M'Ilraith (London: Temple Company, n.d.), vii.

46. Ibid., 171–72.

47. Ibid., 1.

48. Ibid., ix.

49. See Anderson, *The Living Word*, 53, "The notion that the Bible is *only* story, or that revelation (if we dare use the term) is only a mental event, sounds suspiciously like a new kind of docetism."

50. Harrisville and Sundberg, *Bible in Modern Culture*, 103.

51. Ibid., 103–4.

52. There is some value in this approach. However, when the vehicle that carries the concept is always deemed inferior to the concept, as Thompson and others would maintain, I believe important content can be lost.

53. Gilkey, as quoted in Anderson, *The Living Word*, 55..

54. Ibid., 53.

55. Rudolf Bultmann et al., *Kerygma and Myth: A Theological Debate*, ed. Hans Werner Bartsch, trans. Reginald H. Fuller (London: S.P.C.K., 1960), 3, emphasis in original.

56. Ibid., 3–4. This does not mean that Bultmann would necessarily deny the historicity of all scripture. He would not deny the probability that the unmiraculous passages could be historical.

57. Harrisville and Sundberg, *Bible in Modern Culture*, 222–23, emphasis in original.

58. Ibid., 210.

59. Ibid., 211.

60. Joseph Smith, *Teachings of the Prophet Joseph Smith*, comp. Joseph Fielding Smith (Salt Lake City: Deseret Book, 1938), 351.

61. I suspect that the proposition that God is either transcendent or immanent is a false dichotomy. The Restoration may be offering us another alternative to this either/or proposition, and we have never articulated it.

62. Leonard J. Arrington, "Why I Am a Believer," *Sunstone* 10, no. 1 (January 1985): 38.

63. Ibid., 37.

64. See also the commentary on this verse in the *Lectures on Faith* (Salt Lake City: Deseret Book, 1985), 7:12.

65. *Teachings of the Prophet Joseph Smith*, 256.

66. Ibid., 135–36. See also D&C 101:4–5, which states that the members of the Church "must needs be chastened and tried, even as Abraham, who was commanded to offer up his only son. For all those who will not endure chastening, but deny me, cannot be sanctified."

67. *Journal of Discourses* (London: Latter-day Saints' Book Depot, 1886), 24:197.

68. I thank Robert L. Millet of Brigham Young University for this reference.

69. Arrington, "Why I Am a Believer," 37.

70. Such is the stated opinion of a friend and former colleague; typescript in the possession of the author.

71. For this myth, see any newer translation, such as Stephanie Dalley, *Myths from Mesopotamia: Creation, the Flood, Gilgamesh, and Others* (Oxford: Oxford University Press, 1992), 154–62. In fact, recently Simo Parpola equated parts of the "Descent of Ishtar" with what Latter-day Saints would call the "Plan of Salvation." He wrote, "The first half of the myth outlines the soul's divine origin and fall, the latter half its way of salvation through repentance, baptism and gradual ascent toward its original perfection" (*Assyrian Prophecies,* State Archives of Assyria IX [Helsinki: Helsinki University Press, 1997], p. xv).

Joseph Smith and the Historicity of the Book of Mormon

5

Kent P. Jackson

Latter-day Saints accept the fact that the Book of Mormon is the word of God, brought to light through the Prophet Joseph Smith. Yet some writers claim that while the Book of Mormon is "true," it is not historical, meaning that the events it describes never took place and the people described in it never existed. But relegating the Book of Mormon to inspired parable or morally uplifting allegory presents serious problems of logic. The book itself announces its historicity repeatedly. Can it really be true in any sense if it consistently misrepresents its origin? Joseph Smith also was consistent in maintaining that the book describes real events and real people. And the voice of God in the Doctrine and Covenants adds the clear and unambiguous witness of the Book of Mormon's historicity. Can these sources be relied on for anything if they unfailingly misrepresent the nature of the "keystone" of the Latter-day Saint faith? In the end, the Book of Mormon can only be what it claims to be, or it is a delusion or a fraud. History and reason leave no other viable options.

It has been suggested by some, even among members of the Church, that the Book of Mormon is a nineteenth-century book, either written by Joseph Smith or received through revelation, and that it has no basis in any real, ancient, historical events. Some who hold this point of view hasten to add that though the book is not historical, it is nonetheless "the word of God," "inspired," and/or "true."[1] This appears to mean that it qualifies as such while the events that it describes never took place. A variation on the suggestion is that it comes from God or is otherwise "true" but that it does not matter if the events that are described in it ever happened.[2]

Typical dictionary definitions of *true* include: "consistent with fact; agreeing with the reality; representing the thing as it is,"[3] "actual state of affairs."[4] The word *historical* means: "of, relating to, or having the character of history especially as distinguished from myth or legend," "true to history."[5] Similarly, *historicity* is defined as "the quality or state of being historic[al] especially as distinct from the mythological or legendary."[6]

This paper will not be an attempt to define words. But it will be an effort to examine what the Book of Mormon says about itself, what Joseph Smith said about it, and what the Lord said about it in the revelations of the Doctrine and Covenants; and it will attempt to reconcile those statements with the notion that the Book of Mormon does not need to be historical to be the inspired word of God.

Those who argue in favor of the true-but-not-historical thesis sometimes invoke the analogy of good literature or the parables of Jesus. The parables, they would suggest, are nonhistorical literary creations that Jesus used to teach true principles. They would suggest that while the parables are not meant to portray events that actually transpired, they are nonetheless true in the sense that they enlighten us, lift us, educate us, and teach us about life. Like good literature in general, the parables are true because their *message* is true, despite the nonhistorical nature of the events and persons who are mentioned in them.[7]

Using the parables-are-true-but-not-historical model, friendly critics of the Book of Mormon's historicity argue that it does not matter whether the events and individuals in the Book of Mormon are historical, because the aims of the book are achieved independently of its historicity. In other words, like parables or other good works of literature, the Book of Mormon can teach its true principles even if the events in it never happened.[8] Thus it can still be the word of God.[9]

In my opinion, Latter-day Saints cannot accept these ideas regarding the Book of Mormon. Its historicity is fundamental to what it is and what it intends to accomplish. A perspective that sees it as unhistorical is, in my view, a rejection not only of it and everything else about it but of much more as well.

To determine whether the Book of Mormon must be historically genuine in order to be the "true" "word of God," I will examine four sources of potential evidence that may bear on our subject: (1) the internal evidence provided within the Book of Mormon itself, (2) the evidence from the Prophet Joseph Smith, (3) the evidence from the Doctrine and Covenants, and (4) the evidence from the Three and Eight Witnesses. This evidence is not brought forth to prove the truth of the Book of Mormon, because that is something that is unprovable using the tools of scholarship and reasoning. But I believe that it can be demonstrated that the book *cannot* be both unhistorical and true at the same time. That is the objective of this paper.

Evidence from the Book of Mormon

The Book of Mormon is a thoroughly self-conscious book. Throughout its pages, its authors recorded not only the history of their people and the revelations of their prophets but also the process of the composition of the book. A few examples will suffice:

> I [Nephi] have received a commandment of the Lord that I should make these plates, for the special purpose that there should be an account engraven of the ministry of my people.
> Upon the other plates should be engraven an account of the reign of the kings, and the wars and contentions of my people; wherefore these plates are for the more part of the ministry; and the other plates are for the more part of the reign of the kings and the wars and contentions of my people.
> Wherefore, the Lord hath commanded me to make these plates for a wise purpose in him (1 Ne. 9:3–5).

> I, Jarom, do not write more, for the plates are small. But behold, my brethren, ye can go to the other plates of Nephi; for behold, upon them the records of our wars are engraven, according to the writings of the kings, or those which they caused to be written.
> And I deliver these plates into the hands of my son Omni, that they may be kept according to the commandments of my fathers (Jarom 1:14–15).

> And now, my son Helaman, I [Alma] command you that ye take the records which have been entrusted with me;
> And I also command you that ye keep a record of this people, according as I have done, upon the plates of Nephi, and keep all these things sacred which I have kept, even as I have kept them; for it is for a wise purpose that they are kept (Alma 37:1–2).

These are representative samples of dozens of such passages. The nouns *record* and *records* are used in almost one hundred verses with respect to the Book of Mormon itself and the documents that went into it.[10] The word *plates* is used almost one hundred times with respect to the Book of Mormon and the plates that went into it.[11] The words *write* and *writing* are used in over one hundred fifty verses, all having to do with the writing of the Book of Mormon record.[12] Other words, such as *book,*[13] *account,*[14] and *engravings*[15] appear in dozens of places in the book, all chronicling the writing of the records that became the Book of Mormon. Following is a list of passages in which the Book of Mormon refers to itself, the process of its creation, or the writings that comprise it.

1 Ne. 1:1–3, 16–17; 6:1, 3–6; 8:30; 9:1–5; 10:1, 15; 13:35–36; 14:25, 28, 30; 17:6; 19:1–6, 18

2 Ne. 3:12, 18–19, 23; 4:14–15, 25; 5:4, 12, 29–33; 11:1–3; 25:1, 3, 6, 8, 21–23, 26; 26:15, 17; 27:6–26, 29; 28:2; 29:10, 12–13; 30:3; 31:1–2; 33:1, 3–5, 11

Jacob 1:1–4; 3:13–14; 4:1–4; 7:26–27

Enos 1:13–16, 23

Jarom 1:1–2, 14–15

Omni 1:1, 3–4, 8–9, 11, 14, 18, 25, 30

W of M 1:1–6, 9–11

Mosiah 1:6, 8, 16; 8:1, 12–13, 19; 12:8; 17:4; 21:27–28, 35; 28:9, 11, 17–20

Alma 3:12; 5:2; 8:1; 9:34; 11:46; 13:31; 18:36, 38; 22:1, 35; 23:5; 28:8–9; 35:13, 16; 37:1–2, 8–9, 21; 43:3; 44:24; 45:2; 47:1; 50:38; 63:17

Hel. 2:13–14; 3:13–17; 8:3; 14:1; 16:25

3 Ne. 1:2–3; 2:9; 5:8–11, 14–19; 7:17; 8:1; 10:19; 16:4; 17:15–17, 25; 18:37; 19:32, 34; 23:4, 6–8, 11–14; 24:1; 26:6–8, 11–12, 18; 27:23–26; 28:18, 25; 30:1

4 Ne. 1:19, 21, 47–49

Morm. 1:1–4; 2:17–18; 3:17–20; 4:23; 5:9, 12; 6:1, 6; 7:8–9; 8:1, 3–5, 12, 14, 23; 9:31–35

Ether 1:1–6; 2:12–13; 3:17, 22–24, 27; 4:1, 3–5, 17; 5:1–2; 6:1; 8:20, 26; 9:1; 12:20, 23–25, 40; 13:1, 13–14; 15:11, 33–34

Moro. 1:1, 4; 7:1; 9:7, 24; 10:1–2, 27, 29

I know of no book that discusses itself so much and so thoroughly. The authors wrote about the smallness of their plates, the difficulty of engraving in metal, their primary sources in other books, and, more than anything else, the messages that they wanted their distant readers to learn from what they recorded.

This information is very important for our discussion of the historicity of the Book of Mormon. The book presents itself so completely as an actual historical record written in ancient times that in my view there can be only two options for evaluating its claims:

Option 1. It is a fraud.
Option 2. It is a genuine ancient book.

The Book of Mormon does not present itself as a historical novel, nor does it intend to be viewed as such. The parables of Jesus, on the other hand, do not make claims about their historicity. But the Book of Mormon repeatedly makes bold and certain claims that it is an ancient book, and those claims are central to its message and its intent.

Evidence from Joseph Smith

Since Joseph Smith was the publisher of the Book of Mormon, we can rightly assign some measure of credit for its existence to him, assuming that he was not entirely subject to some force independent of his own agency. It will not be necessary to repeat the whole story of Moroni's coming, the plates, and the Book of Mormon, but we will view some selections of Joseph Smith's public and private statements about its origin and content.[16]

1832 draft history

When I was seventeen years of age, I called again upon the Lord, and he showed unto me a heavenly vision. For behold, an angel of the Lord came and stood before me, and it was by night. . . . And he revealed unto me that . . . there were plates of gold upon which there were engravings which were engraven by Moroni and his fathers, the servants of the living God in ancient days, and deposited by the commandments of God. . . . I immediately went to the place and found where the plates were deposited, as the angel of the Lord had commanded me, and straightway made three attempts to get them. And then, being exceedingly frightened, I supposed it had been a dream of vision, but when I considered, I knew that it was not. . . . The angel appeared unto me again and said unto me, "You . . . cannot now obtain them, for the time is not yet fulfilled. . . . In [God's] own due time thou shalt obtain them." For now I had been tempted of the Adversary and sought the plates to obtain riches, and kept not the commandment that I should have an eye single to the glory of God. Therefore I was chastened and sought diligently to obtain the plates, and obtained them not until I was twenty-one years of age.[17]

Note the deliberate historical detail in the account: the Prophet's age at the time of the angel's first visit, time of day, metal of plates, who engraved them and when, physical attempts to obtain them, certainty that it was not a dream, temptation to profit from the plates, and age when Joseph Smith finally obtained them.

Letter to a newspaper, January 1833

> The Book of Mormon is a record of the forefathers of our western tribes of Indians, having been found through the ministration of an holy angel [and] translated into our own language by the gift and power of God after having been hid up in the earth for the last fourteen hundred years; containing the word of God which was delivered unto them. By it we learn that our western tribes of Indians are descendants from that Joseph that was sold into Egypt, and that the land of America is a promised land unto them.[18]

Some historical details: book written by ancestors of Indians, translated into English, duration of plates' burial in ground, Israelite ancestry of Indians.

Letter to Emma Smith, June 1834 (describing the countryside in Missouri)

> The whole of our journey, in the midst of so large a company of social, honest, and sincere men, wandering over the plains of the Nephites, recounting occasionally the history of the Book of Mormon, roving over the mounds of that once beloved people of the Lord.[19]

Journal entry, November 1835

> When I was about seventeen years old, I saw another vision of angels. In the night season after I had retired to bed, I had not been asleep but was meditating upon my past life and experience. . . . An angel appeared before me. His hands and feet were naked, pure and white, and he stood between the floors of the room, clothed with purity inexpressible. He told me of a sacred record which was written on plates of gold. I saw in the vision the place where they were deposited. He said the Indians were the literal descendants of Abraham. . . . also that the Urim and Thummim was hid up with the record, and that God would give me power to translate it with the assistance of this instrument. . . . After the vision had all passed, I found that it was nearly daylight. . . . I went and found the place where the plates were, according to the direction of the angel. [I] also saw them, and the angel as before. . . . The angel told me . . . to come again in one year from that time. I did so but did not obtain them, also

the third and the fourth year, at which time I obtained them and translated them into the English language by the gift and power of God.[20]

Some historical details: age, time of day, dress of angel, location above the floor, metal of plates, burial place, Indians are descendants of Abraham, instruments to aid in translation, yearly visits, translation into English.

1838 "History of Joseph Smith" (JS–H 1)

29 On the evening of the . . . twenty-first of September [1823[21]], after I had retired to my bed for the night, . . .

30 . . . Immediately a personage appeared at my bedside, standing in the air, for his feet did not touch the floor.

31 He had on a loose robe. . . . His hands were naked, and his arms also, a little above the wrist; so, also, were his feet naked, as were his legs, a little above the ankles. His head and neck were also bare. I could discover that he had no other clothing on but this robe, as it was open, so that I could see into his bosom. . . .

34 He said there was a book deposited, written upon gold plates, giving an account of the former inhabitants of this continent, and the source from whence they sprang. He also said that the fulness of the everlasting Gospel was contained in it, as delivered by the Savior to the ancient inhabitants;

35 Also, that there were two stones in silver bows—and these stones, fastened to a breastplate, constituted what is called the Urim and Thummim—deposited with the plates; . . . and that God had prepared them for the purpose of translating the book. . . .

42 Again, he told me, that when I got those plates of which he had spoken . . . I should not show them to any person; neither the breastplate with the Urim and Thummim. . . . The vision was opened to my mind that I could see the place where the plates were deposited, and that so clearly and distinctly that I knew the place again when I visited it. . . .

46 [He] added a caution to me, telling me that Satan would try to tempt me (in consequence of the indigent circumstances of my father's family), to get the plates for the purpose of getting rich. . . .

51 Convenient to the village of Manchester, Ontario county, New York, stands a hill of considerable size. . . . On the west side of this hill, not far from the top, under a stone of considerable size, lay the plates, deposited in a stone box. This stone was thick and rounding in the middle on the upper side, and thinner towards the edges, so that the middle part of it was visible above the ground, but the edge all around was covered with earth.

52 Having removed the earth, I obtained a lever, which I got fixed under the edge of the stone, and with a little exertion raised it up. I looked in, and there indeed did I behold the plates, the Urim and Thummim, and the breastplate, as stated by the messenger. The box in which they lay was formed by laying stones together in some kind of cement. In the bottom of the box were

laid two stones crossways of the box, and on these stones lay the plates and the other things with them. . . .

59 At length the time arrived for obtaining the plates, the Urim and Thummim, and the breastplate. . . .

60 By the wisdom of God, they remained safe in my hands, until I had accomplished by them what was required at my hand. When, according to arrangements, the messenger called for them, I delivered them up to him; and he has them in his charge until this day, being the second day of May, one thousand eight hundred and thirty-eight. . . .

I wish to mention here, that the Title Page of the Book of Mormon is a literal translation, taken from the very last leaf, on the left hand side of the collection or book of plates, . . . the language of the whole running same as all Hebrew writing in general; and that said Title Page is not by any means a modern composition either of mine or of any other man's who has lived or does live in this generation. . . . The Title Page of the English Version of the Book of Mormon . . . is a genuine and literal translation of the title-page of the Original Book of Mormon, as recorded on the plates.[22]

Some historical details: exact date, time of day, angel at bedside, standing in air, detailed description of clothing, metal of plates, description of Urim and Thummim, prohibition against showing, temptation to profit from plates, description of burial location, detailed description of box, physical exertion to open it, content of box, angel retrieves plates, origin of title page, direction of writing.

Newspaper article, July 1838

Moroni, the person who deposited the plates, . . . being dead and raised again therefrom, appeared unto me and told me where they were and gave me directions how to obtain them. I obtained them and the Urim and Thummim with them, by the means of which I translated the plates. And thus came the Book of Mormon.[23]

1842 "Church History"

On the evening of the twenty-first of September, a.d. 1823, . . . on a sudden a light like that of day, only of a far purer and more glorious appearance and brightness, burst into the room. Indeed, the first sight was as though the house was filled with consuming fire. The appearance produced a shock that affected the whole body. In a moment a personage stood before me, surrounded with a glory yet greater than that with which I was already surrounded. . . .

I was also informed concerning the aboriginal inhabitants of this country. . . . I was also told where there were deposited some plates on which was engraven an abridgement of the records of the ancient prophets that had existed on this continent. . . . On the morning of the twenty-second of September a.d. 1827, the angel of the Lord delivered the records into my hands.

These records were engraven on plates which had the appearance of gold, each plate was six inches wide and eight inches long and not quite so thick as common tin. They were filled with engravings . . . and bound together in a volume, as the leaves of a book with three rings running through the whole. The volume was something near six inches in thickness, a part of which was sealed. The characters on the unsealed part were small, and beautifully engraved. The whole book exhibited many marks of antiquity in its construction and much skill in the art of engraving. With the records was found a curious instrument which the ancients called "Urim and Thummim," which consisted of two transparent stones set in the rim of a bow fastened to a breastplate.

Through the medium of the Urim and Thummim I translated the record by the gift, and power of God. . . .

We are informed by these records that America in ancient times has been inhabited by two distinct races of people. The first were called Jaredites and came directly from the tower of Babel. The second race came directly from the city of Jerusalem, about six hundred years before Christ. They were principally Israelites, of the descendants of Joseph. The Jaredites were destroyed about the time that the Israelites came from Jerusalem, who succeeded them in the inheritance of the country. The principal nation of the second race fell in battle towards the close of the fourth century. The remnant are the Indians that now inhabit this country. . . . The last of their prophets who existed among them was commanded to write an abridgement of their prophesies, history, and so forth, and to hide it up in the earth, and that it should come forth and be united with the Bible for the accomplishment of the purposes of God in the last days.[24]

Some historical details: time of day, exact date, description of glory, existence and location of people in record, date and time of day of reception of plates, detailed description of plates, description of Urim and Thummim, discussion of groups of people in book, origin of Jaredites and Lehites, date of Lehite departure, date of Nephite demise, Indian descent, abridgment and burial of record.

Newspaper article, May 1842 (concerning some mummified remains of Native Americans that had been found)

The Book of Mormon gives an account of a number of the descendants of Israel coming to this continent; and it is well known that the art of embalming was known among the Hebrews. . . .

This art was no doubt transmitted from Jerusalem to this continent by the before-mentioned emigrants, which accounts for the finding of the mummies, and at the same time is another strong evidence of the authenticity of the Book of Mormon.[25]

Journal entry, May 1844 (from a conversation with some Sac and Fox Indians)

> The Great Spirit has enabled me to find a book [showing them the Book of Mormon], which told me about your fathers.[26]

Joseph Smith thus spoke and wrote in some detail about the coming forth of the Book of Mormon. He stated that an angel appeared in his room, stood above the floor, and spoke of ancient people who once lived in the Americas—the ancestors of today's Native Americans. He stated that the angel told him about their written record. They had migrated to America from the Old World and were descendants of ancient Israelites. The Prophet described the angel's appearance and clothing. He described in detail the physical characteristics of the plates, the interpreters, and the box in which they were contained. He stated that this event was not a dream but the actual appearance of a man who once lived, had died, and had been raised again from the dead.

In a consistent way, over the course of his lifetime, Joseph Smith continued to tell and to stand by this same story. I see the following logical possibilities for evaluating what he stated concerning the Book of Mormon and the words that he attributed to the angel Moroni:

> *Option 1.* Joseph Smith was an impostor who lied about the coming of the angel and the origin of the Book of Mormon.
>
> *Option 2.* Joseph Smith sincerely believed that an angel appeared to him, and he believed that his English Book of Mormon text was translated from a golden book. But none of it was true.
>
> *Option 3.* An angel really appeared to Joseph Smith, but there were no plates and the Book of Mormon is not historical.
>
> > a. Hence what Joseph Smith reported that the angel said is not true, or
> >
> > b. what the angel told Joseph Smith was not true. (It was either an angel of the devil or a less-than-honest angel.[27])

Option 4. An angel really appeared to Joseph Smith, and there really were gold plates, but the Book of Mormon is not historical.

    a. Hence what Joseph Smith reported that the angel said is not true, or

    b. what the angel told Joseph Smith was not true.

Option 5. The whole story is true: an angel really appeared to Joseph Smith, there really were gold plates, and the Book of Mormon is historical, as both Joseph Smith and the angel asserted.

Evidence from the Doctrine and Covenants

According to God in the revelations of the Doctrine and Covenants, Nephites, Jacobites, Josephites, Zoramites, Lamanites, Lemuelites, and Ishmaelites (that is, peoples known only from the history in the Book of Mormon) are living today (D&C 3:16–18). The Book of Mormon is "the testimony of their fathers." They are "in unbelief because of the iniquity of their fathers." They will "come to the knowledge of their fathers . . . [and] the promises of the Lord" (3:17–20). God's "other sheep" were a branch of the house of Israel. He would bring forth "their marvelous works, which they did in [his] name," as well as his gospel, "which was ministered unto them" (10:60–62).

According to God in the Doctrine and Covenants, the Book of Mormon is an account "engraven upon the plates of Nephi" (10:38–41, 45). It is "the record of Nephi" (10:42), "an abridgment of the account of Nephi" (10:44). Joseph Smith was to "translate [the] first part of the engravings of Nephi" (10:45).

According to God in the Doctrine and Covenants, the Book of Mormon contains what God's ancient "holy prophets" and "disciples" "desired in their prayers should come forth" to us in our day. In ancient times, God promised them that it would be so "according to their faith in their prayers" (10:46–47). They had faith that the gospel that was given them to "preach in their days" would come to "their brethren the Lamanites" in our day. And it was "their faith in their prayers" that it would be made known also to other nations who would possess this land (10:48–49). Those ancient "prophets" and "disciples" (10:46) left "a blessing on this land in their prayers," that whoever would believe the gospel in their record would "have eternal life" (10:50). According to the "faith in [the] prayers" of those ancient persons, God would bring forth "this part of [his] gospel to the knowledge of" His people in our time (10:52).

According to God in the Doctrine and Covenants, Joseph Smith had the plates (5:1). He was not allowed to show them to anyone unless God told him (5:3). God would show the plates to three witnesses and would declare their truth to them (5:11–13). Their testimony will condemn those who do not believe them (5:18). Martin Harris would see the plates and "know of a surety that they are true" (5:25–26). Joseph Smith had the "Urim and Thummim" (10:1). He had to finish "the remainder of the work of translation" (10:3) but was not to retranslate what was lost (10:30–31).

According to God in the Doctrine and Covenants, the Three Witnesses would see the plates, the breastplate, the sword of Laban, the Urim and Thummim, and the Liahona (17:1–2). After those witnesses will "have seen them with [their] eyes," they would testify of them (17:3). They would testify that they had seen them, just as Joseph Smith had seen them (17:5).

According to God in the Doctrine and Covenants, "as your Lord and your God liveth [the Book of Mormon] is true" (17:6). It "contains the truth and the word of God" (19:26). Today's Native Americans are "a remnant" of the Jews (19:27). Moroni appeared to Joseph Smith (20:6). He "gave him power from on high, by the means which were before prepared, to translate the Book of Mormon" (20:8), which "contains a record of a fallen people" (20:9). God sent Moroni to Joseph Smith (27:5). He was "an angel from heaven" (128:20).

Thus the Lord's words in the Doctrine and Covenants bear a straightforward and consistent testimony concerning the historicity of the Book of Mormon, with repeated reference to its ancient authors. I see four logical possibilities for evaluating these statements in the Doctrine and Covenants concerning the Book of Mormon:

> *Option 1.* Joseph Smith was an impostor and made up these so-called revelations.

Option 2. Joseph Smith sincerely believed that these were revelations, but none of them came from God, and none of them are true.

Option 3. These are real revelations from God, but what God told Joseph Smith in them is not true.

Option 4. These are real revelations from God, and what God told Joseph Smith in them is true.

It seems to me that if one believes that the revelations in the Doctrine and Covenants do indeed come from God, one will be compelled to accept His statements concerning the historicity of the persons and events discussed in the Book of Mormon.

Evidence from the Three and Eight Witnesses

Since the Lord, by revelation, designated the witnesses to be independent evidence for the truth of the Book of Mormon (D&C 17:3–6), we do well when we take their accounts seriously. They were, after all, selected not for their own sake but for the sake of adding further testimonies about the Book of Mormon to that of Joseph Smith.

The testimonies of the witnesses are an important part of the coming forth of the Book of Mormon, because now there were others who could state with Joseph Smith, "We . . . have seen the plates. . . . And we also know that they have been translated by the gift and power of God, for his voice hath declared it unto us. . . . And we declare with words of soberness, that an angel of God came down from heaven, and he brought and laid before our eyes, that we beheld and saw the plates."[28]

Given the range of logical possibilities for the origin of the Book of Mormon, the fact that witnesses claimed to see the angel and the plates might not be sufficient evidence for critics who maintain that there may well have been an angel and maybe even some plates but that the content of the book is not historical. But there is more to the testimony of the witnesses. In the June 1829 revelation in which the Lord designated the Three Witnesses, he told them that they would see, in addition to the plates, "the sword of Laban, the Urim and Thummim, which were given to the brother of Jared upon the mount, when he talked with the Lord face to face, and the miraculous directors which were given to Lehi while in the wilderness, on the borders of the Red Sea" (D&C 17:1). The significance of these items is that they are all objects that are mentioned in the account in the Book of Mormon text itself. They are not external to the narrative but are artifacts from the *history* in the book. This means that if the experience of the Three Witnesses took place as they said it did, they saw evidence not only that there was a divinely revealed book but also that the account in it is historical. Accordingly, the Three Witnesses saw, along with the Book of Mormon plates (according to David Whitmer), "the sword of Laban, the Directors (i.e. the ball which Lehi had) and the Interpreters."[29] In addition, they also saw "the Brass Plates,"[30] another artifact discussed in the text itself. Thus the Three Witnesses were shown a collection of souvenirs from the history recorded in the Book of Mormon. And all of this was part of God's merciful plan to provide us with witnesses for the book.

Since the beginning of the Church, the testimonies of the witnesses have been a problem for those who reject Joseph Smith. These men's lives are well documented. They were respected in their communities and were considered by their contemporaries to be not only of sound character but also of sound mind. Sadly, in the late 1830s each of the Three Witnesses left the Church, becoming disillusioned with Joseph Smith personally over matters of doctrine and administration. Two were later rebaptized, yet all three continued to maintain, even in their days of disassociation from the Church, that their published testimony was a true account of an actual supernatural event in which they had been participants.[31] Ironically, the disaffection of the witnesses adds to the credibility of their testimonies. Had the experience been fraudulent, the witnesses no doubt would have seized the opportunity to expose the Prophet as an impostor. But they remained true to their statements even when they felt personal animosity toward Joseph Smith.

The following logical possibilities can be used to evaluate the testimonies of the Three and Eight Witnesses:

> *Option 1.* The eleven men—otherwise well-known and respected citizens—each lied about their experiences

with great consistency over the course of their lifetimes. The events never took place.

Option 2. The eleven men—otherwise well-known and respected citizens—sincerely believed throughout their lives that the events took place. But the events never really happened.

Option 3. The events took place as described by the eleven men.

Today, while some say that the Book of Mormon is somehow "true" but not historical, the testimonies of the witnesses expose their point of view as nonsense by providing evidence that cannot be dismissed. Reasonable men claimed throughout their lives that they saw an angel, handled the plates and other artifacts from the account in the book, and heard the voice of God. It is no wonder that the witnesses were foreknown by revelation and prepared by the Lord to perform their important calling to bear testimony of His work (D&C 17:1–9; Ether 5:1–4). The Book of Mormon still contains their "words of soberness" that are as valid today as they were in 1830 when the book first came off the press.

Judging the Evidence

Our evidence compels us to judge the credibility of the argument against the historicity of the Book of Mormon, or, on the other hand, the credibility of the evidence discussed above.

Given all the clear and consistent claims in favor of historicity made by the Book of Mormon itself, by Joseph Smith, by other witnesses, and by the revelations of God to Joseph Smith, what credibility could any of these sources have if the book is not historical?

Can the Book of Mormon indeed be "true," in *any* sense, if it lies repeatedly, explicitly, and deliberately regarding its own historicity? Can Joseph Smith be viewed with *any* level of credibility if he repeatedly, explicitly, and deliberately lied concerning the historicity of the book? Can we have *any* degree of confidence in what are presented as the words of God in the Doctrine and Covenants if they repeatedly, explicitly, and deliberately lie by asserting the historicity of the Book of Mormon? If the Book of Mormon is not what it claims to be, what possible cause would anyone have to accept *anything* of the work of Joseph Smith and The Church of Jesus Christ of Latter-day Saints given the consistent assertions that the Book of Mormon is an ancient text that describes ancient events?

This is not an invitation for anyone to leave the Church. It is, instead, an invitation to abandon the fallacious and logically impossible argument that the Book of Mormon can be true, though not historical, while Joseph Smith, the revelations of God, and the book itself claim in clear and unmistakable terms the opposite.

As one chooses to embrace the gospel, the other line of reasoning must be pursued. The book's repeated assertion of its historicity, the faithful testimony of the Prophet Joseph Smith concerning it, and the voice of God speaking to us of it through the Doctrine and Covenants join with the spirit of personal revelation and testimony in bearing witness that the Book of Mormon is a genuine historical record of ancient origin.

Kent P. Jackson is professor of ancient scripture, Brigham Young University.

Notes

1. According to Anthony A. Hutchinson, "Members of The Church of Jesus Christ of Latter-day Saints should confess in faith that the Book of Mormon is the word of God but also abandon claims that it is a historical record of the ancient peoples of the Americas. We should accept that it is a work of scripture inspired by God . . . but one that has as its human author Joseph Smith, Jr." "The Word of God is Enough: The Book of Mormon as Nineteenth-Century Scripture," *New Approaches to the Book of Mormon: Explorations in Critical Methodology,* ed. Brent Lee Metcalfe (Salt Lake City: Signature Books, 1993), 1. A similar notion that is even more intellectually inconsistent is found in Blake T. Ostler, "The Book of Mormon as a Modern Expansion of an Ancient Source," *Dialogue: A Journal of Mormon Thought* 20, no. 1 (spring 1987), 66–123.

2. According to Hutchinson, "Ultimately whether the Book of Mormon is ancient really does not matter." Hutchinson, 16. According to Mark D. Thomas, "In the final analysis the book's authority cannot depend on its age. If the Book of Mormon's message is profound, that alone should be sufficient reason for serious analysis and

dialogue." "A Rhetorical Approach to the Book of Mormon: Rediscovering Nephite Sacramental Language," Metcalfe, 53.

3. *The Oxford English Dictionary,* 2d ed., s.v. *true* (regarding "a statement or belief").

4. *Webster's New International Dictionary,* 3d ed., s.v. *true.*

5. Ibid., s.v. *historical.*

6. Ibid., s.v. *historicity.*

7. Though I do not know personally if any or all of the parables are historical or not, for the sake of this discussion, I am willing to concede that their impressive teaching capacity is not dependent on whether the persons or events in them depict real history.

8. Following the same argument, Joseph Smith's status as a true prophet is not dependent on the historicity of events in the Book of Mormon.

9. This is the argument of Hutchinson, 1–19.

10. *Record(s):* 1 Ne. 1:2–3, 17; 6:1; 19:1–2, 4; 2 Ne. 5:29; Jacob 7:26; Enos 1:13–16; Jarom 1:14; Omni 1:9, 11; W of M: 1:1–3, 5–6, 9–10; Mosiah 1:6; 8:12–13; 12:8; 21:27; 28:11, 20; Alma 3:12; 5:2; 18:36, 38; 23:5; 35:16; 37:1–2, 9; 44:24; 45:2; 47:1; 50:38; Hel. 3:13, 15; 16:25; 3 Ne. 1:2–3; 2:9; 5:9–11, 14–18; 8:1; 17:25; 23:7–8; 28:18; 4 Ne. 1:19, 21, 47–49; Morm. 1:1–2; 2:17; 4:23; 6:1, 6; 7:8; 8:1, 4–5, 12, 14; 9:32–33; Ether 1:3, 6; 2:13; 4:17; 6:1; 9:1; 12:20; 13:1, 14; 15:11, 33; Moro. 9:24; 10:2.

11. *Plates:* 1 Ne. 1:17; 6:1, 3, 6; 9:1–5; 10:1; 19:1–6; 2 Ne. 4:14–15; 5:4, 29–33; Jacob 1:1–4; 3:13–14; 4:1–3; 7:26–27; Jarom 1:2, 14–15; Omni 1:1, 3, 8, 11, 14, 18, 25, 30; W of M 1:3–6, 9–10; Mosiah 1:6, 16; 8:19; 21:27; 28:11; Alma 37:9, 21; 44:24; 3 Ne. 5:10–11; 26:7, 11; 4 Ne. 1:19, 21; Morm. 1:4; 2:17–18; 6:6; 8:5, 14; 9:33; Ether 1:2, 4; 4:4; 5:2.

12. *Write* and cognates: 1 Ne. 1:16; 6:1, 3, 5; 8:30; 9:1; 10:15; 13:35–36; 14:25, 28, 30; 17:6; 19:3, 6, 18; 2 Ne. 3:12, 18–19; 4:14–15, 25; 5:4, 12; 11:1–2; 25:1, 3, 6, 8, 21–23, 26; 26:15, 17; 28:2; 29:10, 12; 30:3; 31:1–2; 33:1, 3–5, 11; Jacob 1:2; 3:13; 4:1–2, 4; 7:26–27; Enos 1:23; Jarom 1:1–2, 14; Omni 1:1, 4, 9, 11; W of M 1:2–3, 5, 11; Mosiah 1:8; 8:1; 17:4; 28:11, 19; Alma 8:1; 9:34; 11:46; 13:31; 44:24; Hel. 2:14; 8:3; 14:1; 3 Ne. 5:8, 18; 7:17; 16:4; 17:15, 17; 19:32, 34; 23:4, 6, 11–12; 24:1; 26:6, 8, 11–12, 18; 27:23–24; 28:25; 30:1; 4 Ne. 1:21; Morm. 3:17–20; 5:9, 12; 7:9; 8:1, 3–5, 23; 9:31–35; Ether 1:4; 2:12; 3:17, 22–24, 27; 4:1, 4–5; 5:1; 8:20, 26; 12:23–25, 40; 13:1, 13; 15:33–34; Moro. 1:1, 4; 7:1; 9:7, 24; 10:1, 27, 29.

13. *Book(s):* 1 Ne. 10:15; 2 Ne. 3:23; 26:17; 27:6–12, 14–15, 17, 19, 22, 29; 28:2; 30:3; Omni 1:4, 9; Mosiah 1:8; 8:1; Alma 9:34; 13:31; Hel. 2:13–14; 16:25; 3 Ne. 5:8; 7:17; 26:6; 4 Ne. 1:21; Morm. 1:1; Ether 1:2.

14. *Account:* 1 Ne. 1:16–17; 6:3; 9:2–4; 10:1; 19:4–5; W of M 1:3; Mosiah 21:35; 28:9; 28:17–19; Alma 22:1, 35; 28:8–9; 35:13; 43:3; 63:17; Hel. 2:14; 3:14, 17; 3 Ne. 5:9, 16, 19; 10:19; Morm. 2:18; 5:9; Ether 1:1–6; 3:17; Moro. 1:1.

15. *Engrave* and cognates: 1 Ne. 9:3, 4; 19:1–2; 2 Ne. 5:30–32; Jacob 1:1–4; 4:1, 3; Jarom 1:14; Omni 1:11; Mosiah 21:27–28; Morm. 1:3–4; 3 Ne. 5:10; 26:11.

16. In the following texts, I have provided modern punctuation and spelling.

17. Dean C. Jessee, ed., *The Papers of Joseph Smith* (Salt Lake City: Deseret Book, 1989–92), 1:7–9.

18. Joseph Smith to editor, *American Revivalist and Rochester Observer,* 4 January 1833; Jessee, ed., *The Personal Writings of Joseph Smith* (Salt Lake City: Deseret Book, 1984), 273.

19. Joseph Smith to Emma Smith, 4 June 1834; Jessee, *Personal Writings,* 324.

20. Joseph Smith Diary, 9 November 1835; Jessee, *Papers,* 2:69–71.

21. The year is identified in verse 28.

22. Jessee, *Papers,* 1:276–81, 283–84, 300–1. All but the last paragraph is in the Joseph Smith–History in the Pearl of Great Price.

23. *Elders' Journal* 1, no. 3 (July 1838), 42–43.

24. *Times and Seasons* 3, no. 9 (1 March 1842): 707–8.

25. *Times and Seasons* 3, no. 13 (2 May 1842): 781–82.

26. Joseph Smith, *History of The Church of Jesus Christ of Latter-day Saints,* ed. B. H. Roberts, 2d ed. rev. (Salt Lake City: Deseret Book, 1957), 6:402.

27. But angels "speak the words of Christ" (2 Ne. 32:3), and thus they do not lie.

28. "The Testimony of Three Witnesses," Book of Mormon.

29. Interview with Orson Pratt and Joseph F. Smith, 7–8 September 1878, Joseph F. Smith Diary, LDS Church Archives; Lyndon W. Cook, ed., *David Whitmer Interviews* (Orem, Utah: Grandin, 1991), 26; see also George Q. Cannon interview, 27 February 1884; Cook, 108.

30. Cook, 25.

31. See Richard Lloyd Anderson, *Investigating the Book of Mormon Witnesses* (Salt Lake City: Deseret Book, 1981).

Historicity and the Truthfulness of God

6

Robert J. Matthews

While some may argue that gospel truth is separate from historical truth, the gospel cannot be true unless it is also historical. This means that events such as the Creation, Fall, Atonement, and Restoration all truly took place in an identifiable time and place, even if that time and place are not known to us. If these or any gospel events were not historically true, God could not render a righteous judgment on any person.

Unless the conditions of the gospel are historically true and are founded in both time and place, God could not render an honest and fair judgment on humankind.

It all begins with what a person thinks God is, what he thinks the devil is, what salvation is, what truth is, and what one's own existence is. Without some knowledge of these things, one has no frame of reference with which to understand oneself, what this mortal life is, or even what truth is. In order to have any firm grasp on these basic concepts, one has to recognize and accept the existence of *absolute* truth, that is, the existence of a body of truth or facts that are unvarying and everlasting, absolutely grounded in actual existence in both time and place. The scriptural definition of truth is knowledge of "things as they really are, and . . . as they really will be" (Jacob 4:13; D&C 93:24).

Finite mortal man cannot of himself obtain a knowledge of the absolutes because they are beyond his mortal capabilities of research. Methods and tools of human origin are too crude to measure infinite things. The acquisition of absolute truth requires revelation from an absolute, unchanging, infinite God. When a revelation from God has been obtained, one has tapped into the limitless reservoir of divine knowledge, intelligence, and experience of eternity that transcends what any human mind could conceive of on its own. Even if the mind could formulate a concept of eternity, the mind could not be certain whether it was a figment of its own imagination or whether it was actual fact. Certitude can be possible only by the light of divine revelation.

The Prophet Joseph Smith stated that revelation from God is "the most glorious principle of the Gospel of Jesus Christ."[1] He also explained that without divine revelation no person can know anything about God or the devil: "If it requires the Spirit of God to know the things of God; and the spirit of the devil can only be unmasked through that medium, then it follows as a natural consequence that unless some person or persons have a communication, or revelation from God, unfolding to them the operation of the spirit, they must eternally remain ignorant of these principles; for I contend that if one man cannot understand these things but by the Spirit of God, ten thousand men cannot; it is alike out of the reach of the wisdom of the learned, the tongue of the eloquent, the power of the mighty."[2]

Since God is a God of truth, his revelations are always true. Each revelation does not contain the whole truth, but each will always be in accord with the absolute and be given from the perspective of the whole truth. I have often heard talk about the difference between spiritual truth and historical truth, but that is meaningless. Usually people talk about these so-called two areas of truth because they want to harmonize some concept the world has accepted with the revelations of God. They feel this approach will enable them to believe in the gospel without differing with the world. But it appears to me that it is not possible that there could be spiritual truth separate and apart from historical truth. Truth *is* historical or it is not truth. The nature of truth makes philosophical reasoning unnecessary to establish its existence.

Some examples may be helpful. First, let us consider the character of God. The seven *Lectures on Faith,* first delivered in Kirtland, Ohio, in the fall of 1834, explain that God's character and personal attributes are, and of necessity must be, absolute. He is holy, just, truthful, merciful, knowledgeable, powerful, and unchangeable. He is absolute in every characteristic, and He is permanent. If He were anything less, He would not be God.[3]

The Significance of Time and Place

Let us consider next the Creation, the Fall, and the Atonement. In both ancient and modern scripture, this absolute God declares that He created the earth and man for a wise purpose. He has not explained the entire process, but He has given us to understand that He was the authorizing agent in the Creation. He further declared that He placed Adam and Eve, real people who were not subject to death, in a Garden and gave them commandments, which they transgressed and thereby brought about a process of physical, spiritual, and moral degeneration resulting in death. This is called the Fall. We are duty bound to accept the fact of Adam's Fall, because a truthful God has spoken it.

To be historically true, the Creation has to fit into some identifiable time and place. The time and the place may not be identifiable to finite man, but they *are* known to God. Likewise to be historical, the Fall of Adam (whatever the process) had to occur at some actual geographical location that can be defined by such coordinates as longitude, latitude, and altitude and could be recorded chronologically.

Jesus Christ claims to be the Son of God in the flesh. In that way His precise lineage is superior to the lineage of other men. Because God the Father is the Father of Jesus' earthly body, Jesus was a God while on earth in the flesh, and therefore He could conquer death. We are duty bound to believe precisely these things about Jesus, because they were revealed in a serious manner by a truthful God. God revealed also that Jesus Christ did not commit any sin on earth, that He shed His blood for a ransom of humankind, and that He died on the cross and rose from the dead with His glorified, tangible body of flesh and bones. Each of these events had to occur in both time and place, so literally that they could be recorded by a chronometer, placed on a calendar, and marked on a map. Therefore we are duty bound to believe in them.

The same is true of Joseph Smith's First Vision, the coming forth of the gold plates of the Book of Mormon, the restoration of the priesthood by angels, and a large number of other events. All these are historical and geographical events with a history in both time and place.

The Lord could have given Joseph Smith the Book of Mormon without the gold plates, or the Book of Abraham without use of the papyrus. He could have manufactured the finished products in heaven and handed them to us. But I think such would have seriously impaired our responsibility to understand how the Lord works. Since the earth is tangible, and we are tangible, it is consistent with God's ways and His plainness and openness that His work be made available to us in a plain, simple, and tangible manner as far as possible—without artificial magic, unnecessary mystery, or any deception. God is indeed a worker of miracles, but there seems to be a law that miraculous ways are not used if the matter can be accomplished without them. There were real plates, real papyrus, real angels with real hands to confer priesthood, and a real Savior who suffered real pain and shed real blood. Such literalness gives the gospel substance, justifies the believer, and more fully leaves the unbeliever without excuse.

Historicity and Judgment

The events we have listed above (such as Creation, Fall, Atonement, Resurrection) are the very foundation of the gospel of Jesus Christ, both anciently and in The Church of Jesus Christ of Latter-day Saints today. Furthermore, the Lord has spoken and instructed us as follows: "Ye shall be holy; for I am holy" (Lev. 11:44), and "I would that ye should be perfect even as I, or your Father who is in heaven is perfect" (3 Ne. 12:48). If the foundational events of the gospel of Jesus Christ did not literally occur—if there were no gold plates, no Urim and Thummim, no angel Moroni, no Father and Son in the Sacred Grove, no Fall of Adam, no resurrection of Jesus Christ—then nothing is true, and even God Himself has not told the truth and is therefore neither holy nor perfect. Our Judge cannot hold *us* to righteousness on the Day of Judgment, if *He* has not been truthful Himself.

Judgment would be a sham, and eternity would be chaos, if every aspect of the gospel is not totally and completely true. Consider the predicament that would arise at the judgment bar if the founding events of the Christian faith did not happen. A righteous judgment could not be rendered against any part of humankind who did not believe the gospel if the plan is based on any falsehood. On the other hand, what about those who *did* believe the gospel if that gospel is not totally true? Could God in all honesty bless and reward them for believing a lie? That would make mockery of faith; for faith is to hope for things that "are not seen, which are true" (Alma 32:21). Or in other words, faith is the assurance that the gospel of Jesus Christ is true (JST Heb. 11:1). It is my conviction that God has not been playing games with us. The revelations and the founding events of the gospel are historically true, both in time and in place. I expect that the unbelieving portion of humankind will find on the day of judgment that what the Lord and His prophets have said about the plan of salvation is literally and historically true. Therefore, the way in which we respond to these events while in our mortal probation will exert a permanent influence in our final examination. If we have not believed the facts of the gospel of Christ, our lives have been built on a sandy foundation instead of on a rock. Everything about the judgment must be fair and open. There must never come a time when anyone can justifiably say that our Heavenly Father was unfair, or that any incompleteness or deception existed in the plan of salvation. God will be totally vindicated in every particular.

Of course I know that there are figurative statements in the scriptures, but such things are obviously figurative. Such expressions as "I am the door," or "ye are the salt of the earth," enrich the language and add layers of meaning that would be impossible to duplicate without the use of symbols. Nevertheless, actual historical events are not spoken of in such figurative terms.

The marvelous and wonderfully logical Paul spoke of the integrity of the gospel when he wrote:

> Now if Christ be preached that he rose from the dead, how say some among you that there is no resurrection of the dead? But if there be no resurrection of the dead, then is Christ not risen: And if Christ be not risen, then is our preaching vain, and your faith is also vain. Yea, and we are found false witnesses of God; because we have testified of God that he raised up Christ: whom he raised not up, if so be that the dead rise not. For if the dead rise not, then is not Christ raised: And if Christ be not raised, your faith is vain; ye are yet in your sins. Then they also which are fallen asleep in Christ are perished. If in this life only we have hope in Christ, we are of all men most miserable.

> But now is Christ risen from the dead, and become the first fruits of them that slept (1 Cor. 15:12–20).

Father Lehi, a doctrinal giant, was thinking along the same lines when he explained to his son Jacob that unless the Gospel is literally true, the earth

> must needs have been created for a thing of naught; wherefore there would have been no purpose in the end of its creation. Wherefore, this thing must needs destroy the wisdom of God and his eternal purposes, and also the power, and the mercy, and the justice of God. . . . But behold, all things have been done in the wisdom of him who knoweth all things. Adam fell that men might be; and men are, that they might have joy. And the Messiah cometh in the fulness of time, that he may redeem the children of men from the fall. And because that they are redeemed from the fall they have become free forever, knowing good from evil; to act for themselves and not to be acted upon, save it be by the punishment of the law at the great and last day, according to the commandments which God hath given (2 Ne. 2:12, 24–26; see also 2 Ne. 11:7).

The Miracle of Salvation

The salvation that God promises is not simply the acquisition of some knowledge, manners, and learned responses. It is not a coating of intellectual polish, or a veneer of sophistication. It involves some of that, but the salvation that comes through Jesus Christ is considerably more. It includes: (1) a mighty change of heart, (2) a cleansing from past sins by a baptism of water and the Holy Ghost, or of fire, and (3) a sanctification of the very tissues of the body. Salvation involves being born again, becoming a new creature in Jesus Christ, having the dross purged by the Holy Ghost, and having an eye single to the glory of God. Attainment of knowledge, although an *aid* to salvation, will not sufficiently change and purge the heart of man. It takes the Spirit of God speaking to man's spirit to give a testimony, and it takes a cleansing by the Holy Ghost to change a person from a natural man into a saint. Without that divine change, a person is not saved. All of these processes are miraculous because they cannot be accomplished by the laws of the mortal world, but they are real, and they are historical.

For these very reasons we understand that the gospel is more than a system of ethics, a social order, or a mental exercise. Without the historical divine birth of Jesus Christ, His actual sinless life, the historical shedding of His precious blood in Gethsemane, His literal death on the cross, and His literal physical resurrection from the grave, there could have been no redemption from sin or from death even if we had the same set of gospel rules, the same gospel ordinances, and the same ethics that we now have. The plan would lack power without the ultimate triumph over sin and death by Jesus Christ. Nothing is more basic to the gospel than the historical fact of Jesus' Atonement. He came to atone for the Fall of Adam, as well as for our personal sins. By His life, His death, and His blood, He paid for a broken law. Without that payment, nothing we could do would save us in this life or the next. If Christ had not made the Atonement and risen from the dead, nothing man could do could ever make up the loss, and the Day of Judgment would be indescribably dreadful. But the historical nature of the Atonement of Jesus Christ makes the inevitable judgment a day of rescue, ransom, and redemption.

When our personal standard is revealed truth, we have no difficulty with the matter of historicity. The Prophet Joseph Smith explained that the same sociality will exist among people in eternity as exists among us now. That situation calls for reality and tangibility (D&C 130:1–3). Eternity, based on reality, leads to a literal view of heaven. This was magnificently expressed by Elder Orson Pratt:

> A Saint, who is one in deed and in truth, does not look for an immaterial heaven, but he expects a heaven with lands, houses, cities, vegetation, rivers, and animals; with thrones, temples, palaces, kings, princes, priests, and angels; with food, raiment, musical instruments, &c; all of which are material. Indeed, the Saints' heaven is a redeemed, glorified, celestial, material creation, inhabited by glorified material beings, male and female, organized into families, embracing all the relationships of husbands and wives, parents and children, where sorrow, crying, pain, and death will be known no more. Or to speak still more definitely, this earth, when glorified, is the Saints' eternal heaven. On it they expect to live, with body, parts, and holy passions: on it they expect to move and have their being; to eat, drink, converse, worship, sing, play on musical instruments, engage in joyful, innocent, social amusements, visit neighboring towns and neighboring worlds: indeed, matter and its qualities and properties are the only beings or things with which they expect to associate.[4]

If these are the true riches of eternity (D&C 38:20, 39), a real world in physical space, and if the historical relationships we enjoyed here continue there, only on a much higher plane, then the historicity of central gospel events takes on even deeper meanings. Indeed, the historicity of key scriptural events will form one unbroken chain from the premortal existence, through the Creation, Fall, Atonement, Resurrection, and Judgment to our eternal reward.

Before his retirement, Robert J. Matthews was professor of ancient scripture, Brigham Young University.

Notes

1. Joseph Smith, *Teachings of the Prophet Joseph Smith,* comp. Joseph Fielding Smith (Salt Lake City: Deseret Book, 1938), 298–99.

2. Ibid., 205.

3. See Larry E. Dahl and Charles D. Tate Jr., eds., *The Lectures on Faith in Historical Perspective* (Provo, Utah: Religious Studies Center, Brigham Young University, 1990).

4. *Millennial Star* 28, no. 46 (17 November 1866): 722.

No Middle Ground:
The Debate over the Authenticity
of the Book of Mormon

7

Louis Midgley

The authenticity of the Book of Mormon has been under attack since before the book was published. While the Book of Mormon has been called everything from fiction and fraud to the product of demonic possession, the current argument against its authenticity seeks to find a "middle ground" between these claims and what the Book of Mormon itself claims to be—inspired writings of ancient prophets. The "middle-ground" genre of attack professes that the Book of Mormon can still be scripture, in that it inspires and motivates, even though the people and events detailed therein, and Joseph Smith's account of angelic visitors and gold plates, are not historically true. This type of argument is invalid because we cannot accept as simply motivational that which claims to be historical reality.

There is no middle ground on the question of whether the Book of Mormon is an authentic ancient text. On this—but not of course on every issue—we are confronted with an either/or possibility. Why? The Book of Mormon claims to be a record largely written and/or edited by Mormon, an ancient prophet and military leader who, according to the book itself, lived from approximately A.D. 327 to 385 somewhere in the New World. In fashioning his account, Mormon included or drew upon records begun by Nephi thirty years after his family traveled from Palestine to the New World, soon after 600 B.C.

There is nothing in the Book of Mormon (or in Joseph Smith's account of its coming forth) that suggests that it should be read as anything other than historical fact. On the other hand, critics of the Book of Mormon have always insisted that it is a product of the nineteenth century—that it reflects the thinking and the world of Joseph Smith (or one of his contemporaries) immediately prior to its publication. I will sketch some of the permutations of these two large categories of competing approaches to the Book of Mormon. The focus has always been on whether the Book of Mormon is what it and the Latter-day Saints declare it to be: an authentic ancient record of divine revelations to peoples called by God out of the wicked societies in which they found themselves in a providential effort to keep alive the covenants made with their fathers. The publication of the Book of Mormon constitutes for faithful Latter-day Saints a crucial, initial generative or founding event of the restoration of the fulness of the gospel of Jesus Christ and the reestablishment of the kingdom of God on earth.

The Book of Mormon and the story of its coming forth provoked some of Joseph Smith's contemporaries to attempt to demonstrate that it is fraudulent—that it is not an authentic ancient history and therefore that its teachings are a deception, if not blasphemy. The first critics insisted that the Book of Mormon must be read as a modern book—as somehow a product of the time and place in which it was initially published; they have thus striven to provide plausible alternative explanations of the Book of Mormon precisely because of its crucial role in both grounding and forming the content of the faith and memory of Latter-day Saints. Hence, from at least 1831, the Saints have been confronted with literature that criticizes the Book of Mormon—the crux of which has been an attack on its historicity.[1] From virtually the moment the Book of Mormon appeared in print, both the Saints and their critics have seen it as either what it claims to be or as essentially fraudulent.

The historicity of the Book of Mormon has thus been a crucial issue for both the Saints and the critics of Joseph Smith and the restored gospel. The critics, with few exceptions, still insist that both its narrative structures and prophetic teachings are essentially a muddled hodgepodge. Sectarian anti-Mormons on the most extreme fringe of Protestant evangelical religiosity insist that the book is demonic and that Joseph Smith was under the influence of what they describe as Satanic forces.[2] A more moderate faction of evangelical anti-Mormons has been at war with their extremist colleagues.[3] Only recently have the sectarian criticisms of the Book of Mormon tended to move away from the old, discredited attacks that were set in place during the first decades after its publication.

The explanation for such shifts seems to be that it is no longer possible to gain the attention of knowledgeable Latter-day Saints with the old, frenzied attacks on the Book of Mormon once common in sectarian circles. This fact has yielded a shift in the approach to the Book of Mormon among its more thoughtful sectarian critics. And better-informed non-LDS observers of Mormon things now recognize the importance of the Book of Mormon to the faith of the Saints; they sense something of its subtle complexity; they respect the way it both grounds and forms the content of the faith and memory of the Saints; and they also sense its power to fill the lives of the Saints with an understanding of their relationship with God.[4]

An Ancient or a Modern Book?

"The Book of Mormon," according to Hugh Nibley, "must be read as an ancient, not as a modern book. Its mission, as described by the book itself, depends in great measure for its efficacy on its genuine antiquity."[5] When confronted with the Book of Mormon and the story of its coming forth, the decisive question is whether it is—as it claims—an account of the inspired teachings of ancient prophets initially led from Jerusalem through Lehi's prophetic guidance soon after 600 B.C., and hence also an authentic history of some of the inhabitants of the New World.

When the Book of Mormon is read as a modern book, Joseph Smith must be seen as a liar who knowingly made up a preposterous tale with which he may have intended to attract and manipulate gullible followers. Or he must be pictured as unable to distinguish between actually encountering an angel, eventually possessing plates, interpreters, and so forth, and not having had those experiences, in which case the Book of Mormon would turn out to be a bizarre product of his abnormal psychology. The issues surrounding the historical authenticity of the Book of Mormon thus come down to an either/or choice not only regarding its truth claims but also regarding whether or not Joseph Smith was a genuine prophet. On this crucial issue there is simply no middle ground. Critics of the restored gospel have understood this from the beginning. The not-prophet explanations have ranged from attempts to demonstrate that Joseph Smith perpetrated a conscious fraud, to efforts to portray him as someone sincere about his illusions, or perhaps in some way psychologically dissociative and hence delusional, or to some combination of these explanations.

Against these alternative explanations, the Saints maintain that the Book of Mormon is precisely what it purports to be—a divinely inspired, providentially recorded and preserved account of ancient peoples separated from the inhabitants of the Old World, recorded on metal plates and revealed to Joseph Smith by an angel who was also once a participant in the events it records. Joseph Smith is also seen as a genuine prophet by the Saints. Both the Saints and the more thoughtful critics have thus understood that the explanation for the Book of Mormon must be consistent with its prophetic and historical contents. This is true whether one reads it as an authentic ancient text or as a nineteenth-century fabrication and hoax.

Both sectarian and secular critics of the Book of Mormon begin with the assumption that Mormon (who claimed to have provided the final redaction) and the Nephite prophets and scribes named in the volume were not its true authors; critics have therefore had to identify its modern author (or authors). They are thus faced with the task of fashioning an explanation that plausibly accommodates all that is known about the book and its coming forth; they have also had to take into account its complex and subtle narrative structure and teachings.

From the beginning, critics have been faced with the question of who wrote the Book of Mormon. Was it Joseph Smith? That was the first explanation,[6] and it immediately collapsed. Was it written by someone else—a contemporary of Joseph Smith?[7] Exactly how was this accomplished? Those who reject the Mormon explanation must also explain how and why it was composed. In whatever way the critics tell the story and whatever the motives they attribute to Joseph Smith (or to those involved in a supposed conspiracy), they must explain both the existence and contents of the Book of Mormon. Since earlier attempts to credit its composition to someone other than Joseph Smith have floundered,[8] we are currently confronted with a return to the stance of its original critics who insisted that it was written by

Joseph Smith.[9] Those who now fashion naturalistic explanations of the Book of Mormon are faced with the task of uncovering in Joseph Smith's immediate environment or in the workings of his psyche all of the sources for its complicated narrative structure, style, cast of characters, prophetic teachings, and so forth.[10]

In addition to the usual array of sectarian criticisms of the Book of Mormon, believers are now also confronted with secular explanations that dogmatically and systematically remove the divine from the natural world and, more importantly, from history. Thus, "in our day," according to one recent attempt to account for historical understanding, "of course, the deity is absent."[11] When historians approach the Book of Mormon with such a dogma, every effort will be made to deny that it is authentic. However, to begin with that assumption, and it is clearly an assumption and not somehow the conclusion of a demonstration, is to beg all the important questions raised by the existence of a text such as the Book of Mormon.

In one way or another, recent attempts to remove the mighty acts of God either overtly or inadvertently from the Saints' understanding of the past undermine the grounds for, and also radically alter the content of, the faith of the Saints. They do so by treating what they believe is the actual presence of the divine in human affairs as mere instances of sincere though mistaken illusion or delusion, or as the product of outright fraud.

Secular Assumptions and Revisionist Accounts

The role of secular, naturalistic assumptions in undermining or transforming the supernatural or the miraculous in the interpretation of the Bible is well known.[12] What is less well known is the role of such assumptions in efforts to tell the story of religion generally. Historians are often either not aware of or are silent about their guiding assumptions, though they sometimes divulge them. For example, in the 1975 edition of his massive two-volume history of religion in America, Sydney E. Ahlstrom grants that no one can "say that he can in one lifetime write an American religious history 'from the sources.'"[13] Anyone taking on such a task would have to rely on a vast number of secondary works. A history of American religion must be synthetic, depending on the assimilation of essays written by others who specialize in the parts which are then assembled into the larger picture on the basis of some controlling theme, idea, or explanatory hypothesis.

When the paperback edition of his book first appeared, Professor Ahlstrom could "see no grounds for expecting drastic changes in the Western historiographical tradition. . . . This tradition began to free itself from ecclesiastical surveillance and providential interpretations during the Renaissance; and ever since then, despite the pride and petulance of historians and interference from both church and state, the overall accuracy, coherence, and plausibility of its explanations have improved. Historiography may be an ideal construction in constant need of revision; but it is not a trick or a fable. So the work goes on. Fads and fashions come and go."[14]

Ahlstrom added that "the ideas of even the most magisterial thinkers, like Marx and Freud, are only very slowly assimilated. Yet week by week, in seminars, classrooms, and scholars' studies the effort is sustained."[15] Apparently the great leap forward in understanding religion in America involves, at least from Ahlstrom's perspective, the assimilation of assumptions and explanations that reduce religion to delusion, in the case of Karl Marx,[16] or illusion, in the case of Sigmund Freud.[17] Presumably these are not the "fads and fashions [that] come and go," but bedrock truths that must be "very slowly assimilated."

To his credit, Ahlstrom also sensed that "the present, after all, is but a thin film on the past, an imaginary figment; while the future exists only as a possibility—or a negation. In a certain sense, therefore, we all live and have our being in the past."[18] He then insisted, and correctly, that a people or "a nation that is unaware of its past bears an alarming similarity to a person suffering from amnesia: a crucial element of its being is lacking."[19] He also noted that Americans have experienced a break in the continuity they previously had with the past.[20] Why? Partly because they, much like various communities of believers, have either forgotten their past or have had it interpreted or reinterpreted out from under them by historians whose explanations have transformed it under the relentless pressure of the dominant ideas of the age in which they live. Are not at least religious communities insulated from the corrosive effects of secular assumptions by their own beliefs and understandings—their faith? Not in the least. Why?

Ahlstrom sensed that "the historian cannot claim divinely inspired sources of insight, nor can he place one body of holy scripture above another."[21] But are they really all that neutral and unable to pass judgment? Have not secular notions advanced by the likes of Marx and Freud—those magisterial thinkers Ahlstrom seems to celebrate, and their many followers—had their impact on the work of historians?

The faith and memory of believing peoples has not fared very well when it has been explained from within the categories of secular modernity. This is the larger issue. The stories told by secularized historians have had profoundly corrosive impacts on communities of faith.[22] For Christians in general, the corrosive effect of secular categories and explanations has been on the understanding of the miraculous elements in the accounts contained in the Bible. For Latter-day Saints, however, the question is primarily how naturalistic explanations of the Book of Mormon impact faith.[23]

C. S. Lewis has pointed out that "what cannot be trusted to recur is not material for science: that is why history is not one of the sciences. . . . Thus hand over miracles from science to history (but not, of course, to historians who beg the question by beginning with materialist assumptions)."[24] Those secular critics who dogmatically reject the historicity of the Book of Mormon approach the text with what amounts to essentially naturalistic assumptions. With these in place they typically avoid taking seriously the possibility that it is an authentic ancient text and that Joseph Smith was therefore a genuine prophet. This means that much of the literature critical of the historicity of the Book of Mormon involves in various and sometimes subtle ways the logical fallacy of question begging—that is, critics make the desired conclusion work as their beginning premise.

But it is a mistake to begin with naturalistic assumptions that rule out in advance the possibility of divine revelation. Critics of the historicity of the Book of Mormon regularly begin with naturalistic assumptions that set in place exactly the conclusion they wish to reach. When confronted with an account in which a nonnatural (or in that sense "supernatural") element is present in a prophetic truth claim, as it clearly is in the case of the Book of Mormon, the wise course is to avoid the fallacy of question begging.

C. S. Lewis was also right in holding that "history is not one of the sciences" precisely because "what cannot be trusted to recur is not material for science."[25] But the enormous reputation of the natural sciences has generated a kind of secular "religion" that can be called scientism—the belief that naturalistic explanations can (or should eventually be able to) explain everything, including alleged instances of divine special revelations. Hence, what Lewis described as "miracle" is present in what are believed to be real events. It is found in the mighty acts of God, the appearance of divine messengers, theophanies, the presence of the divine on the stage of human history, and so forth; it is not, from the perspective of the believers, mere illusion or delusion or subjective emotional responses to presumably "natural" environmental forces. If the believers are wrong about this, their faith is simply in vain. Hence, what Lewis called miracle, understood this way, is a necessary or essential element of the faith and memory of Latter-day Saints.

Reading the Book of Mormon
with Naturalistic Assumptions

Whatever else might be said about them, secular, naturalistic assumptions effectively remove the divine from the stage of human history. Is it possible to find ways of preserving some modicum of religiosity in the face of secular fashions? When the miraculous has been removed, can a sentimental something be retained? One writer reports that in 1835 David Friedrich Strauss, the author of the famous *Das Leben Jesu,* denied "the historicity of all miracles, the resurrection, and most of the contents of the gospels." But Strauss also thought it possible "to save the eternal truths contained in the historically dubious record through the concept of myth." It turns out that in the background assumptions of secularized intellectuals such as Strauss, "reason destroys truth by its naturalistic explanations; the use of myth allows the preservation of truth in the face of rationalism."[26] How?

For example, treating the writers of the Gospels as purveyors of fables and myths presumably saves them from being seen as base deceivers.[27] It does this by entirely deliteralizing the content of the teachings found in the Gospels. Jesus, for example, is no longer seen as having been resurrected; Paul only "saw" Jesus *in a new light* on the road to Damascus. So it turns out that much like liberal biblical critics who strive to find some way of salvaging something from what is left when the miraculous is dogmatically removed, both historians generally and now also a few Mormon historians have struggled to find a way of salvaging something when they have reduced the divine to myth and fable in their highly secularized accounts.

Accordingly, we have an explanation for the recent spate of efforts to read the Book of Mormon as merely a kind of extended parable, a kind of morality tale or fable, as inspiring or inspired "frontier fiction,"[28] and thereby for efforts to turn Joseph Smith's prophetic charisms into instances of magic, myth, and mysticism.[29]

The faith and memory—the very identity—of Latter-day Saints is compromised and radically transformed and even logically undercut when certain crucial texts are read with naturalistic assumptions or when naturalistic explanations are employed to explain away the accounts of the divine in those texts by explanations that rule out in advance the possibility that divine revelations are a genuine feature of a real, and not merely a mythical or a fictional, past.

When historians write about the Latter-day Saint past in merely "human and naturalistic terms," they are clearly employing a vocabulary and also a set of secular assumptions that are well-known to those who, for example, debate the reality of the resurrection of Jesus of Nazareth. And it has been clearly established that to begin a historical inquiry into the resurrection with naturalistic assumptions rules out in advance the resurrection as a historical reality, thus begging the crucial question.[30] C. S. Lewis was right in holding that explanations resting on naturalistic assumptions, whatever else one might say about them, end up involving a fallacy, since they beg the crucial questions.

"The Broad, Promising Middle Ground"?

Critics of the Book of Mormon who ground their accounts on naturalistic assumptions generally hold that Joseph Smith is an outright fraud. Recently, however, a few critics have objected to the either-prophet-or-fraud stance. In 1974, one Mormon historian suggested that the scholars "should begin to explore the broad, promising middle ground" between genuine prophet and fraud.[31] What might this middle ground be? It has been suggested that Joseph Smith was sincere in his illusions or delusions, that he was a magic-saturated, superstitious frontier mystic. They hold that the Saints should abandon the old and presumably fallacious either-prophet-or-fraud alternatives by simply abandoning the notion that Joseph Smith was either intentionally involved in fraud or he was the genuine prophet that the Saints have always believed him to be. The crucial theoretical issue confronting Latter-day Saints who wish to examine the Book of Mormon and Joseph Smith's prophetic truth claims is the propriety of what are typically designated naturalistic explanations.

One historian insists that the Book of Mormon "is probably best understood, at least in part, as a trance-related production."[32] Thus the Book of Mormon is not "history in any sense." Instead, it is "an unusually sophisticated product of unconscious and little-known mental processes."[33] Such an explanation would supposedly provide a middle ground somewhere between anti-Mormon critics who see the Book of Mormon as an intentional fraud and believers who see it as a genuine ancient text.

These critics often do not understand why Latter-day Saints refuse to accept their essentially secular, naturalistic explanations. There are, no doubt, numerous issues in Latter-day Saint history upon which some middle ground between alternative accounts will turn out to be the most likely explanation. But there is simply no possible middle ground on the question of whether Joseph Smith was a genuine prophet, as Latter-day Saints understand such matters. Likewise, on the question of whether the Book of Mormon is an authentic ancient history, there is simply no middle ground.

Though being a Latter-day Saint involves more than accepting the Book of Mormon, it is also not an exaggeration to say, as one prominent non-LDS writer has done, that "non-Mormons become Mormons when they respond to Mormonism's fundamental truth claims by taking the Book of Mormon at face value."[34] The obvious corollary is that Latter-day Saints become mere cultural Mormons when they begin to invoke naturalistic explanations of the Book of Mormon, that is, explanations that deny that there really was a Lehi colony and that Joseph Smith actually encountered heavenly messengers. Faithful Latter-day Saints, as distinguished from mere dissidents or cultural Mormons, are such precisely because they believe that the Book of Mormon is exactly what it claims to be and also that Joseph Smith's account of its coming forth is simply true.

Because of the crucial role the Book of Mormon (and the account of its recovery) plays in providing both the ground and content for the faith and memory of the Saints, critics of the Restoration, beginning even before the book's publication, flatly denied even the remote possibility that angels could make a book available.[35] Since the 1960s, it has been common for some Mormon historians to insist that Mormon history and culture can and should be studied in naturalistic terms. In 1980, when I started examining the programmatic statements of Mormon historians, it became obvious that we would soon be faced with an overt effort by cultural Mormons to read the Book of Mormon as the mere product of nineteenth-century culture. Some revisionist historians, for example, hint that the Book of Mormon should be read as a nineteenth-century fable (reflecting what Joseph Smith was thinking prior to 1830), or they strive to see his account of his encounters with heavenly messengers merely as an embellishment of a half-forgotten dream that later took on theological significance. Joseph Smith is now also pictured by revisionist historians as a profoundly superstitious magician, a village mystic, a kind of dissociative, inventive "genius," and finally as deeply involved in occult lore and practices.[36] The Book of Mormon is thus turned into Joseph Smith's imaginative effort to set forth his theological speculations in narrative form.

The Book of Mormon clearly flies in the face of some of the dominant secular ideas of our culture; it challenges certain fundamental assumptions of modernity. And it is controversial. For some with roots in the Restoration, it is a puzzle and an offense. Is there some way to render the Book of Mormon harmless? Some of its critics have striven to find a plausible way of reading it as a product of some primitive superstition or mysticism. They have believed that they could thereby skirt the issue of its historicity. Would reading the Book of Mormon as fiction, as an extended parable or myth of some sort, not reduce at least some of the chagrin experienced by cultural Mormons over the traditional prophetic truth claims upon which the faith of the Latter-day Saints has always rested?

As far as I have been able to determine, during the century and a half after the publication of the Book of Mormon, no effort was made to distinguish its prophetic truth claims—its core message and related teachings—from its claim to be an authentic ancient history. And those who insisted on reading the Book of Mormon as fable and fiction and who insisted on seeing magic, superstition, and imposition in Joseph Smith thought of themselves (and were seen by others) as outside the community of Saints. But it is now not uncommon for critics of the Book of Mormon to want to be seen as sympathetic with those they picture as simplistic believers. And some critics even insist that they are Mormons in at least a cultural sense, even when they are no longer believing Latter-day Saints or in some cases even members of the Church.[37] In the last decade or so we have seen efforts by a few people to argue that the sectarian and secular critics of Joseph Smith have always been right—the Book of Mormon is merely the fiction of a highly imaginative farm boy. But, they add, it can be read as either inspiring or perhaps even in some way "inspired," as a work of a "religious genius," and so forth.

Whatever else one might say about such stances, they clearly compete with the traditional reading of the Book of Mormon and with the traditional understanding of the Latter-day Saint past. Hence, it is not uncommon for those anxious to legitimize a revisionist reading of the Book of Mormon to use the pejorative label "traditionalist" to describe those who they see clinging to the notion that there was a Lehi colony. These critics have appropriated the label "revisionist" to describe a "new Mormon history," or a "revisionist Mormon history," which often includes and even features attacks on the historicity of the Book of Mormon.[38]

In the past fifteen years, several revisionist readings of the Book of Mormon have appeared in magazines and books. Efforts have been made to legitimize reading the Book of Mormon as fiction, inspiring or otherwise, and also to promote the view that Joseph Smith was essentially a mystic or a practitioner of magic. There is, it seems to me, an alliance between those who see fraud and hence nothing of value in the Book of Mormon and those who see it as an inspired or inspiring fable or as the product of mysticism, magic, and the occult.

Though the Book of Mormon (coupled with the account of its coming forth) is an essential element in the faith of Latter-day Saints, it is a target for those with sectarian religious commitments and tends to be an annoyance and even an embarrassment to cultural Mormons, including some of those on the fringes of the Mormon academic community who have adopted a naturalistic ideology and therefore dogmatically reject anything that appears "supernatural." These people are consequently especially offended by its links to an angel and would like to find some way to turn it into harmless, though perhaps "inspiring" nineteenth-century fiction. In so doing they reduce what they call "religion" to the advice of theologians on how to live, thereby denying divine, special revelations. It has therefore become increasingly popular among critics of the Book of Mormon to make a distinction between its historicity and its prophetic teachings. One reason is that it simply will no longer do for critics to dismiss it as a jumble or as blasphemy. In addition, some of those who strive to make such a distinction have been trained in liberal (usually Protestant) divinity schools where the historical reality of much or all of the miraculous in the Bible has been jettisoned and where for the most part only moral sentiments have been retained. Or, in a few instances, those without such formal training have still managed to appropriate some version of this ideology.

Faithful Disbelief

Even before and immediately after the founding of the Mormon History Association in 1965, a few cultural Mormons were hinting at their misgivings about the historicity of the Book of Mormon.[39] Eventually some of these historians began to suggest, sometimes in rather ambiguous language, that the Book of Mormon should not be read as an authentic ancient history. But it has only been within the last three decades that those who deny that the Book of Mormon is authentic history have attempted to make a distinction between its historicity and the soundness of its teachings. Some writers have characterized the Book of Mormon "not as literal history, but as inspired allegory" fashioned by Joseph Smith.[40] And the dogmatic rejection of the possibility of the historical authenticity of the Book of Mormon has been taken up by some who claim that such a stance "may offer hope to the 'closet doubters' who might agree that 'you don't get books from angels and translate them by miracles.'"[41] Hope for what? A community of cultural "Mormons" consisting of those who disbelieve? One writer describes this position as an instance of "faithful disbelief."[42]

There are several reasons for the recent attempts to reject the historical authenticity of the Book of Mormon while still claiming to see in it some advice on how to live. Some claim "that all of the hassling over the authenticity of the Book of Mormon is just a waste of time."[43] These critics read the Book of Mormon as a mythology fashioned by Joseph Smith that might contain some nice teachings but not the word of God. However, this entails disposing of the traditional understanding that Joseph Smith was visited by angels and so forth. Some writers have claimed that since the debate over its authenticity has been inconclusive, the conclusions reached have not been based on evidence but on whether one is or is not a believer. They then brush aside the entire debate over the historical authenticity on the grounds of what they sometimes describe as a "heavy-handed either/or approach."[44]

If historians, as some want us to believe, cannot say anything about sacred matters, if they are prevented from advancing opinions on such things, then they should say exactly nothing about prophetic truth claims; they should not dogmatically assume that prophetic truth claims are false. They should at least leave such questions open, which is exactly what they refuse to do. Why? Is it that they believe that unless historians can finally resolve historical issues, they have no business investigating them? Do they not see that arguing that the Book of Mormon is a nonhistorical "sacred text" entails advancing the proposition that Joseph Smith was not a genuine prophet? To take that position is to take a stand on what are clearly historical matters. So it turns out that the so-called middle-ground explanations of the Book of Mormon merely brush aside the crucial issues raised by the Book of Mormon, which have constituted the content and grounds of the faith and memory of the Latter-day Saints.

Such writers reject an either/or position on the Book of Mormon and turn instead to a middle-ground explanation of the text because they seem less concerned with actual historical events and more concerned with what is traditionally known as "theology." Latter-day Saints, they complain, "do not so much have a theology as they have a history."[45] This is, of course, right. The faith of Latter-day Saints is not the product of speculation traditionally known as "theology," that is, the speculation about the divine flowing from a philosophical culture. Latter-day Saints have always looked to events, to accounts of actual encounters with God, for their understanding of divine things, and not to speculation, which they consider to be the primary source of apostate corruption of divine revelation.

Is "Theology" the Answer?

Cultural Mormons have brushed aside divine revelations and are left with nothing but theology. Hence they complain that the Saints confuse history with theology. By looking to prophetic encounters with the divine, rather than the reasoning of theologians, Latter-day Saints find both the content and grounds of faith in accounts of the past. In order to genuinely trust God, to take hold of the forgiveness made available through the Atonement of Christ, one certainly must affirm a number of things about Jesus of Nazareth, including that he was resurrected and that he appeared to the ancient Nephites and eventually to Joseph Smith. Of course, these are believed to be events in time and space and not merely theological speculations. And hence for the Latter-day Saint faith to be true, the Book of Mormon must be exactly what it claims to be. For the Saints, a teaching about Jesus of Nazareth being the Messiah or Christ simply makes no sense apart from essentially historical claims, including that he was killed and then rose again. To take away from faith what are clearly historical claims is to reduce religion to some advice about how to live that is shorn of any real link with God.

Why have critics of the Restoration had an interest in turning the Book of Mormon into fiction? By so doing they feel confident that they have shown that it is fraudulent, and the community of faith for which it serves as a canon is thus grounded on fraud. What is not clear is why a Latter-day Saint would want to read the Book of Mormon as a fable. Nor is it at all clear how the Book of Mormon, read as merely Joseph Smith's theological speculation cast in fictional form, can be the word of God. Some writers, however, now insist on seeing the Book of Mormon as Joseph Smith's "theology" and not as history at all. The "theology" they have appropriated is found in both the explanations and in the background assumptions at work in the most "liberal" portion of contemporary biblical studies, or in the more philosophically grounded efforts to fashion a theology.

Some writers who advance a fashionable middle-ground explanation of the Book of Mormon admit that the basic content of the Christian message must necessarily be grounded in historical fact. The incarnation and resurrection are thus presumably historical. But once one starts down the road of accepting naturalistic explanations, it becomes ever more difficult to protect any historical element of Christian faith from the acids of modernity. And those who want some element of historical content or grounding for their faith—something like the Resurrection of Jesus—end up having to fashion arguments much like those I have proposed to accomplish their ends. But when they do that, they set in place arguments that confront their own secular, naturalistic assumptions.

Moreover, those who, for whatever reason, wish to preserve some modicum of historical content for themselves, as they brush aside the historicity of the Book of Mormon, sometimes argue that contemporary "liberal" theology provides the proper tools for uncovering genuine history rather than mere mythology. Theology is not a scriptural concept; rather, it is a term borrowed by Christians (and others) from Greek philosophy. Theology is words about God—but whose words? For Plato (in the second book of his *Republic*) it was the words of poets in a well-ordered city. What is called "natural theology" is that branch of the study of the nature of First Things. Hence, the natural theology of the Stoics pictured God as the World Soul in an essentially pantheistic picture of divine things. Christians borrowed what they could from the natural theology of the pagans to systematize their beliefs but especially to deliteralize what they found objectionable in the Bible.[46]

Currently, we can see exactly this same sort of thing going on when scholars brush aside Paul's epiphany on the road to Damascus. The result is that natural theology is not what God reveals to man, nor is it found in the accounts of the encounters of prophets with divine things. It is found instead in the speculation of those whose categories and modes of explanation are borrowed from a philosophical culture that sees only scandal in prophetic charisms. Thus, natural theology is not what God reveals to prophets but what theologians claim to have discovered by unaided human reason.

On the other hand, divine revelation, as Latter-day Saints understand it, necessarily involves accounts of God's mighty acts and in that sense is history. But it is not a secular history written with what C. S. Lewis called materialist assumptions that leave out the possibility of miracles. To put the matter bluntly, theology involves arguments about God and not encounters with God. These arguments are about the nature of First Things, where God is thought of as the First Thing. Theology deliteralizes and mythologizes and then attempts to demythologize, that is, render in the currently fashionable secular terms the messages found in the biblical accounts. And when such a program is followed, we end up being told that the Book of Mormon must be read, if we are to follow the tastes and fashions of others, as a myth understood as fable and not as fact.

An objection to grounding faith on historical claims is that history is notoriously inconclusive. One reason is that the stories we tell rest on assumptions we bring to the texts from which we strive to fashion our accounts. In addition, the sources are far too abundant for any mortal to master them all, and they are far too slim to even begin to settle the more interesting questions about the past. For these and other reasons, philosophers have urged Christians and Jews to turn away from history and strive instead for a religion within the limits of reason alone—to discover what is rationally warranted about divine things. It is in such an endeavor that we presumably will find the certainty for which we long. It must be granted that history will not—cannot—provide certainty. But does faith need or expect the kind of certainty that philosophers (or theologians) insist it must have? I doubt it. Certainly faith needs reasons, even good reasons. For me, and I believe for faithful Latter-day Saints generally, the accounts of the prophets and the record of God's mighty acts are sufficient for both the ground and content of faith. Faith is, after all, not merely believing something but trusting God. And our ability to trust God, to live by faith in love and with a genuine hope for the future, rests upon our appropriation of the stories of God's mighty acts, of our remembering and keeping the commandments—the terms of the covenants that make us the children of Christ.

The task of reframing our lives from the perspective of the gospel, a process that addresses the extremities of our life, accomplishes two tasks at once. On the one hand, by supplanting amnesia with memory, it gives us a past in which the divine is present in various ways; it directs the Saints as a community back to an unknown or perhaps forfeited past. On the other hand, by genuinely supplanting despair with hope, it leads the Saints to a future both as a community here and now and also as individuals in the hereafter in the kingdom of heaven. The gifts of memory and hope mediated by texts are not a great, coherent system of theology. The gifts, rather, are given one text at a time, texts both old and alien to us, evoking a world not domesticated by our modernity.

Before his retirement, Louis Midgley was professor of political science, Brigham Young University.

Notes

1. These attacks began with Alexander Campbell's "Delusions," *The Millennial Harbinger* 2, no. 2 (7 February 1831): 85–96; reprinted as *Delusions: An Analysis of the Book of Mormon; with an Examination of its Internal and External Evidences and a Refutation of Its Pretenses to Divine Authority* (Boston: Benjamin H. Greene, 1832).

2. Loftes Tryk, *The Best Kept Secrets in the Book of Mormon* (Redondo Beach, Calif.: Jacob's Well Foundation, 1988) is an example of this literature. Other better-known examples of the extreme wing of Protestant evangelical attacks on the Book of Mormon can be found in the writings of James Spencer, William J. Schnoebelen, and Ed Decker.

3. Sandra and Jerald Tanner (the current leaders of this less extreme wing of evangelical anti-Mormonism) have countered the likes of Decker and Tryk. For reviews of the literature, see Daniel C. Peterson, "A Modern *Malleus maleficarum,*" *Review of Books on the Book of Mormon* 3 (1991): 231–60; and Massimo Introvigne, "The Devil Makers: Contemporary Evangelical Fundamentalist Anti-Mormonism," *Dialogue* 27, no. 1 (spring 1994): 153–69; see also Introvigne, "Old Wine in New Bottles: The Story behind Fundamentalist Anti-Mormonism," *BYU Studies* 35, no. 3 (1995–96): 45–73.

4. Jan Shipps provides an instructive example. She appears to have recently abandoned her earlier efforts to explain the Book of Mormon in naturalistic terms. For an account of the gradual development of her understanding of Mormon things, see Louis Midgley, "The Shipps Odyssey in Retrospect," *Review of Books on the Book of Mormon* 7, no. 2 (1995): 219–52.

5. Hugh Nibley, *An Approach to the Book of Mormon,* Collected Works of Hugh Nibley, vol. 6 (Salt Lake City: Deseret Book and F.A.R.M.S., 1988), 1 (same pagination in 1957, 1964, 1976 editions).

6. Initially advanced by Alexander Campbell. See note 1.

7. See Eber D. Howe, *Mormonism Unvailed, or, A Faithful Account of That Singular Imposition and Delusion, From Its Rise to the Present Time: With Sketches of the Characters of Its Propegators, and a Full Detail of the Manner in Which the famous Gold Bible was Brought Before the World, to Which are Added, Inquiries into the Probability that the Historical part of the Said Bible was Written by One Solomon Spalding, More than Twenty Years Ago, and by Him intended to have been Published as a Romance* (Painesville, Ohio: printed and published by the author, 1834). This has turned out to be the mother of all anti-Mormon books.

8. The standard explanation for the Book of Mormon in non-LDS circles from 1834 to 1945 was the idea that it had been written by someone other than Joseph Smith—by Sidney Rigdon—who borrowed the names and narrative structure of the book from an old and presumably lost romance written by Solomon Spalding. This explanation has fallen on hard times. Only a very few sectarian writers still push this long-discredited explanation of the Book of Mormon. For a summary of the details concerning this explanation of the Book of Mormon, see Lester E. Bush Jr., "The Spaulding Theory Then and Now," *Dialogue* 10, no. 4 (autumn 1977): 40–69.

9. See Fawn M. Brodie, *No Man Knows My History: The Life of Joseph Smith, the Mormon Prophet* (New York: Knopf, 1945; rev. ed., 1971). For two recent treatments of Brodie's book, see Newell G. Bringhurst, ed., *Reconsidering No Man Knows My History: Fawn M. Brodie and Joseph Smith in Retrospect* (Logan, Utah: Utah State University Press, 1996); and Louis Midgley, "F. M. Brodie—'The Fasting Hermit and Very Saint of Ignorance': A Biographer and Her Legend," *F.A.R.M.S. Review of Books* 8, no. 2 (1996): 147–230. For a review of the positions advanced on the authorship of the Book of Mormon, see Midgley, "Who Really Wrote the Book of Mormon? The Critics and Their Theories," *Book of Mormon Authorship Revisited: The Evidence for Ancient Origins,* ed. Noel Reynolds (Provo, Utah: F.A.R.M.S., 1997), 101–39.

10. See, for example, Robert N. Hullinger, *Joseph Smith's Response to Skepticism* (Salt Lake City: Signature Books, 1992); Hullinger, *Mormon Answer to Skepticism: Why Joseph Smith Wrote the Book of Mormon* (St. Louis, Mo.: Clayton, 1980); or Dan Vogel, *Indian Origins and the Book of Mormon: Religious Solutions from Columbus to Joseph Smith* (Salt Lake City: Signature Books, 1986).

11. Hans Kellner, "Introduction: Describing Redescriptions," in *A New Philosophy of History,* ed. Frank Ankersmit and Hans Kellner (Chicago: University of Chicago Press, 1995), 15.

12. A glance at a history of biblical criticism reveals the problem posed by naturalistic assumptions in dealing with the Bible. See, for example, Robert M. Grant and David Tracy, *A Short History of the Interpretation of the Bible,* 2d ed. (Philadelphia:

Fortress, 1984); or Edgar Krentz, *The Historical-Critical Method* (Philadelphia: Fortress, 1975).

13. Sydney E. Ahlstrom, "Preface," *A Religious History of the American People* (Garden City, N.Y.: Doubleday, 1975), 23.

14. Ibid., "Preface to the Image Book Edition," 16–17.

15. Ibid., 17.

16. See especially, Karl Marx, "Towards a Critique of Hegel's *Philosophy of Right*: Introduction," in *Karl Marx: Selected Writings,* ed. David McLellan (Oxford: Oxford University Press, 1977), 63–74.

17. Sigmund Freud, *The Future of an Illusion* (Garden City, N.Y.: Anchor Books, 1964).

18. Ahlstrom, "Preface to the Image Book Edition," 15.

19. Ibid.

20. Ibid., 16.

21. Ibid., "Preface," 22.

22. For an account of the corrosive impact of secularized historiography on the faith and identity of Jews, see Yosef Hayim Yerushalmi, *Zakhor: Jewish History and Jewish Memory* (Seattle: University of Washington Press, 1982).

23. For an insightful view by a Roman Catholic of the recent debate over the historicity of the Book of Mormon, see Massimo Introvigne, "The Book of Mormon Wars: A Non-Mormon Perspective," *Journal of Book of Mormon Studies* 5, no. 2 (1996): 1–25; and in a shortened version in *Mormon Identities in Transition,* ed. Douglas J. Davies (London: Cassell, 1996), 25–34.

24. C. S. Lewis, "Religion without Dogma?" in *God in the Dock: Essays on Theology and Ethics,* ed. Walter Hooper (Grand Rapids, Mich.: Eerdmans, 1970), 134.

25. Ibid.

26. Krentz, 26.

27. Ibid.

28. For examples of such secularized treatments of the Book of Mormon, see the essays contained in *New Approaches to the Book of Mormon: Explorations in Critical Methodology,* ed. Brent Lee Metcalfe (Salt Lake City: Signature Books, 1993). The Metcalfe volume has been criticized extensively in the *Review of Books on the Book of Mormon* 6, no. 2 (1994), and elsewhere.

29. Such efforts became a rather popular undertaking when Mark Hofmann was busy forging what he claimed were authentic early Mormon documents. For a review of the literature, see Midgley, "The Challenge of Historical Consciousness: Mormon History and the Encounter with Secular Modernity," in *By Study and Also by Faith: Essays in Honor of Hugh W. Nibley on the Occasion of His Eightieth Birthday, 27*

March 1990, ed. John M. Lundquist and Stephen D. Ricks (Salt Lake City: Deseret Book and F.A.R.M.S., 1990), 2:502–51; and Midgley, "The Acids of Modernity and the Crisis in Mormon Historiography," in *Faithful History: Essays on Writing Mormon History,* ed. George D. Smith (Salt Lake City: Signature Books, 1992), 189–225.

30. For the use of the adjective *naturalistic* in exactly the way it has been used by certain Mormon historians (both in and out of the Church), see, for example, Stephen T. Davis, *Risen Indeed: Making Sense of the Resurrection* (Grand Rapids, Mich.: Eerdmans, 1993), 20, 32–34, 37–39, 170, 186–88; Gary R. Habermas and Anthony G. N. Flew, *Did Jesus Rise from the Dead? The Resurrection Debate,* ed. Terry L. Miethe (San Francisco: Harper & Row, 1987); and also essays by Stephen T. Davis, "Is it Possible to Known that Jesus was Raised from the Dead?" *Faith and Philosophy* 1, no. 2 (April 1984): 147–59; Gary R. Habermas, "Knowing that Jesus' Resurrection Occurred: A Response to Stephen Davis," *Faith and Philosophy* 2, no. 3 (July 1985): 295–302; Stephen T. Davis, "Naturalism and the Resurrection: A Reply to Gary Habermas," *Faith and Philosophy* 2, no. 3 (July 1985): 303–8, among many others that could be cited.

31. Marvin S. Hill, "Secular or Sectarian History? A Critique of *No Man Knows My History,*" *Church History* 43, no. 1 (March 1974): 96, reprinted in *Reconsidering No Man Knows My History,* 83.

32. Lawrence Foster, *Religion and Sexuality: The Shakers, the Mormons, and the Oneida Community* (Chicago: University of Illinois Press, 1984), 296. He also argues that Joseph Smith, like Jesus of Nazareth and other founders of religious movements, suffered from manic depression, which explains the religious "genius" behind the founding of religious movements. See Foster, "The Psychology of Religious Genius: Joseph Smith and the Origins of Religious Movements," *Dialogue* 26, no. 4 (winter 1993): 1–22.

33. Ibid., 297.

34. Jan Shipps, "An 'Insider–Outsider' in Zion," *Dialogue* 15, no. 1 (spring 1982): 154.

35. For a recent expression of this dogma, see Sterling M. McMurrin and L. Jackson Newell, *Matters of Conscience: Conversations with Sterling M. McMurrin on Philosophy, Education, and Religion* (Salt Lake City: Signature Books, 1996), 368–69; and compare with "An Interview with Sterling McMurrin," *Dialogue* 17, no. 1 (spring 1984): 25; or "The History of Mormonism and Church Authorities: An Interview with Sterling M. McMurrin," *Free Inquiry* 4, no. 1 (winter 1983–84): 34.

36. D. Michael Quinn's *Early Mormonism and the Magic World View* (Salt Lake City: Signature Books, 1987), and John L. Brooke's *The Refiner's Fire: The Making of Mormon Cosmology, 1644–1844* (Cambridge: Cambridge University Press, 1994) are the two most recent books in this genre.

37. For example, a former Mormon historian has claimed that he is "still a Mormon for the same reasons that secular Jews (even the atheists among them) are still

Jewish." See D. Michael Quinn, "Dilemmas of Feminists & Intellectuals in the Contemporary Church," *Sunstone* 17, no. 1 (June 1994): 68.

38. For the pejorative use of the label "traditional Mormon history" and the corresponding appropriation of the label "revisionist Mormon history," see D. Michael Quinn, "Editor's Introduction," *The New Mormon History: Revisionist Essays on the Past* (Salt Lake City: Signature Books, 1992), vii–xx. See Louis Midgley, *John Whitmer Historical Association Journal* 13 (1993): 118–21, for a response to Quinn's ideology in a review of his book that is focused primarily on his tendentious remarks in his "Editor's Introduction."

39. See, for example, Marvin S. Hill, "The Historiography of Mormonism," *Church History* 28, no. 4 (December 1959): 418–19. See also Klaus J. Hansen, "Jan Shipps and the Mormon Tradition," *Journal of Mormon History* 11 (1984): 135–45.

40. George D. Smith, "Joseph Smith and the Book of Mormon," *Free Inquiry* 4, no. 1 (winter 1983–84): 27; reprinted in *On the Barricades: Religion and Free Inquiry in Conflict*, ed. Robert Basil, Mary Beth Gehrman, and Tim Madigan (Buffalo, N.Y.: Prometheus Books, 1989), 147. For details on Prometheus Books and the magazine *Free Inquiry*, see Louis Midgley, "Atheists and Cultural Mormons Promote a Naturalistic Humanism," *Review of Books on the Book of Mormon* 7, no. 1 (1995): 229–38; and see also Midgley, "George Dempster Smith, Jr., on the Book of Mormon," *Review of Books on the Book of Mormon* 4 (1992): 5–12.

41. George D. Smith, letter to editor, *Seventh East Press*, 8 February 1983, 11 (quoting "An Interview with Sterling McMurrin," 25).

42. Ibid.

43. "An Interview with Sterling McMurrin," 25; and compare McMurrin, *Matters of Conscience*, 210–11; and Roger D. Launius, "From Old to New Mormon History: Fawn Brodie and the Legacy of Scholarly Analysis of Mormonism," in Bringhurst, *Reconsidering No Man Knows My History*, 206.

44. Launius, 219.

45. Ibid., 198.

46. For a detailed treatment of "theology," see Midgley, "Directions that Diverge: 'Jerusalem and Athens' Revisited," *F.A.R.M.S. Review of Books* 11, no. 1 (1999): 58–72.

The Historical Jesus:
A Latter-day Saint Perspective

8

Robert L. Millet

By the nineteenth century, some scholars had begun to question the origins of the New Testament. Few scholars doubt that Jesus lived, but some doubt the historicity of much that is recorded about Him. They concede that Jesus was a good teacher, but they deny His miracles and His divine mission, and they discredit words traditionally attributed to Him in the New Testament. Each critical viewpoint approaches the Bible differently: Historical criticism compares the New Testament to its contemporary documents and setting; textual criticism aims at the discovery of the oldest and most authentic manuscripts; source criticism tries to determine the sources of the New Testament, including the hypothetical Q document; form criticism focuses on the importance of oral transmission; and redaction criticism looks at the Gospel writers as editors. While these may be legitimate fields of study, the stance of some Bible critics precludes supernatural agency. Through Joseph Smith's First Vision, the Book of Mormon, and other revelations, the Restoration provides a powerful additional witness of Christ's divinity and of the New Testament.

I would like to begin by relating how I first encountered the matter of historicity in my doctoral program.[1] My memories of the first class I took in religion at an eastern university are still very much intact. It was a course entitled "Seminar in Biblical Studies" and dealt with such issues as scripture, canon, interpretation, authorship, eschatology, prophecy, and like subjects. We were but weeks into the seminar when the professor was confronted by a question from an Evangelical Protestant student on the reality of miracles among ancient Israel. The response was polite but brief: "I'm not going to state my own position on the matter in this class. Let me just say that I feel it doesn't really matter whether the Israelites actually crossed the Red Sea on dry ground as a result of some miracle performed by Moses. What matters is that the Israelites then and thereafter saw it as an act of divine intervention, and the event became a foundation for a people's faith for centuries."

About a year later I found myself in a similar setting, this time in a seminar entitled "Critical Studies of the New Testament," the first half of a two-semester encounter with a literary–historical study of the New Testament. The composition of the students in the seminar made for fascinating conversation: a Reformed Jew, two Methodists, two Southern Baptists, a Roman Catholic, a Nazarene, and a Latter-day Saint. The professor was a secular Jew. By the time we had begun studying the passion narratives in the Gospels, the question of "historical events" vs. "faith events" had been raised. The professor stressed the importance of "myth" and emphasized that miraculous events in the New Testament (because in them the narrative detaches itself from the ordinary limitations of time and space such that the supernatural "irrupts" into human history) should be relegated to the category of faith events or sacred story. And then came the punch line, a phrase that had a haunting familiarity: "Now, for example: Whether or not Jesus of Nazareth came back to life—literally rose from the dead—is immaterial. What matters is that the Christians thought he did. And the whole Christian movement is founded on this faith event."

Few people doubt that Jesus Christ lived. His appearance on the stage of history is too well attested to doubt. But what is so often doubted is His divinity—His divine Sonship, His miracles, His ability to forgive sins and heal and regenerate human souls, His power over life and death.

In recent years the so-called "Jesus Seminar" has focused our attention on the words of Jesus.[2] Several New Testament scholars have concluded that 82 percent of the words traditionally attributed to Jesus in the four Gospels were not really spoken by Him. They have published a new translation of the Gospels called the Scholars Version. In it they have employed a system of color coding in which the words formerly attributed to our Lord are classified according to color: (1) Words in red indicate what was definitely spoken by Jesus; (2) words in pink are those that the scholars are less certain may be traced back to Jesus or are words that have suffered modification in transmission; (3) words in gray did not originate with Jesus, though they may well reflect his ideas; and (4) words in black are those that were put into the mouth of Jesus in the stories prepared by His followers or admirers (or, in some cases, by his enemies) and are therefore inauthentic. All references to Christ as the Son of God have been declared inauthentic, as have all places that refer to His messiahship, His preexistence, His resurrection, His forgiveness of sins, and His miraculous healings. For that matter, the Gospel of John has been printed in black.

My initial reaction to this whole undertaking was a form of quiet rage: How dare they? Who do they think they are? What audacity to suppose that they know enough about our Lord and Savior to set us straight, to tell the world what Jesus said and what He did not say! My next reaction was more somber: What a pity! How disheartening, how sad that what began as the Quest for the Historical Jesus has brought us to the point where we have sheared the Savior of divinity and reduced to myth and metaphor His capacity to come into the world and transform fallen humanity. How unfortunate it is that basically good men and women, people who have at least an affection or an admiration for holy writ, should wander so far afield. How did we come to this?

What is known by scholars as the "Old Quest" for the Historical Jesus began around 1775. It entailed a concern with the religious personality of Jesus of Nazareth, a focus on His environment and how that environment affected His beliefs, and a desire to dismiss and tear away the veneer with which the Early Church and thereafter Christian theologians had covered Jesus. Albert Schweitzer is best known for his major work on this subject. His book, *The Quest of the Historical Jesus* (German 1906, English 1910), contains a lengthy review of the quest to his own time.[3] Schweitzer concluded that it was in fact impossible to discover the historical quest, thus bringing to an end the initial quest.

With Rudolph Bultmann, a new approach to "Jesus Studies" was undertaken (see his *History of the Synoptic Tradition,* published in 1963).[4] He suggested that theology did not depend upon the varying conclusions of historians; it was perverse, he felt, to require that theology be founded on our history. Besides, he added, we know so little about the historical figure of Jesus that it is fruitless to attempt to understand Him historically. Jesus was something, or rather someone, to be experienced personally, existentially. This came to be known by some as the "no quest" period.

The third or "new quest" was led by one of Bultmann's students, Ernst Käsemann, who contended that we could indeed reconstruct enough of the historical record to come to a real understanding of Jesus, especially of Jesus' Jewishness.[5] The members of the Jesus Seminar are an outgrowth of the new quest, as are other more respected scholars who find the Jesus Seminar—approach as well as conclusions—to be inane. Scholars like James H. Charlesworth,[6] E. P. Sanders,[7] and Geza Vermes[8] come to mind. They choose not to address the divine Sonship or the matter of Christ's divinity and focus instead on His social surroundings and milieu.

In 1966 Elder Gordon B. Hinckley said: "Modern theologians strip [Jesus] of his divinity and then wonder why men do not worship him. These clever scholars have taken from Jesus the mantle of godhood and have left only a man. They have tried to accommodate him to their own narrow thinking. They have robbed him of his divine sonship and taken from the world its rightful King."[9] Some five years later, President Harold B. Lee explained to a group of students at Utah State University:

> Fifty years ago or more when I was a missionary, our greatest responsibility was to defend the great truth that the Prophet Joseph Smith was divinely called and inspired and that the Book of Mormon was indeed the word of God. But even at that time there were the unmistakable evidences that there was coming into the religious world actually a question about the Bible and about the divine calling of the Master himself. Now, fifty years later, our greatest responsibility and anxiety is to defend the divine mission of our Lord and Master, Jesus Christ, for all about us, even among those who claim to be professors of the Christian faith, are those not willing to stand squarely in defense of the great truth that our Lord and Master, Jesus Christ, was indeed the Son of God.[10]

Biblical Criticism

To what extent have we accepted uncritically the tenets and canons of biblical criticism? Why should we be so willing to jettison time-honored beliefs and sacred values on the basis of someone else's doubts or a system of scholarship that from the outset precludes the essentials of the Christian message? I want to take the time here to examine critically some of the universally held presuppositions and approaches of New Testament criticism. Such an analysis is fundamental to any serious effort to address the question of historicity in the life and ministry of Jesus Christ.

For centuries men have been concerned with the meaning and historical reliability of valuable texts. In particular, treasured works and collections like the Bible have been the center of attention of persons with both sacred and secular motives and outlooks. Biblical criticism is the science and methodology associated with taking a critical (close and precise) look at the holy scriptures. Elder John A. Widtsoe observed:

> To Latter-day Saints there can be no objection to the careful and critical study of the scriptures, ancient or modern, provided only that it be an honest study—a search for truth. The Prophet Joseph Smith voiced the attitude of the Church at a time when modern higher criticism was in its infancy. "We believe the Bible to be the word of God as far as it is translated correctly." This article of our faith is really a challenge to search the scriptures critically. Moreover, the Church had just been established, when Joseph Smith under divine direction, set about to revise or explain the incorrect and obscure passages of the Bible. The work then done is a powerful evidence of the inspiration that guided the Prophet. Whether under a special call of God or impelled by personal desire, there can be no objection to the critical study of the Bible.[11]

Though questions of authorship and authority of scriptural books have been raised for hundreds of years,[12] most critical inquiry into the origins of the New Testament belongs to the nineteenth and twentieth centuries. Obviously, not all biblical critics are motivated by the same interests or feel a commitment to values beyond their training or discipline. Unfortunately, many with linguistic and literary skills have taken positions regarding the New Testament that tend (directly or indirectly) to cast doubt on accepted and traditional religious concepts: revelation, miracles, and a belief in the overall hand of Deity in the formation and preservation of the scriptures. It would appear that here, as in all studies, identifying one's presuppositions—recognizing a scholar's orientation—is crucial.

Donald Guthrie has noted that "there is a decided difference between a scholar who accepts the divine origin of Scripture and inquires into its historical and literary origins and a scholar who begins his critical inquiries with the assumption that there is nothing unique about the text and who claims the right to examine it as he would any other book. The former is not simply submitting the text to the bar of his own reason to establish its validity, but assumes that the text will authenticate itself when subject to reverent examination. His stance of faith and his critical inquiry in no way invalidate each other."[13]

Historical Criticism

One approach to a study of the New Testament is what is known in German as *Religionsgeschichte,* a history of religions approach. Here scholars have sought, for example, to examine the influence of contemporary religious ideas on early Christian texts—the supposed influence of the Essenes on John or Jesus, the impact of the Greek mystery religions on Christian ordinances or ritual, or the supposed pervasive influence of the Gnostics on Paul's letters.[14] One obvious presupposition of this perspective is that an event or a movement is largely (if not completely) a product of its surroundings, the result of precipitating factors in the environment.

Though it is certainly valuable to be able to look critically at the setting—for nothing takes shape in an intellectual or religious vacuum—and though it is true that many elements impinge upon a moment in history, we need not suppose a causal connection between any two factors in an environment. Simply because A precedes B, we need not conclude that A caused B; we need not be guilty of the logical fallacy of *post hoc, ergo propter hoc.* Nor need we conclude that because A and B coexist they are necessarily related. Thus one of the flaws in the reasoning of some historical critics is an overreliance on a linear view of history, an acceptance of the principle that phenomena evolve from previously existing circumstances. Such is certainly not the case in all situations; many events or movements in history were more revolutionary than evolutionary.[15]

Another "history of religions" approach to the Gospels consists in stressing similarities between the Gospels and other contemporary documents, and in so doing minimizing the uniqueness of the canonical books.[16] But what is it that one has established when one demonstrates that the idea of a "virgin birth" was known to the Greeks, that many Greeks accepted the idea of a God-man, that the crux of many of Jesus' sayings is to be found also among Jewish rabbis before the first century A.D., or that the concepts of martyrdom and ascension into heaven were not new to the world of Jesus of Nazareth? Latter-day Saints are blessed with an understanding of the plan of salvation that informs our thinking regarding antiquity. We know that Christ's eternal gospel has been preached from the beginning, and that Christian prophets have taught Christian doctrine and administered Christian ordinances since the days of Adam.[17] Should we be surprised that elements of that doctrine or semblances of the ordinances or rituals (albeit in fragmentary and even apostate form) should be found in cultures throughout the world?[18]

Textual Criticism

One of the major reasons for the variety of Bibles today is that the different versions are not necessarily translated from the same manuscripts. Unfortunately, today there are no original manuscripts of the New Testament, only copies of copies of copies. Scribal errors came early in the process of transmission; even careful scribes were prone to the mistakes associated with human limitations (eyes, ears, physical strength, and faulty judgment).[19] When an error in copying went undetected, it was preserved in successive copies. Through comparing variant readings and grouping together documents with similar readings, manuscript or textual "families" became apparent, each family of manuscripts possessing certain distinct characteristics in common. One reason various English versions of today's Bible differ is that they represent translations of different textual families.

"Textual criticism, commonly known in the past as 'lower' criticism in contrast to the so-called 'higher' (historical and literary) criticism, is the science that compares all known manuscripts of a given work in an effort to trace the history of variations within the text so as to discover its original form."[20] The method of textual criticism, observes Bruce Metzger, "involves two main processes, recension and emendation. Recension is the selection, after examination of all available material, of the most trustworthy evidence on which to base a text. Emendation is the attempt to eliminate the errors which are found even in the best manuscripts."[21] Some of the principles or criteria for choosing among readings (and scholars would disagree as to the relative weighting of each of these factors) are as follows:

1. The earliest manuscript is likely to be the most correct.
2. The shorter reading is to be preferred to the longer.
3. The text supported by the most authorities (manuscripts and early quotations) is likely to be the most nearly correct.
4. The manuscripts with the widest geographical distribution are preferred.[22]

Textual criticism, a science dedicated to the discovery of the oldest and most accurate and authentic manuscripts (and thus the most ancient messages), has certainly proven to be one of the most valuable approaches to a study of the New Testament. There are, however, some precautions that must be taken by Latter-day Saints who are sincerely intent on discovering things as they were in antiquity. First of all, the Book of Mormon is a powerful witness that the world has never had a complete Bible, that plain and precious truths were taken away or kept back from the Old and New Testaments long before the time of their compilation and canonization (see 1 Ne. 13:20–40). "The problem which lies before the textual critic," Frederic Kenyon observed, "is now becoming clear. The original manuscripts of the Bible, written by the authors of the various books, have long ago disappeared."[23] In discussing theologically motivated alterations of the texts, Bart D. Ehrman has written recently: "The New Testament manuscripts were not produced impersonally by machines capable of flawless reproduction. They were copied by hand, by living, breathing human beings who were deeply rooted in the conditions and controversies of their day. Did the scribes' polemical contexts influence the way they transcribed their sacred Scriptures?" Ehrman contends that they did, "that theological disputes, specifically disputes over Christology, prompted Christian scribes to alter the words of Scripture in order to make them more serviceable for the polemical task."[24]

Textual variants occur in many ways, both the unplanned and the planned ones. The unplanned—errors of the hand, the eye, the ear, and of judgment—will probably not occur in the same place in each copy. Such errors are dealt with without extreme difficulty; they may be corrected through a comparison with other copies. "It is the planned changes," Robert J. Matthews has noted, "that are the most damaging." These come about

> when the copyist or the translator begins to think for himself and deliberately makes his copy differ from the written document. In this manner, substantial changes may occur in a very short time and can result in added material or in the loss of material. Even these changes could be corrected if one had the original to refer to for comparison, but if the master copy is unavailable, the corrupted texts perpetuate the errors. All subsequent copies made from the altered text will bear the same shortcomings because there is no master copy or archetype with which to correct it. . . .
>
> As we read the words of the angel [in 1 Nephi 13], we discover that the world never has had a complete Bible, for it was massively, even cataclysmically, corrupted *before* it was distributed. If this is true, and since the originals disappeared early from the scene (thus preventing a correction from that source), what does this passage from Nephi mean to us about Bible textual criticism? . . .
>
> The great scholars, employing the science of textual criticism, seem to be effectively correcting the errors made by the carelessness and weakness of man. By extensively searching the available manuscripts, such as the Vaticanus, Sinaiticus, Alexandrinus, and lesser fragments, the text of the Bible may yet be recovered to the condition it was in *after* it was cataclysmically corrupted as spoken in 1 Nephi. . . .
>
> It appears to me that the world has mistakenly identified the text of the second or third generation as being the same as the original. . . . Thus the great manuscripts so highly regarded are indeed precious for their antiquity and beauty, but they represent the depleted text not the original. The plain and precious missing parts have not yet been made known through manuscripts and scholars, but are available only through the Book of Mormon, the Joseph Smith Translation, and modern revelation through the instrumentality of a prophet.[25]

Source Criticism

Source criticism, once known as literary criticism, is that scholarly study that seeks to identify the possible sources for scriptural books. A close comparative study of the Synoptic Gospels (Matthew, Mark, and Luke—literally those that take a "similar look" at Christ), for example, is most revealing. We find, for example, that essentially 606 of the 661 verses of Mark appear in Matthew and that 380 of Mark's verses reappear with only slight alteration in Luke. From another perspective, "of the 1,068 verses of Matthew, about 500 contain material also found in Mark; of the 1,149 verses of Luke, about 380 are paralleled in Mark." There are only 31 verses in Mark not found in Matthew or Luke: only 7 percent of the Gospel of Mark is exclusive.[26]

What is one to make of such statistics? What is the chronological and literary relationship between the Synoptic Gospels? The issues underlying the relationships between these three Gospels constitute what biblical critics have come to know as the "Synoptic Problem." Since the nineteenth century, many scholars have concluded that the solution of the Synoptic Problem was to be found by stressing the priority of Mark, the shortest of the Gospels. The general consensus has been that Mark was the first Gospel written and that Matthew and Luke drew upon Mark in preparing their own.[27] This approach, known as the "Markan Hypothesis," or the "Two-Document Hypothesis," contends that Matthew relied on (a) Mark, on (b) a "sayings source" or collection of sayings by Jesus (the Q Document, from the German word *Quelle,* "source"), and (c) added his own peculiar style, perspective, and experiences (called M) in preparing the Gospel which we know as Matthew. Luke relied on (a) Mark, on (b) Q, and (c) added his own unique perspective (called L). In short, the Two-Document Hypothesis for the composition of Matthew and Luke is as follows:

Matthew = Mark + Q + M
Luke = Mark + Q + L

The Two-Document Hypothesis has been accepted by most of the New Testament scholarly world since the last century. The discovery of Gnostic Christian materials in the Nag Hammadi Library in Upper Egypt in the late 1940s revealed, among other important things, a collection of 114 sayings, known as the "Gospel According to Thomas," which many scholars felt to be supportive of the proposition that "Jesus-sayings" (like Q) were afloat for many years before the formation of the canonical Gospels.[28] Others have wondered whether the reverse was not true: perhaps documents like the Gospel of Thomas simply drew on or copied from older materials, like the Gospel of Matthew.[29]

Though it is a common presupposition of some biblical critics to prefer the shortest document as the oldest (thus assuming that the longer ones contain embellishments and additions), Latter-day Saints should take seriously Nephi's vision of the corruption of the biblical texts in this regard. Is it not just as reasonable to suppose that Mark, having before him the longer Matthew or the longer Luke, chose to prepare an abbreviated Gospel, placing less stress on sermons and parables and more stress on the movements and actions of our Lord?[30]

William R. Farmer, for example, has argued for the primacy of Matthew, an approach that goes a long way toward eliminating the need for a hypothetical sayings source. Some of Farmer's suggestions as to the inadequacy of the Two-Document Hypothesis to resolve the Synoptic Problem include the following: (1) the failure of the Markan Hypothesis "to account for Mark's selection of items in relation to Matthew and Luke from the presumably rich storehouse of tradition available to him"; (2) another "inadequacy . . . is that it requires us to believe that Matthew and Luke are independent of one another." This does not explain the "numerous agreements between Matthew and Luke in passages where they are supposed to be independently copying Mark"; in a related manner, "there are at least twenty topics that Matthew and Luke have in common. These cannot be explained through a dependence upon Mark, because Mark does not contain several of these topics. For example, Mark does not have birth narratives, a genealogy, a temptation story, the Sermon on the Mount, or large collections of parables," all of which are found throughout Matthew and Luke; (3) all the church fathers who mention the sequence of the Gospels indicate that Matthew was written first. "The earliest statement regarding sequence was made by Clement of Alexandria who indicates that both Matthew and Luke were written before Mark"; and (4) there is the question of the relation between the historical spread and development of the Christian Church and the formation of the Gospels:

> Let us put the matter another way. Jesus and his disciples were Jews living in Palestine. In due time the community that began with Jesus and his disciples spread out into the Mediterranean world. As the extra-Palestinian expansion of the community took place, more and more gentiles sought membership in it until finally it developed into a community that was predominantly gentile.
>
> How does this affect our view of the Gospels? All would agree, of course, that Matthew is the most Jewish Gospel in the canon. It is also the Gospel that best reflects the Palestinian origins of the Christian church. Luke too is very Jewish, but there are many passages where, by comparison, this Gospel is better adapted for use by gentiles outside of Palestine. While unmistakably retaining traditions of Jewish and Palestinian origin, Mark is the best adapted of the three for gentile readers who are not acquainted with Palestinian culture. Thus, in terms of historical development, we can begin easily enough with Matthew

and go on to Luke and/or Mark. But historically speaking, it is difficult to reverse the process and to place Matthew after either one or both of the others.[31]

The above is not presented to denigrate the Two-Document Hypothesis as a heuristic device, but rather to suggest other alternatives.[32] It may well be that the Gospel of John, long believed to be the latest of the Gospels, took shape much earlier than we had supposed; perhaps, as some contend, it is the earliest! The discovery of the Dead Sea Scrolls has certainly shown the Gospel of John to be as "Jewish" in content as the other Gospels.[33]

Form Criticism

Form criticism is the science that attempts to identify the origins of literary materials in the Gospels. One approach to this method assumes that oral traditions in different forms—stories and sayings—were woven together by the Gospel writers to produce a more complete written tradition about Jesus and the events of His life.[34] In short, "the main purpose for the creation, the circulation, and the use of these forms was not to preserve the history of Jesus, but to strengthen the life of the church. Thus these forms reflect the concern of the church, and both the form and content have been influenced by the faith and theology of the church, as well as by her situation and practice."[35]

A serious student of the New Testament must feel some sense of gratitude for the focus that form criticism has given to the importance of oral transmission. There can be no doubt that much good has come to the world as a result of a closer look at this almost neglected dimension of literary development. Acceptance of Christ and His gospel was accomplished first through the power of verbal human testimony. Much of the earliest scripture in the meridian dispensation (as perhaps in all dispensations) existed in an oral and unrecorded form.[36] The *kerygma* (proclamation of the gospel), the *logia* (sayings of Christ), and the *agrapha* (unwritten things) circulated as the witness of the apostles spread from Jerusalem to the ends of the known world.

On the other hand, although form critics like Martin Dibelius and Rudolph Bultmann would suggest an evolutionary development in the Gospels from an oral stage to written document,[37] such need not to have been the case. Surely these oral testimonies spread at the same time that written documents were being prepared and circulated concerning the works and words of the Master.[38] In our own day, genuine faith-promoting stories circulate in the Church orally at the same time that written accounts of the events are readily available. It does not require a severe stretch of the imagination to suppose that in the first-century Church, written documents recounting many of the events of the life of Jesus were contemporaneous with the Saints' reminiscences and personal oral testimonies. The manner in which oral traditions were valued is highlighted, for example, in a statement by Papias, bishop of Hierapolis in Asia Minor (ca. A.D. 130–40): "But I shall not be unwilling to put down, along with my interpretations, whatsoever instructions I received with care at any time from the elders, and stored up with care in my memory, assuring you at the same time of their truth. . . . If, then, any one who had attended on the elders came, I asked minutely after their sayings—what Andrew or Peter said, or what was said by Philip, or by Thomas, or by James, or by John, or by Matthew, or by any other of the Lord's disciples." And then Papias added: "For I imagined that what was to be got from books was not so profitable to me as what came from the living and abiding voice."[39]

Not all biblical scholars are as enamored with form critical assumptions or methods as was once the case. Richard L. Anderson observed:

> But one can be just as skeptical of form criticism as form criticism is of the Gospels. Investigating how the Gospel accounts have changed begs the question of *whether* they have changed. The Gospels present parallel stories of Jesus' life with occasional contradictions in details, but each Gospel represents a rich supplement to the information on the life of Jesus available in any other Gospel. Form criticism assumes a creativity on the part of the early Christian community different from the "continuity of revelation" creativity I spoke of; it is, instead, "invention" creativity—the assumption that the early Christian community adapted these stories to their preaching needs at any given time. . . .
>
> In my view, form criticism is also badly out-of-date in its assumption that there was a period of oral transmission of the stories of Jesus. The recovery of hundreds of fragments and of books from Qumran shows an intense religious creativity accompanied by an equally intense fanaticism for the writing of commentaries and handbooks of community living. The Qumran community is, of course, a slightly pre-Christian reformation movement of Judaism. Just the other side of the first century we have the letters of the apostolic fathers,

the orthodox bishops of the early second century. We also have the fertile inventions of Gnostic dissidents which developed and continued a tradition from the same time period.

We also have twenty-one letters of the New Testament, proving the capability and inevitability of writing output in the earliest Christian Church. With such impressive evidence of writing among Jewish reformists, orthodox Christians, and sectarian Christians, why should one assume a period of oral transmission divorced from the stability of written records?[40]

Form criticism, in the words of F. F. Bruce, has made a singular contribution: we now know "no matter how far back we may press our researchers into the roots of the gospel story, no matter how we classify the gospel material, we never arrive at a non-supernatural Jesus."[41]

Redaction Criticism

Redaction criticism of the Gospels is a sub-discipline of biblical study that focuses attention on the role of the Gospel writers as redactors or editors. In dealing with the Synoptic Gospels, the redaction critic presupposes certain results from both source criticism (the Markan or Two-Document Hypothesis) and form criticism (the transmission of forms or units of tradition). This branch of study draws attention to the role of the Gospel writers in shaping and forming the Christian traditions into a document that would (a) meet the prevailing needs of the given Christian community, and (b) reflect the particular theological perspective of the Gospel writer.

In regard to the latter function, Norman Perrin has written concerning the work of Matthew, Mark, and Luke in preparing the resurrection narratives: "The resurrection narratives are . . . literary expressions of the evangelists' understanding of what it means to say 'Jesus is risen.' They are narrative expressions of a distinctive theological viewpoint. . . . [The Gospel writer] intends to convince his readers that Jesus is the Messiah, that he is the Son of God, and that his life and fate have changed forever the possibilities for human life in the world. To this end he composes his narrative account of the sequence of events which began with the ministry of John the Baptist . . . and reached its climax in the women's discovery of the empty tomb." Perrin then makes this observation regarding the role of the Gospel writer: "He has taken traditional material circulating in the early Christian communities. . . . He has edited that material and composed it into a new whole—he may even have created some new narratives of his own on the basis of traditional sayings of Jesus and the interpretation of scripture—and everything that he has done, he has done in the service of his overriding conviction that he has a gospel to preach to his readers."[42]

There should be no doubt among Latter-day Saints that the canonical Gospels were compiled, composed, and written under the spirit of revelation. At the same time, we do not detract from the spiritual significance of the writers to suggest that Matthew, Mark, Luke, and John were also divinely directed editors as well as creative authors. Moses was a choice seer and a man open to the revelations of the Lord. He was also a gifted compiler and editor of earlier records.[43] Likewise, Mormon was an inspired author/editor whose "and thus we see" passages in the Nephite record help to demonstrate the wisdom of the ways of the Lord.

Like other writers—inspired or uninspired—Matthew, Mark, Luke, and John had particular messages, styles, and points of view; a format characterizes their work that may be studied in light of some of their more evident literary characteristics. Their Gospels were certainly shaped by such factors as their own backgrounds and the intended audiences of the documents.[44] A recognition of these factors, however, need not lead us to interpretive extremes. Being a theologian does not preclude being a historian. "There is no reason . . . to suppose," writes one conservative scholar, "that theological interest must take precedence over historical validity." Further, "it is difficult to think of the narration of bare facts without some interpretation. But there is no reason to suppose that the interpretation made by each evangelist was his own creation."[45]

Who Was Jesus of Nazareth?

To what degree can we trust the canonical Gospels in regard to what Jesus said and did? Has the Christian Church transformed a lowly Nazarene into a God? Is it possible to tear away the faithful film of believing tradition and get back to the way things really were? Can we excise from the biblical text those theological perspectives that preclude an "accurate" view of Jesus? Indeed, the question of the ages is, "What think ye of Christ?" (Matt. 22:42).

I add my voice to the growing throng of thousands of believing Christians and an increasing number of religious leaders and serious scholars who certify the following:

Jesus was and is who He and the Gospel writers say he was—the literal Son of God, the Only Begotten Son in the flesh of the Eternal Father.

We have every reason to believe that the four Gospels are true and accurate and that the essential message of historical Christianity—that Christ lived, taught, lifted, strengthened, renewed, healed, prophesied, communed with Deity, suffered, died, rose from the dead, appeared thereafter to hundreds, and will come again in glory—is to be taken seriously.

Efforts to demythologize or debunk Jesus will in time be shown to be what they in actuality are—shams and charades on the part of people who dare not believe and who work endlessly to proselytize others to share their doubts. Too often the undergirding assumption of those who cast doubt on the historical Jesus as set forth in scripture, in whole or in part, is a denial of the supernatural and a refusal to admit prophecy, revelation, and divine intervention.

We have been too hasty to apply supposed scientific methodology to sacred texts, because a strict application of the scientific method to sacred events, holy words, and miraculous doings is not possible. Some things are not observable or measurable by this world's tools or devices, and some things may only be felt and understood by those possessed of a believing heart (see Mosiah 26:1–4; Morm. 9:25; D&C 90:24). Stephen Robinson has pointed out the following:

> The exclusion of any supernatural agency (including God) from human affairs is fundamental to the methodology of most biblical scholarship. The naturalistic approach gives scholars from different religious backgrounds common controls and perspectives relative to the data and eliminates arguments over subjective beliefs not verifiable by the historical–critical method. However, there is a cost to using the naturalistic approach, for one can never mention God, revelation, priesthood, prophecy, etc., as having objective existence or as being part of the evidence or as being possible causes of the observable effects. . . .
>
> Naturalistic explanations are often useful in evaluating empirical data, but when the question asked involves nonempirical categories, such as "Is the Book

of Mormon what it purports to be?", it begs the question to adopt a method whose first assumption is that the Book cannot be what it claims to be. This points out a crucial logical difficulty in using this method in either attacking or defending the Church.[46]

Simply stated in regard to the New Testament, why should we be surprised that many biblical scholars conclude that Jesus was not divine, that the miracles did not really occur, that he did not rise from the dead, when the template they place over their reading of the New Testament is a naturalistic one, a distant objectivity, a detachment that precludes by its very nature such things?

But is it not the case that the biblical scholar who ignores the canonical Gospels and pushes instead toward an unavailable record like the hypothetical 'Q' document is relying upon that which is basically unseen and unknown? Does it not require a greater leap of faith to operate one's professional life around documents we do not possess than to accept what we do possess? It is, for example, much easier for me to believe in gold plates, Urim and Thummim, and angels than in some of the ludicrous explanations for vital Restoration events offered by some alternate voices. One has to work almost as hard to accept alternative explanations for Jesus' divinity.

C. S. Lewis, in speaking of biblical critics, observed: "These men ask me to believe they can read between the lines of the old texts; the evidence is their obvious inability to read (in any sense worth discussing) the lines themselves. They claim to see fernseed and can't see an elephant ten yards away in broad daylight." Lewis also noted that the typical biblical scholar does not have immediate access to the truth any more than the average man on the street. "Scholars, as scholars," he added, "speak on it with no more authority than anyone else. The canon 'If miraculous, unhistorical' is one they bring to their study of the texts, not one they have learned from it. If one is speaking of authority, the united authority of all the Biblical critics in the world counts here for nothing. On this they speak simply as men; men obviously influenced by, and perhaps insufficiently critical of, the spirit of the age they grew up in."[47] Indeed, why should modern biblical scholars scoff at the findings of the Jesus Seminar? Is not this the logical extension of what began as the quest of the historical Jesus? Have we not now come face to face with where the naturalistic presuppositions eventually bring us?

Is Christianity based on "faith-events" rather than actual historical incidents? Other questions follow: How is my belief in presentday healing, for example, affected by what did or did not take place in the first century? Can I believe that the power to heal is real in our own day if in fact such powers were not operative in the days of Jesus or Joseph Smith, if the biblical stories of the healing are prevarications? Faith is based on evidence, and the stronger the evidence the stronger the faith. To what extent can I trust in a power of redemption if in fact Jesus was not the Savior of humankind? How should I view death if in fact Jesus did not rise from the tomb? To what degree do my religious beliefs need to be both true and reasonable? One Protestant theologian observed:

> There is an excellent objective ground to which to tie the religion that Jesus sets forth. Final validation of this can only come experientially [we would say, by revelation]. But it is desperately important not to put ourselves in such a position that the event-nature of the resurrection depends wholly upon "the faith." It's the other way around. The faith has its starting point in the event, the objective event, and only by the appropriation of this objective event do we discover the final validity of it. . . .
>
> The Christian faith is built upon Gospel that is "good news," and there is no news, good or bad, of something that didn't happen. I personally am much disturbed by certain contemporary movements in theology which seem to imply that we can have the faith regardless of whether anything happened or not. I believe absolutely that the whole Christian faith is premised upon the fact that at a certain point of time under Pontius Pilate a certain man died and was buried and three days later rose from the dead. If in some way you could demonstrate to me that Jesus never lived, died, or rose again, then I would have to say I have no right to my faith.[48]

Indeed, to what degree can we exercise saving faith in something that did not happen? The prophets declare that "faith is not to have a perfect knowledge of things; therefore if ye have faith ye hope for things which are not seen, which are true" (Alma 32:21).

Can Jesus be a wise teacher and not the Son of God? Is there a difference between the "historical Jesus" and the "Christ of faith"? Do the extant sources allow such a distinction? Did Jesus?

There is a simple syllogism that applies to Jesus. It goes something like this: He was a great moral teacher. He claimed to be the Son of God. He was not the Son of God. Therefore, He could not be a great moral teacher. Robert Stein has written:

On the lips of anyone else the claims of Jesus would appear to be evidence of gross egomania, for Jesus clearly implies that the entire world revolves around himself and that the fate of all men is dependent on their acceptance or rejection of him. . . . There seem to be only two possible ways of interpreting the totalitarian nature of the claims of Jesus. Either we must assume that Jesus was deluded and unstable with unusual delusions of grandeur or we are faced with the realization that Jesus is truly One who speaks with divine authority, who actually divided all of history into B.C.–A.D., and whose rejection or acceptance determines the fate of all men.[49]

One of the most famous statements on this matter, one that forces the issue and exposes the shallowness of many a person's thinking, was made by C. S. Lewis:

I am trying here to prevent anyone saying the really foolish thing that people often say about Him: "I'm ready to accept Jesus as a great moral teacher, but I don't accept His claim to be God." That is the one thing we must not say. A man who was merely a man and said the sort of things Jesus said would not be a great moral teacher. He would either be a lunatic—on a level with the man who says he is a poached egg—or else he would be the Devil of Hell. You must make your choice. Either this man was, and is, the Son of God: or else a madman or something worse. You can shut Him up for a fool, you can spit at Him and kill Him as a demon; or you can fall at His feet and call Him Lord and God. But let us not come with any patronizing nonsense about His being a great human teacher. He has not left that open to us. He did not intend to.[50]

Stripped of His divinity, His teachings concerning His own Godhood, forgiveness of sins, resurrection, and the Second Coming, why would Jesus of Nazareth be so controversial? Why would people dislike such a man? Why on earth would he be crucified?

I have wondered over the years how so many who read the same New Testament I do could conjure up a Jesus who is basically a simple, nondirective counselor, a sensitive ecologist who came to earth to model quiet pacifism. Given, Jesus of Nazareth was indeed the caring, compassionate, forgiving, serving man described by Matthew, Mark, Luke, and John. He was also, however, God incarnate, the discerning, fearless, assertive, confrontive, excoriating, and at times sarcastic being who had little patience with hypocrisy and self-righteousness. John Meir observed:

While I do not agree with those who turn Jesus into a violent revolutionary or political agitator, scholars who favor a revolutionary Jesus do have a point. A tweedy poetaster who spent his time spinning out parables and Japanese koans, a literary asthete who toyed with 1st-century deconstructionism, or a bland

Jesus who simply told people to look at the lilies of the field—such a Jesus would threaten no one, just as the university professors who create him threaten no one. The historical Jesus did threaten, disturb, and infuriate people—from interpreters of the Law through the Jerusalem priestly aristocracy to the Roman prefect who finally tried and crucified him. . . . A Jesus whose words and deeds would not alienate people, especially powerful people, is not the historical Jesus.[51]

In addition, as Scot McKnight pointed out, "A social revolution-ary would have been crucified (and this partly explains Jesus' death, in my view), but it is doubtful that such a revolutionary would have given birth to a church that was hardly a movement of social revolu-tion."[52]

Conclusion

There is another question we must ask: What does the restored gospel offer us in our quest to know and understand the man Jesus who is the Christ?

Joseph Smith's First Vision represents the beginning of the revelation of God to man in this final dispensation. It is also a remarkable confirmation of the bodily resurrection and immortal, living nature of Jesus Christ.

The Book of Mormon stands as a monumental testimony, a companion scriptural witness with the Bible, to the divine Sonship of Jesus, as well as to the divine powers centered in and exercised by Him and His anointed servants.

The revelations of the Restoration, including the teachings and testimonies of latter-day prophets and seers, attest to the person and powers of Jesus of Nazareth and confirm that the Jesus of history is in fact the Christ of faith.

The Latter-day Saints extend the same invitation that Jesus offered a group of fishermen almost two thousand years ago: "Come and see" (John 1:39). The final great test is the test of spirit, the test of individual revelation, with the assurance that all can know. For some it is a leap of faith, a faith "that bridges the chasm between what our minds can know and what our souls aspire after."[53]

Must one be held hostage by the traditional mode of thinking or even subscribe to the majority opinion? Jesus stood against the majority opinion in His day; He challenged the religious establishment. If the Latter-day Saints have anything to offer the religious world, it is a firm conviction that the scriptures mean what they say and say what they mean. They are to be trusted. Latter-day Saints would do well to ensure that theirs is a "critical" look at biblical critical presuppositions, methodologies, and conclusions; some things we simply need not swallow. A firm belief in prophecy, revelation, divine intervention, and absolute truth precludes an overwhelming and undiscriminating acceptance of many of the underlying principles of the science of biblical criticism.

"We have no right to take the theories of men," Elder Orson F. Whitney noted in 1915, "however scholarly, however learned, and set them up as a standard, and try to make the Gospel bow down to them, making of them an iron bedstead upon which God's truth, if not long enough, must be stretched out, or if too long, must be chopped off—anything to make it fit into the system of men's thoughts and theories! On the contrary, we should hold up the Gospel as the standard of truth, and measure thereby the theories and opinions of men."[54] What the world may view with an almost reverent attitude as established fact in these areas of study should be viewed by Latter-day Saints with an enlightened perspective—perspective informed by the supplementary and unique Latter-day Saint resources of additional scriptural records and living oracles—recognizing the approaches and conclusions of others as "scaffolding useful for research purposes,"[55] but centering one's full loyalty and trust in the modern prophetic word.

President Howard W. Hunter noted:

> There are those who declare it is old-fashioned to believe in the Bible. Is it old-fashioned to believe in Jesus Christ, the Son of the Living God? Is it old-fashioned to believe in his atoning sacrifice and the resurrection? If it is, I declare myself to be old-fashioned and the Church to be old-fashioned. . . .
>
> In this world of confusion and rushing, temporal progress, we need to return to the simplicity of Christ. We need to love, honor, and worship him. To acquire spirituality and have its influence in our lives, we cannot become confused and misdirected by the twisted teachings of the modernist. We need to study the simple fundamentals of the truths taught by the Master and eliminate the controversial. Our faith in God needs to be real and not speculative. The restored gospel of Jesus Christ can be a dynamic, moving influence, and true acceptance gives us a meaningful, religious experience. . . . We can be modern without giving way to the influence of the modernist. If it is

old-fashioned to believe in the Bible, we should thank God for the privilege of being old-fashioned.[56]

Robert L. Millet is professor of ancient scripture, Brigham Young University.

Notes

1. The following two paragraphs are taken, with minor changes, from my published article, "The Book of Mormon, Historicity, and Faith," *Journal of Book of Mormon Studies* 2, no. 2 (fall 1993): 1–2.

2. See Robert W. Funk, Roy W. Hoover, and the Jesus Seminar, trans. and eds., *The Five Gospels: The Search for the Authentic Words of Jesus* (New York: Polebridge, 1993).

3. Albert Schweitzer, *The Quest of the Historical Jesus,* trans. W. Montgomery (Great Britain: A & C Black, 1910).

4. Rudolph Bultmann, *The History of the Synoptic Tradition,* trans. John Marsh (New York: Harper & Row, 1963).

5. E.g., Ernst Käsemann, *New Testament Questions of Today* (Philadelphia: Fortress, 1969).

6. James H. Charlesworth, *Jesus within Judaism: New Light from Exciting Archaelogical Discoveries,* The Anchor Bible Reference Library (Garden City, N.Y.: Doubleday, 1988).

7. E. P. Sanders, *Jesus and Judaism* (Philadelphia: Fortress, 1985).

8. Geza Vermes, *Jesus and the World of Judaism* (Philadelphia: Fortress, 1983).

9. Gordon B. Hinckley, *Conference Report,* April 1966, 85.

10. LDS Student Association Fireside, Utah State University, 10 October 1971, cited in Paul R. Cheesman, ed., *The Book of Mormon: The Keystone Scripture* (Provo, Utah: Religious Studies Center, Brigham Young University, 1988), 23.

11. John A. Widtsoe, *In Search of Truth: Comments on the Gospel and Modern Thought* (Salt Lake City: Deseret Book, 1963), 81–82.

12. For example, in the Patristic period, Dionysius of Alexandria discussed the authorship of the book of Revelation; Abraham Ibn Ezra, a medieval Jewish commentator, doubted the Mosaic authorship of the Pentateuch; Martin Luther questioned the value of the epistle of James.

13. Donald Guthrie, "The Historical and Literary Criticism of the New Testament," in *Biblical Criticism: Historical, Literary and Textual,* ed. R. K. Harrison, B. K.

Waltke, D. Guthrie, and G. D. Fee (Grand Rapids, Mich.: Zondervan, 1978), 87. An excellent study of all phases of New Testament biblical criticism is Raymond F. Collins, *Introduction to the New Testament* (Garden City, N.Y.: Doubleday, 1983).

14. See, for example, C. H. Dodd, *The Interpretation of the Fourth Gospel* (Cambridge: Cambridge University Press, 1953); W. Schmithals, *Gnosticism in Corinth* (Nashville: Abingdon, 1971).

15. See Thomas Kuhn, *The Structure of Scientific Revolutions*, 2d ed., enl. (Chicago: University of Chicago Press, 1970); see also David Hackett Fischer, "Fallacies of Causation," in *Historians' Fallacies: Toward a Logic of Historical Thought* (New York: Harper & Row, 1970), 164–86.

16. An illustration of this can be found in David R. Cartlidge and David L. Dungan, *Documents for the Study of the Gospels* (Philadelphia: Fortress, 1980).

17. See Robert L. Millet, "A Small Book that Spans Eternity," in *Studies in Scripture, Vol. 2: The Pearl of Great Price,* ed. Robert L. Millet and Kent P. Jackson (Salt Lake City: Randall Book, 1985), 6–8; Milton R. Hunter, *The Gospel Through the Ages* (Salt Lake City: Bookcraft, 1945).

18. This represents one of many possible answers to the question of cultural and religious similarities throughout world history. See Spencer J. Palmer, "Mormon Views of Religious Resemblances," *BYU Studies* 16, no. 4 (summer 1976): 660–81; see also Milton R. Hunter, 39–40; Hugh Nibley, *The World and the Prophets,* ed. John W. Welch, Gary P. Gillum, and Don E. Norton (Salt Lake City: Deseret Book and F.A.R.M.S., 1987), 234–37; Robert L. Millet, "The Eternal Gospel," *Ensign,* July 1996, 48–56.

19. For an excellent summary of the causes of error in the transmission of texts, see Bruce M. Metzger, *The Text of the New Testament: Its Transmission, Conception, and Restoration,* 2d ed. (New York: Oxford University Press, 1968), 186–206.

20. Gordon D. Fee, "The Textual Criticism of the New Testament," in Harrison et al., 127.

21. Metzger, 156.

22. See a brief article by E. J. Epp, "Textual Criticism, NT," in *The Interpreter's Dictionary of the Bible* (Nashville: Abingdon, 1976), supplementary vol. 891–95.

23. Frederic Kenyon, *Our Bible and the Ancient Manuscripts* (New York: Harper, 1958), 53.

24. Bart D. Ehrman, *The Orthodox Corruption of Scripture: The Effect of Early Christological Controversies on the Text of the New Testament* (New York: Oxford University Press, 1993), 3–4.

25. Robert J. Matthews, "The Book of Mormon as a Co-Witness with the Bible and as a Guide to Biblical Criticism," *The Sixth Annual Church Educational System Religious Educators' Symposium on the Book of Mormon* (Salt Lake City: The Church of Jesus Christ of Latter-day Saints, 1982), 56–57. Bruce Metzger has written: "The manuscripts of the New Testament preserve traces of two kinds of

dogmatic alterations: those which involve the elimination or alteration of what was regarded as doctrinally unacceptable or inconvenient, and those which introduce into the Scriptures 'proof' for a favorite theological tenet of practice" (201).

26. These figures are found in F. F. Bruce, *The New Testament Documents: Are They Reliable?* 5th ed. (Grand Rapids, Mich.: Eerdmans, 1960), 31.

27. For excellent treatments of the dating, formation, and areas of stress of the Gospels of Mark and Luke, see S. Kent Brown, "The Testimony of Mark," in *Studies in Scripture, Vol. 5: The Gospels,* ed. Kent P. Jackson and Robert L. Millet (Salt Lake City: Deseret Book, 1986), 61–87; Richard Lloyd Anderson, "The Testimony of Luke," in *Studies in Scripture, Vol. 5,* 88–108.

28. See *The Nag Hammadi Library in English,* ed. James M. Robinson, rev. ed. (San Francisco: Harper & Row, 1988), 124–38; F. F. Bruce, *Jesus and Christian Origins Outside the New Testament* (Grand Rapids, Mich.: Eerdmans, 1974), 110–56.

29. For further possibilities concerning the Gospel of Thomas, see S. Kent Brown, "The Nag Hammadi Library: A Mormon Perspective," in *Apocryphal Writings and the Latter-day Saints,* ed. C. Wilfred Griggs (Provo, Utah: Religious Studies Center, Brigham Young University, 1986), 260, 275 n. 37.

30. See C. S. Mann, *Mark,* Anchor Bible 27 (Garden City, N.Y.: Doubleday, 1986), 47–66.

31. William R. Farmer, *Jesus and the Gospel: Tradition, Scripture, and Canon* (Philadelphia: Fortress, 1982), 3–7.

32. Some scholars have also been critical of the notion of a single sayings source. "It is not in the least necessary, we think, to suppose that there was a *single* block of material on which both Matthew and Luke drew. The vitality of oral tradition, the varying emphases cherished by various groups in the early Church, the care that was taken (to which the Johannine letters bear witness) to ascertain from reliable sources precisely what did happen in the public and private ministry of Jesus, the urgent need felt to preserve Christ's teachings in writing in the face of the difficult times—all these will have led to more than one tentative collection of oral material." Further, they contend that it is "far simpler to suppose that both Matthew and Luke used their own sources than to assume that one evangelist saw the other's work and proceeded to some radical editorial revision." W. F. Albright and C. S. Mann, *Matthew,* Anchor Bible 26 (Garden City, N.Y.: Doubleday, 1971), xlvii, li.

33. See the comments of Frank M. Cross Jr. in *The Ancient Library of Qumran and Modern Biblical Studies* (Grand Rapids, Mich.: Baker, 1980), 215–16, regarding the relationship of pre-Christian Essene motifs of light and darkness and the same elements in John's Gospel. One of the more interesting yet controversial books published in some time is John A. T. Robinson, *Redating the New Testament* (Philadelphia: Westminster, 1976). Robinson challenges the traditional scholarship that places much of the New Testament in the late first century–early second century A.D. He proposes that the evidence (internal and external) suggests that all New Testament records could very well have been written by A.D. 70. See also Robinson, *The Priority of John,* ed. J. F. Coakley (London: SCM, 1985).

34. See Edgar V. McKnight, *What Is Form Criticism?* (Philadelphia: Fortress, 1969), for a brief treatment of the subject.

35. Norman Perrin, *What Is Redaction Criticism?* (Philadelphia: Fortress, 1969), 15–16. An example of a form critical study is Arland J. Hultgren, *Jesus and His Adversaries* (Minneapolis: Augsburg, 1979).

36. See Bruce R. McConkie, *Doctrinal New Testament Commentary* (Salt Lake City: Bookcraft, 1965–73), 1:55–56.

37. For example, see Martin Dibelius, *From Tradition to Gospel* (New York: Scribners, 1935); Rudolph Bultmann, *The History of the Synoptic Tradition.*

38. See Birger Gerhardsson, *The Origins of the Gospel Traditions* (Philadelphia: Fortress, 1979); Werner H. Kelber, *The Oral and the Written Gospel* (Philadelphia: Fortress, 1983).

39. Papias, "Fragments of Papias," in *The Ante-Nicene Fathers,* ed. Alexander Roberts and James Donaldson (Grand Rapids, Mich.: Eerdmans, 1981), 1:153.

40. Richard Lloyd Anderson, "Types of Christian Revelation," in *Literature of Belief: Sacred Scripture and Religious Experience,* ed. Neal E. Lambert (Provo, Utah: Religious Studies Center, Brigham Young University, 1981), 63–64.

41. Bruce, 33.

42. Norman Perrin, *The Resurrection According to Matthew, Mark, and Luke* (Philadelphia: Fortress, 1977), 3–5. This book is a redaction critical study of the resurrection narratives. For another example, see Reginald H. Fuller, *The Formation of the Resurrection Narratives* (Philadelphia: Fortress, 1980).

43. See Bruce R. McConkie, *A New Witness for the Articles of Faith* (Salt Lake City: Deseret Book, 1985), 402; cf. also the words of Spencer W. Kimball in *President Kimball Speaks Out* (Salt Lake City: Deseret Book, 1981), 55–56.

44. See Millet, "'As Delivered from the Beginning': The Formation of the Canonical Gospels," in *Apocryphal Writings and the Latter-day Saints,* 199–213; "The JST and the Synoptic Gospels: Literary Style," in *The Joseph Smith Translation: The Restoration of Plain and Precious Things,* ed. Monte S. Nyman and Robert L. Millet (Provo, Utah: Religious Studies Center, Brigham Young University, 1985), 147–62.

45. Guthrie, 107–8; see also Hengel, *Acts and the History of Earliest Christianity* (Philadelphia: Fortress, 1980), 56–57.

46. From Stephen E. Robinson, "The 'Expanded' Book of Mormon?" in *Second Nephi: The Doctrinal Structure,* ed. Monte S. Nyman and Charles D. Tate Jr. (Provo, Utah: Religious Studies Center, Brigham Young University, 1989), 393–94.

47. C. S. Lewis, *Christian Reflections* (London: Harper Collins, 1967), 197–98.

48. John Warwick Montgomery, *History and Christianity* (San Bernadino, Calif.: Here's Life, 1983), 107–8.

49. Robert Stein, *The Method and Message of Jesus' Teachings* (Philadelphia: Westminster, 1978), 118–19.

50. Lewis, *Mere Christianity* (New York: Simon & Schuster, 1996), 56.

51. John Meir, *A Marginal Jew: Rethinking the Historical Jesus* (Garden City, N.Y.: Doubleday, 1991), 1:177.

52. Scot McKnight, "Who Is Jesus? An Introduction to Jesus Studies," in *Jesus Under Fire: Modern Scholarship Reinvents the Historical Jesus,* ed. Michael J. Wilkins and J. P. Moreland (Grand Rapids, Mich.: Zondervan, 1995), 61–62.

53. Malcolm Muggeridge, *Jesus: The Man Who Lives* (New York: Harper & Row, 1975), 20.

54. Orson F. Whitney, *Conference Report,* April 1915, 100.

55. Joseph F. Smith, *Gospel Doctrine* (Salt Lake City: Deseret Book, 1986), 38.

56. Howard W. Hunter, *That We Might Have Joy* (Salt Lake City: Deseret Book, 1994), 23, 25–26.

Notes on Historicity and Inerrancy

9

Daniel C. Peterson

Some believe that historicity and inerrancy in scripture are the same. By this argument, when a portion of scripture is found to have errors, the entire record is considered neither historical nor accurate. However, nothing in this imperfect world is inerrant, and although the authors of the scriptural records were prophets and called of God to write their portion of the scriptures, they were not perfect—no one is. So although the authors were not inerrant, their writings are nonetheless historical. By academic standards the scriptures fulfill all the criteria for historically accurate records. With the human errors accounted for, the scriptures are reliable historically and accurate in their testimony of the doctrines of the gospel and the mission of Jesus Christ.

For now we see through a glass, darkly; but then face to face: now I know in part; but then shall I know even as also I am known (1 Cor. 13:12).

Let these things be stated as conjectural only, similar to the reality (Xenophanes of Colophon).[1]

When I agreed originally to discuss "historicity and inerrancy," I was a bit perplexed. One way for me to have dealt with this subject—and, I believe, to have done so quite adequately—would be simply to have observed that *historicity* and *inerrancy* are not the same thing. In fact, I was severely tempted to do only that. Most people would, I suspect, think it *obvious* that they are distinct. But most people, I fear, would be naïve. There *are* individuals who claim that asserting the historicity of the scriptures entails an assertion of their inerrancy. Although the equation of belief in historicity with belief in inerrancy borders on the slanderous—despite its manifest character as a straw man intended to stigmatize those who believe in the essential credibility of the scriptures as unreflective, irrational fundamentalists, and notwithstanding the fact that there is no obvious merit to it but indeed major counterevidence against it—the equation persists in some circles.

I am reminded, for instance, of one well-educated Latter-day Saint writer who can discern no middle ground between fundamentalism, on the one hand, and radical skepticism on the other. "Once one gives up the idea of an inerrant, strictly historical, biblical record," he says, "it must be admitted that there is little in the life of Jesus that can be known with certainty."[2]

From a particular perspective, this claim is unremarkable. It is true that we can know very little in history or anywhere else with absolute certainty. Even divine or angelic revelation of the most spectacular kind can subsequently be doubted by the very people who experienced it and once firmly believed it to be true.[3] Brigham Young, for instance, recalled some of those (clearly beyond the better-known "official" witnesses of the Book of Mormon) "who handled the plates and conversed with the angels of God, [but] were afterwards left to doubt and to disbelieve that they had ever seen an angel." One of the early members of the Quorum of the Twelve, whom President Young described as "a young man full of faith and good works," "prayed, and the vision of his mind was opened, and the angel of God came and laid the plates before him, and he saw and handled them, and saw the angel, and conversed with him as he would with one of his friends; but after all this, he was left to doubt, and plunged into apostasy, and has continued to contend against this work. There are hundreds in a similar condition."[4]

Anything can be doubted. I am unable even to prove that there is a real, objectively existing external world. How do I know that the room in which I wrote this paper and the audience to whom I originally presented it were not simply subjective experiences in my mind? I cannot prove definitively otherwise. Nor can I prove that God did not suddenly create my readers and me ninety seconds ago, equipped with a complete and utterly convincing set of false memories. Furthermore, as the great logician Bertrand Russell noted, no number of past sunrises, however great, logically entails that the sun will, without fail, rise tomorrow.[5]

So there should be little surprise that history, which manifestly operates on a lower level of certainty than those sections of almanacs that predict times of sunrise, can generally furnish plausibility and even a very high degree of probability—but no more than that. But this is true of *all* history, not merely of that area of history that focuses on religion and religious claims. Leopold von Ranke's contention that real, scientific historians can and must describe the past "as it actually happened" is dead. Nobody that I know or read believes that totally objective, scientific history—history written without preconceptions and without prejudgments—is possible.

But I suspect that our selected revisionist skeptic is not merely offering us a banality, a bit of trivia, when he offers us his Hobson's choice between inerrancy and agnosticism. No, his claim seems a different one, and it is one that is both remarkable and wholly indefensible.[6] This becomes instantly apparent if we simply plug different terms into an argument with a structure identical to his, as follows: "Once one gives up the idea of an inerrant, strictly historical [Thucydides], it must be admitted that there is little in the [history of the Peleponnesian War] that can be known with certainty." Or, "Once one gives up the idea of . . . inerrant, strictly historical [records from the late eighteenth century], it must be admitted that there is little in the [history of the American Revolution] that can be known with certainty." Or even, "Once one gives up the idea of an inerrant, strictly historical [memory], it must be admitted that there is little in the [story of one's own life] that [one can know] with certainty." Obviously, such claims would be laughed to scorn in secular historiographical circles, and well beyond. If they were to be accepted, they would destroy historical scholarship; they would destroy the human individual's sense of identity and his or her capacity to act intelligently. Yet to reject thoroughgoing and unjustified doubt in religious studies, our revisionist writer informs us, is to be a fundamentalist.

The Historicity of Jesus

This writer and some of his associates are much taken with the controversial "Jesus Seminar," which has gained a great deal of media notoriety in recent years with its assertions, for example, that real scholarship on the New Testament reveals that the Resurrection of Jesus never occurred, that the Savior never claimed to be divine, and that only about 18 percent of the statements attributed to Christ in the four Gospels are authentic. But the Jesus Seminar scarcely represents mainstream biblical scholarship, let alone mainstream historical scholarship. "Who," asks Duke professor Richard Hays, "are the scholars that make up the membership of the Jesus Seminar? The group's publicity creates the impression that they represent a broad cross-section of this country's leading critical scholars. It is asserted that 'the scholarship represented by the Fellows of the Jesus Seminar is the kind that has come to prevail in all the great universities of the world.' Though the Seminar expects to encounter hostile criticism, its work is said to be under attack principally 'by conservative Christian groups' and by 'those who lack academic credentials.' . . . In fact—let it be said clearly—most professional biblical scholars are profoundly skeptical of the methods and conclusions of this academic splinter group."[7]

More important for our present purposes, the methods of the Jesus Seminar, which are far from the mainstream of biblical scholarship, are even farther from the historiographical mainstream. "No responsible historian," Professor Craig L. Blomberg observes of the Seminar's co-founders, "would ever approach the biographies of Alexander, Augustus, or Apollonius with the approaches of [John Dominic] Crossan or [Robert] Funk."[8]

A good illustration of this is to be found in the case of Julius Caesar's famous crossing of the Rubicon River upon his return from Gaul to Italy in 49 B.C. In doing so, in violating the long-standing rule that no Roman general would ever bring his troops into the immediate vicinity of the city of Rome, he openly challenged the authority of the Roman state as then constituted, committed himself to fight a civil war, and changed the course of history. This event is often used as a textbook illustration of what seems to be an indisputable fact of ancient history. But things are not nearly so neat or so simple. "What is often overlooked," remarks Professor Blomberg, "is that we are not absolutely sure of the date of the crossing or the location of the Rubicon. And, as with the Gospels, we have four accounts of the event from later historians—Velleius Paterculus, Plutarch, Suetonius, and Appian. Only the first of these was even born before the mid-first century *after* Christ."[9]

In other words, three of the four historians were born at least a full century after the event, meaning that they did not *write* about it until perhaps a century and a half afterwards. This contrasts very unfavorably with the four canonical Gospels, which have rarely if ever been dated to a point so long after the ministry of Christ. Even the earliest of the four historians whose extant works discuss the incident, Velleius Paterculus, was born a full three decades too late to have been even an infant eyewitness to it. Professor Blomberg states:

> All apparently relied on one eyewitness source, that of Asinius Pollio, which has disappeared without a trace. Yet the four accounts vary at least as much as the Gospels do when reporting the same event. One writer, Suetonius, attributes Caesar's decision to cross the Rubicon to seeing "an apparition of superhuman size and beauty," who was "sitting on the river bank, playing a reed pipe."
>
> When this kind of miraculous detail appears in a Gospel account, the entire story is usually rejected [by revisionist skeptics] as mythical. Here it appears in an account of an event that is regularly cited as one of the most well-established historical facts of antiquity! Clearly a double standard is at work here. *The Gospels deserve to be treated at least as generously as any other purportedly historical narrative from the ancient world.* The words of the British historian of ancient Rome, A. N. Sherwin-White, though penned a generation ago, remain equally applicable to today's radical criticism: "It is astonishing that while Graeco-Roman historians have been growing in confidence, the twentieth-century study of the Gospel narratives, starting from no less promising material, has taken so gloomy a turn."[10]

Historical Knowledge

A few months ago, while I was a guest on a Salt Lake City radio talk show, a listener called in to protest that nothing that we were talking about in connection with religion could possibly be an object of real knowledge. The only real knowledge, he said, was that of science, in which experiments conducted under controlled conditions can replicate and confirm the results of earlier researchers to the satisfaction of any intelligent observer. Now, I agree that laboratory experimentation offers one very important form of knowledge. The problem is that not even all science conforms to this model—to say nothing of other areas of human knowing. Nor *can* it. Virtually all of astronomy, for example, would be excluded by his rule. Has anybody replicated the Big Bang in a laboratory recently? For that matter, has anyone repeated macroevolution lately or re-created the Grand Canyon? The caller's principle would rule out all history. We can never replicate the career of Ramses II, nor even his historical birth, even if it should someday prove possible to clone the pharaoh's genetic twin. Quite unreasonably, the caller seemed to close ranks with the sort of modern people described by C. S. Lewis, among whom "Pre-Historic Man is labelled 'Science' (which is reliable) whereas Napoleon or Julius Caesar is labelled as 'History' (which is not)."[11] Moreover, the caller's rule would make it impossible for him to prove, thirty seconds afterwards, that he had been on the phone with me. (At least, the confidence that he had been would not be "real knowledge," by his own account.) It would deny the status of "real knowledge" to his memories of his family. Furthermore, it would destroy the basis of such varied kinds of knowledge as mathematics and the principles of ethics. Can one prove in a laboratory that two is an even number, or that it is wrong to torture people for fun? Indeed, the caller's rule would invalidate *itself*, since the principle that "only propositions that can be confirmed in replicatable laboratory experiments constitute real knowledge" is itself a proposition that *cannot* be confirmed in a replicatable laboratory experiment.

Now, again, this may seem obvious. My discussion may seem the academic equivalent of shooting fish in a barrel. But there is an important point to be grasped here: Historical knowledge does not, it is true, attain the same kind or degree of certitude as can be attained in a chemistry lab, or at the end of a geometric proof—though, even those two areas may not deliver quite as much certainty as is commonly thought[12]—but it can attain a plausibility or probability that comes very close to certainty. And we are right to call it, precisely, "historical *knowledge*." Historicity is not the same thing as inerrancy. An inerrant narrative would certainly be historical. But there are plenty of substantially accurate historical narratives that are not inerrant. In fact, there is (so far as I am aware) no other kind. Although nobody in his or her right mind would ever call Josephus or al-Tabari inerrant, much less the author or authors of *The Annals of the Cakchiquels,* we still find these writers indispensable for the reconstruction of what we generally regard as fairly reliable histories of Second Temple Jewry, the early Arab Muslims, and the inhabitants of pre-Columbian Guatemala.

I am not even sure, honestly, what an inerrant historical text would be. For example, no text can possibly be complete. It would take me months just to catalog and describe all the movements and small events that took place in the lecture hall during the reading of this paper. C. S. Lewis makes my point with predictable eloquence:

> Each of us finds that in his own life every moment of time is completely filled. He is bombarded every second by sensations, emotions, thoughts, which he cannot attend to for multitude, and nine-tenths of which he must simply ignore. A single second of lived time contains more than can be recorded. And every second of past time has been like that for every man that ever lived. The past (I am assuming . . . that we need consider only the human past) in its reality, was a roaring cataract of billions upon billions of such moments: any one of them too complex to grasp in its entirety, and the aggregate beyond all imagination. By far the greater part of this teeming reality escaped human consciousness almost as soon as it occurred. None of us could at this moment give anything like a full account of his own life for the last twenty-four hours. We have already forgotten; even if we remembered, we have not time. The new moments are upon us. At every tick of the clock, in every inhabited part of the world, an unimaginable richness and variety of "history" falls off the world into total oblivion. Most of the experiences in "the past as it really was" were instantly forgotten by the subject himself. Of the small percentage which he remembered (and never remembered with perfect accuracy) a smaller percentage was ever communicated even to his closest intimates; of this, a smaller percentage still was recorded; of the recorded fraction only another fraction has ever reached posterity. . . . When once we have realized what "the past as it really was" means, we must freely admit that most—that nearly all—history . . . is, and will remain, wholly unknown to us. And if *per impossible* the whole were known, it would be wholly unmanageable. To know the whole of one minute in Napoleon's life would require a whole minute of your own life. You could not keep up with it.[13]

Thus, any historical record must necessarily be selective. Indeed, most of its selecting has already been done for it, since the vast majority of facts are lost almost immediately. Most utterances are never written down; most actions are never recorded. But even if they were once recorded, the overwhelming majority of the documents of the past, like the overwhelming majority of buildings and artifacts, have disappeared without a trace.[14] To choose an example almost purely at random (simply because I have just been reading about her), virtually every bit of information about the life of the illustrious Greek poet Sappho has disappeared. As Dudley Fitts has observed, what we know about this rough contemporary of Lehi is "nothing but speculation. We have heard a great deal about Sappho, and we know almost nothing. The sands of Egypt have been generous and papyruses are still being found, but unless we are granted a discovery of almost theophanic import we are not likely to learn much more."[15] Relatively few of the plays of even the great Greek tragedians Aeschylus, Sophocles, and Euripides have survived; all of the dialogues of Aristotle have vanished.

But even where the materials or documents still exist, the most important and most sensitive part of the historiographical task remains to be done. In the terminology of the Italian philosopher Benedetto Croce, the raw data of the past, the mere theoretical list of events, isn't even *history* at all. It is what he called *chronicle*. And *chronicle* only comes to life—becomes *history*—when the historian, picking and choosing what is meaningful for his or her *present-day* purposes, relives it in his or her own mind.[16] Sir Karl Popper relates that he once began a lecture to physics students in Vienna with the instructions, "Take pencil and paper; carefully observe, and write down what you have observed!" Not surprisingly, the students found the assignment mystifying. *What* were they supposed to observe? Without some sort of object, at least an implicit one, without limitation and definition, the imperative "Observe!" is meaningless and absurd.[17] The same is clearly true for historiography as well. The German biblical scholar Herbert Niehr notes that "history cannot be found simply in the sources. The sources merely provide the material to be exploited. For writing historiography or the history of a religion, it does not suffice to retell the sources. Explicit working hypotheses have to be formulated that are open to subsequent verification or falsification. It is only within the frame of these working hypotheses that the interpretation of the sources finds its place."[18]

But this is where the dream of an absolutely objective, value-neutral historical record dies. For it brings into play the personality of the author of the record, the selector and organizer of the data, whose beliefs, background information or misinformation, limitations of time and energy, perceptiveness or imperceptiveness, or even individual quirks will inevitably affect the outcome. Such factors play a role even in eyewitness testimony. The story of the discovery of the circulation of blood, and of the role played by the heart in it, will serve well as an example here: Numerous scientists before William Harvey dissected human hearts just as he would do, but they failed to observe the right, the salient, things. Instead, they saw what their theories and expectations had prepared them to see, and they apparently failed to notice the many aspects of the heart, now utterly obvious to even the most slothful student of anatomy and physiology, that were inconsistent with the prevailing doctrines of Galenic medicine.[19] As Karl Popper remarks, "Every witness must always make ample use, in his report, of his knowledge of persons, places, things, linguistic usages, social conventions, and so on. He cannot rely merely upon his eyes or ears, especially if his report is to be of use in justifying any assertion worth justifying. But this fact must of course always raise new questions as to the sources of those elements of his knowledge which are not immediately observational."[20]

Scriptural Historicity

This is so in scripture, as in uninspired historiography. The Book of Mormon, for example, relates that due to fatigue or oversight or a lapse of attention or incomprehension or whatever reason, an important and fulfilled prophecy of Samuel the Lamanite had been omitted from the narrative of his appearance among the Nephites. The Savior was obliged personally to direct its inclusion when he visited the New World after his resurrection (3 Ne. 23:7–13). In the case of the four Gospels, it seems rather unlikely that the fallible pre-resurrection Apostles (who failed to grasp much of what Christ said to them) were suddenly transformed into infallible automatons by his triumph over the grave. Recently published arguments for the impossibility and even the undesirability of historiographical objectivity surely apply to the scriptures and the prophets, as well as to secular or uninspired writers. Prophets are not marionettes. And there is no reason to expect a prophetic narrator to be historically omniscient, any more than there is reason to believe him scientifically omniscient. Moreover, the fact that the narrator of a story or a history knows how it will eventually turn out means that his or her understanding of that narrative will be different from the understanding of those who were involved in the story while it was in the process of unfolding. Knowledge of the broader picture unavoidably must—and should—affect our description of its details. Is it even conceivable, for instance, that the authors of the Gospels remained unaffected by the end of *their* story—the atoning death and triumphant resurrection of Christ—as they sat down to write their narratives of the life of Jesus? For the scriptural writers, as for us, "all observation involves interpretation in the light of our theoretical knowledge. . . . Pure observational knowledge, unadulterated by theory, would, if at all possible, be utterly barren and futile."[21] We need not share the rather extreme mistrust that Professor Niehr has for the Hebrew Bible, nor think the gulf between biblical events and the biblical narrative of those events as vast as he clearly does, to understand the inevitable truth of his assertion that the Hebrew Bible "does not depict the histories of Judah and Israel as they took place, but as they have been reimagined in the mind of the writers."[22] For this is the nature of all historiography, without conceivable exception. If God had wanted inerrant, perfect scriptures, He would not have given them through human beings.

But as we reject the notion of an impossible, completely objective historiography, we must avoid falling into the error of historical relativism, where all is arbitrary and no historical account can ever be rationally preferred over another. We have every reason, for example, to believe that the authors of the Gospels were conscientious and well-intentioned. The King James Version somewhat obscures the situation when it portrays Luke, who was himself a relative newcomer to Christianity, as "having had perfect understanding of all things from the very first" (Luke 1:3). What the Greek says, rather, is that Luke wrote his Gospel (and presumably also its sequel, the Acts of the Apostles) after "having investigated everything carefully from the beginning."[23] In other words, he functioned just the way any conscientious historian functions: he did research. His research may have included the reading of other written accounts, and it evidently relied on the accounts of "eyewitnesses" (*autoptai;* Luke 1:1–2).

Thus, we have in the Gospel narratives inevitable authorial subjectivity, manifested in the decisions the writers had to make about what was or was not important and what was or was not trustworthy, and in their undoubted authorial commitment to a pre-existing belief system. But these are balanced, as in every good piece of history they must be, with careful research and an attempt to get the story right. In this context, it is perhaps significant that the Joseph Smith Translation of the Bible anticipates modern scholarly emphasis on the individual character of the New Testament Gospels by such labels as "the Testimony of St. Matthew" and "the Testimony of John."[24] And, like the testimonies we bear in our church meetings, the testimonies of the Gospel writers, though they are in one important sense subjective, should not (merely for that reason) be dismissed as arbitrary or as not grounded in real experience or history.[25]

President Brigham Young offered another reason why inerrancy is hardly to be sought, even in the scriptures themselves: "I do not even believe," he reflected, "that there is a single revelation, among the many God has given to the Church, that is perfect in its fulness. The revelations of God contain correct doctrine and principle, so far as they go; but it is impossible for the poor, weak, low, grovelling, sinful inhabitants of the earth to receive a revelation from the Almighty in all its perfections. He has to speak to us in a manner to meet the extent of our capacities."[26]

If God had wanted inerrant, perfect scriptures, He would not have wasted them on human beings. For what would be the point, anyway, of inerrant scriptures? We could neither inerrantly recognize them as such, nor inerrantly read them. Already in the sixth century before Christ, the pre-Socratic thinker Xenophanes of Colophon recognized this aspect of the human condition: "And as for certain truth, no man has seen it, nor will there ever be a man who knows about the gods and about all the things I mention. For if he succeeds to the full in saying what is completely true, he himself is nevertheless unaware of it; and Opinion (seeming) is fixed by fate upon all things."[27] In other words, no mortal human being can know the truth absolutely, indubitably, precisely, or beyond any possibility of error or dispute. Humans are fallible and often foolish. Anything can be disputed. Anything can be doubted. Still, despite his awareness of human limitation, Xenophanes did not despair of attaining, perhaps asymptotically, at least a fairly good idea of the truth. "Truly," he said, "the gods have not revealed to mortals all things from the beginning; but mortals by long seeking discover what is better."[28] Neither should we despair, for there is no cause to do so. It is vastly important that the scriptures be reliable guides to salvation and to the nature of God and His purposes. It is far less important that they be entirely accurate on the numbers of Israelites who left Egypt, or on the magnitude of the number π in the construction of Solomon's temple. Historicity is essential. Inerrancy is not. And the two are not the same. Some skeptics want us to abandon our belief in the historicity of the scriptures because the scriptures do not appear to be infallible. But this is a leap we need not take. Some among those skeptics want us to believe that the scriptural stories can still be religiously meaningful even if they are purely fictional. In some cases, of course, this is true. The story of Job illustrates various answers to the problem of evil just as well if it is fictional as it does if it is an accurate historical account. In this regard, it rather resembles Plato's *Republic,* or his *Symposium,* where we really do not care whether Thrasymachus or Alcibiades really said or did the things Plato relates. But Jesus is not Job, and it matters very much whether the story of Christ really happened as the Gospels say it did. Even here, though, we must distinguish the essential from the nonessential.

What Really Matters

Benedetto Croce's contrast between *chronicle* and *history,* mentioned above, roughly resembles the distinction that German and other Christian theologians have long made between *Historie* and *Geschichte.* Both terms, of course, literally mean *history.* But, as Carl Braaten explains the theological and philosophical difference between the two, "*Historie* is the sum total of historical facts lying 'back there' in the past which can be objectively verified; the mode of knowledge appropriate here is impartial investigation and neutral observation. *Geschichte* has to do with phenomena that concern me existentially, that make some demand upon me and call for commitment."[29]

Of course, we should object to the notion of "impartial investigation and neutral observation" as constituting any part of real historical practice. Probably no actual historian passively surveys the data without a question or a thesis or even a hypothesis in mind.[30] Obviously, there can be historical facts that have no life-orientational importance for me or for anyone else. That is to say that *Historie* can exist without *Geschichte*. It is, for example, absolutely insignificant for anyone I can think of that the Caliph 'Umar may have sneezed on the morning of 10 June A.D. 640. But hundreds of millions of Muslims around the world conduct their lives based on acceptance of the proposition that sometime near A.D. 610, the Prophet Muhammad began to receive the revelations that would eventually be compiled in the Qur'ān. And millions of Latter-day Saints believe that Joseph Smith was in a grove of trees in the presence of the Father and the Son in the spring of 1820. Does it matter whether or not these events really happened? Can *Geschichte* be valid without an underlying *Historie?* Manifestly, people can find life-orientational significance in stories that did not actually occur. (Religious people commonly suppose that everybody not of their faith is doing exactly that.) A madman who thought himself Superman might well be moved to heroic behavior by his delusion. But do we not usually regard such motivation as defective? Would we not in most cases seek, however gently, to correct or to treat such mistaken ideas?

My contention, simply, is that sound *Geschichte,* life-orientational history, must rest upon substantially accurate *Historie,* or factual historical data. The underlying history need not be totally correct in every tiny detail, nor must it be complete. Given human limitations and the inevitable disappearance of virtually all human utterances and nearly all human records and artifacts, we can never—in this life—have a wholly true picture of the past. But the story, though told by errant human beings, must be largely true.

If, for example, the intent of the story of the resurrection of Jesus is to illustrate God's love, or how God's purposes triumph over evil—and, surely, these are among its intents—it fails to accomplish those ends if God did not actually resurrect Jesus from the dead. As the British scholar N. T. Wright points out, "Several first-century Jews besides Jesus held, and acted upon, remarkable and subversive views." Accordingly, he asks, "Why should Jesus be any more than one of the most remarkable of them?" He concludes that "the answer must hinge on the resurrection. If nothing happened to the body of Jesus, I cannot see why any of his explicit or implicit claims should

209

be regarded as true. What is more, I cannot, as a historian, see why anyone would have continued to belong to his movement and to regard him as its Messiah. There were several other Messianic or quasi-Messianic movements within a hundred years either side of Jesus. Routinely, they ended with the leader's being killed by the authorities, or by a rival group. If your Messiah is killed, you conclude that he was not the Messiah."[31]

Indeed, if the purpose of the story of Jesus' resurrection is to illustrate divine love or the triumph of good over evil, but Jesus did not in fact rise from the grave, God actually looks worse or less powerful than if the story had not been told at all. For it then serves only to show the vast contrast between what He allegedly *could* have done and what He in reality *did*. The Apostle Paul was vividly aware of what was at stake: "And if Christ be not raised, your faith is vain; ye are yet in your sins. Then they also which are fallen asleep in Christ are perished. If in this life only we have hope in Christ, we are of all men most miserable" (1 Cor. 15:17–19).

However, if Jesus really rose from the dead, it scarcely matters how many angels were standing by His empty tomb when the apostles arrived. Much recent scholarship on the New Testament presupposes that the Gospel narratives are largely fictional or, at any rate, treats them as if they are. Such a presupposition would explain why so much academic attention is lavished on the authors and purported editors of the documents, on their schools and strategies and rhetoric and supposed agendas. It is because we are unconvinced that the Danish prince Hamlet, if he lived at all, has any particular relevance to the play that bears his name that we feel free to concentrate not on him but on the style, the biography, and the technique of William Shakespeare. But if Christ is God come in the flesh, the little details and the narrative strategies of the Gospel accounts, albeit interesting, possess at most merely secondary significance. Important though they are, the Gospels—indeed, all the books of the Bible—are intended to point beyond themselves to what really matters.[32] "The fundamental principles of our religion," said the Prophet Joseph Smith, "are the testimony of the Apostles and Prophets, concerning Jesus Christ, that He died, was buried, and rose again the third day, and ascended into heaven; and all other things which pertain to our religion are only appendages to it."[33]

We must also, of course, apply these principles to our reading of the Book of Mormon. If the emigration of Lehi did not actually happen, then the story of his emigration provides no evidence for God's providential intervention in history. Indeed, quite the contrary, for it would then seem that contrary to the claim of the Book of Mormon, nobody, neither Lehi nor anyone else, was saved by God from the destruction of Jerusalem. But it would hardly matter whether Lehi left under the reign of Zedekiah, as the Nephite record asserts, or whether some mistake had occurred and he really took his departure in the days of Jehoiachin. God's intervention in real space and time would still be attested. The more central question of whether Jesus really appeared to the Nephites is infinitely weightier than whether the figures given for the military units at the close of Nephite history are precisely accurate. No small historical quibbles, even if they call into question the infallibility of the Book of Mormon—an infallibility that the Book of Mormon pointedly refuses to claim for *itself*—are of more than academic interest, so long as they do not cast doubt on the essential historical truth of the book. That is the issue, and it is hugely important. We should not allow ourselves to be distracted from it. The Book of Mormon as an authentic record of a real God's genuine interventions and self-disclosures in literal history is a very different thing from the Book of Mormon as a fictional expression of a nineteenth-century farmboy's touching faith in such an intervening and self-disclosing God.

An ahistorical Book of Mormon makes a hash of the founding narratives of the Restoration, with their descriptions of golden plates brought by an angel. (And, I might add, an ahistorical Book of Mormon runs counter to the considerable *evidence* for the plates and the angel.)[34] A fallible but largely accurate Book of Mormon, however, is consistent with those founding narratives, and with its description of itself as a record of the migrations, wars, reformations, and ultimate demise of an ancient people. It still provides powerful evidence for the existence of a caring God and a redeeming Christ. Otherwise, simply, it does not. And the issues here are as important as they can be. If the universe is truly a closed, naturalistic system, what does this say about the religious hopes of humankind? What comfort for the terminally ill, or for bereaved parents? What point in morality or self-denial? What assurance of eternal purpose, of real goodness, of our being at home in the cosmos?

I want my position to be clearly understood. On essential issues such as the resurrection of Christ, we can trust that the accounts given in the scriptures are fundamentally and significantly correct. And, perhaps even more important, we can trust that the prophets have identified sound lessons for us, that they have given us the real meaning—or, at least, the most significant portion of it, since there is probably no way to exhaust completely the meaning of anything consequential—for the events they narrate. But I will go even beyond that. If I have seemed during this paper to insist only on accuracy in the big picture, while appearing ready to jettison the minor details, I want to make it clear that although I reject inerrancy, I believe that the scriptures are substantially accurate even in the details, that the narratives of the Bible are by and large accurate, that there were Nephites, and that their history is as accurately told in the Book of Mormon as it is humanly possible to tell a story. I believe that considerable evidence can be amassed to support these propositions and to sustain and confirm the witness of the Spirit.

And this, as you well realize, is no small thing. If the Book of Mormon is an authentic account of a real visit of the resurrected Christ to the Americas, miraculously revealed to an unlettered young prophet by a real, tangible angel, then it provides solid reason for a belief that God lives, that Jesus is the Christ, and that revelation has commenced again in modern times. I testify that it is and does just that.

Daniel C. Peterson is associate professor of Arabic, Brigham Young University.

Notes

1. The translation is from Kathleen Freeman, *Ancilla to the Pre-Socratic Philosophers: A Complete Translation of the Fragments in Diels, Fragmente der Vorsokratiker* (Cambridge: Harvard University Press, 1978), 24, where the reference to the original Greek is also given.

2. Stephen E. Thompson, "Searching for the 'Historical Jesus,'" *Sunstone* 16, no. 9 (June 1994): 61.

3. I have personally spoken with several people who have had such manifestations and then doubted; one or two of them I have known rather well. Laman and Lemuel may fall into this category (see 1 Ne. 3:29–31).

4. *Journal of Discourses* (London: Latter-day Saints' Book Depot, 1854–86), 7:164. A number of impressive accounts from "witnesses" to the Book of Mormon beyond the official eleven are collected in Susan Easton Black, ed., *Stories from the Early Saints: Converted by the Book of Mormon* (Salt Lake City: Bookcraft, 1992).

5. Bertrand Russell, *The Problems of Philosophy* (New York: Oxford University Press, 1997), 60–62. I am grateful to my colleague Dennis F. Rasmussen for helping me locate this dimly remembered reference. For a similar point, see David Hume, *Enquiries Concerning the Human Understanding and Concerning the Principles of Morals* (Oxford: Clarendon, 1972), 32–39, and *A Treatise of Human Nature: Being An Attempt to Introduce the Experimental Method of Reasoning into Moral Subjects* (New York: Dolphin, 1961), 79–86, 120–31. Compare Karl R. Popper, *Conjectures and Refutations: The Growth of Scientific Knowledge* (London: Routledge; Kegan Paul, 1969), 41–42 nn. 8, 53.

6. James D. G. Dunn, *The Partings of the Ways Between Christianity and Judaism and their Significance for the Character of Christianity* (London: SCM; Philadelphia: Trinity Press International, 1991), 13, warns against precisely this kind of hyperskepticism. One is indeed tempted to say, on the basis of Thompson's claim, that once one gives up the idea of inerrant radical revisionist skeptics, it must be admitted that there is little in their arguments that can be known with certainty to be either true or useful. Consistency would seem to demand some such verdict.

7. Richard B. Hays, "The Corrected Jesus," *First Things* 43 (May 1994): 47; also 44, 48. Close observers of recent arguments about Latter-day Saint history and scripture will recognize a familiar ring both in the claim that a debunking scholarship is the only true kind of scholarship on scriptural issues and in the would-be revisionists' extensive and skillful use of publicity. I have recently commented on the Jesus Seminar, and on its derivatives and analogues within Mormonism, in my "Editor's Introduction: Triptych (Inspired by Hieronymus Bosch)," *F.A.R.M.S. Review of Books* 8, no. 1 (1996): v–xlv. For an even more recent critique of the Seminar by an evangelical Protestant, see James R. Edwards, "'Who Do Scholars Say That I Am?'" *Christianity Today* 40, no. 3 (4 March 1996): 14–20. In an article that was unavailable to me at the time I wrote my "Editor's Introduction," Birger A. Pearson, an eminent scholar of early Christianity, forcefully challenges the Jesus Seminar's claim to be doing unbiased history. See his "The Gospel according to the Jesus Seminar," *Religion* 25 (1995): 317–38. Paul Rhodes Eddy, "Jesus as Diogenes? Reflections on the Cynic Jesus Thesis," *Journal of Biblical Literature* 115, no. 3 (fall 1996): 449–69, criticizes a position prominently associated with leading Seminar members. I had pointed to the apparent self-validating secular bias of the Jesus Seminar. On pp. 468–69, Professor Eddy notes the same problem in those who argue that Jesus was a Hellenized Cynic philosopher, "a noneschatological Jesus who

preached a pure this-worldly kingdom of values (values, interestingly enough, that foreshadowed the moral worldview of the twentieth-century postmodern liberal academy)." "To what degree," he asks, "is the historical Cynic Jesus essentially a reflection of the thought world and/or values of his modern-day co-constructors?"

8. Craig L. Blomberg, "Where Do We Start Studying Jesus?" in Michael J. Wilkins and J. P. Moreland, eds., *Jesus under Fire: Modern Scholarship Reinvents the Historical Jesus* (Grand Rapids, Mich.: Zondervan, 1995), 27.

9. Ibid., 37.

10. Ibid., 37, citing A. N. Sherwin-White, *Roman Society and Roman Law in the New Testament* (Oxford: Clarendon, 1963), 187 (emphasis in the original). See the discussion of Caesar's crossing of the Rubicon in Paul Merkley, "The Gospels as Historical Testimony," *Evangelical Quarterly* 58 (1986): 328–36.

11. C. S. Lewis, *God in the Dock: Essays on Theology and Ethics,* ed. Walter Hooper (Grand Rapids, Mich.: Eerdmans, 1970), 241.

12. William Barrett, *The Illusion of Technique: A Search for Meaning in a Techno-logical Civilization* (Garden City, N.Y.: Doubleday, 1979), 3–117, describes the effect of cultural and psychological factors upon so rarified a discipline as mathe-matical logic. References on this issue could be multiplied indefinitely. "It is a disturbing fact," wrote Sir Karl Popper, "that even an abstract study like pure epistemology is not as pure as one might think (and as Aristotle believed) but that its ideas may, to a large extent, be motivated and unconsciously inspired by political hopes and by Utopian dreams" (Popper, *Conjectures and Refutations,* 6). Popper's entire corpus of work should be mandatory reading for those tempted to dogmatic scientism.

13. C. S. Lewis, *Christian Reflections,* ed. Walter Hooper (San Francisco: Harper Collins, 1991), 139–40.

14. The house in which I lived for two years as an undergraduate, and which I once rather imagined was destined for designation as a historical monument, was demol-ished to make way for the expansion of a pizza restaurant's parking lot.

15. Dudley Fitts, foreword to Mary Barnard *Sappho: A New Translation* (Berkeley and Los Angeles: University of California Press, 1962), viii.

16. See the discussion in Ronald H. Nash, *Christian Faith and Historical Under-standing* (Grand Rapids, Mich.: Zondervan, 1984), 33–34.

17. Popper, *Conjectures and Refutations,*46.

18. Herbert Niehr, "The Rise of YHWH in Judahite and Israelite Religion: Meth-odological and Religio-Historical Aspects," in *The Triumph of Elohim: From Yahwisms to Judaisms,* ed. Diana Vikander Edelman (Grand Rapids, Mich.: Eerd-mans, 1996), 50.

19. Popper, *Conjectures and Refutations,* 41–42 n. 8.

20. Ibid., 22–23.

21. Ibid., 23; cf. 28, 38 n. 3, 41–42 n. 8, 44–47.

22. Niehr, "The Rise of YHWH," 47.

23. The translation is mine, but such modern renderings as the New American Standard Bible, the New International Version, the New American Bible, and the New Revised Standard Version will bear me out on this.

24. The same idea seems to be present in D&C 88:141.

25. For a discussion of related issues, see David B. Honey and Daniel C. Peterson, "Advocacy and Inquiry in the Writing of Latter-day Saint History," _BYU Studies_ 31, no. 2 (spring 1991): 139–79.

26. _Journal of Discourses,_ 2:314. I am inclined to agree, in at least one sense, with Karl Popper's contention that absolutely pure and untainted sources of knowledge do not, and cannot, exist (Popper, _Conjectures and Refutations,_ 25). Not, at any rate, here in this fallen world.

27. Freeman, _Pre-Socratic Philosophers,_ 24.

28. Ibid., 22.

29. Cited by Nash, _Christian Faith,_ 14.

30. Again, see Honey and Peterson, "Advocacy and Inquiry," 139–79.

31. N. T. Wright, "How Jesus Saw Himself," _Bible Review_ 12 (June 1996): 29. A few lines later, speaking of the writers of the Gospels, Wright remarks, "I cannot make sense of the whole picture, historically or theologically, unless they were telling the truth" about the Resurrection of Christ.

32. We may ultimately find that much scholarship on the Bible and other gospel-related subjects was scarcely more perceptive than my family dog: Whenever I try to direct his attention to something, he inevitably focuses on my finger rather than on the object to which I am alerting him. Similarly, a great portion of contemporary academic study of the scriptures appears to be obsessed with the signifier while utterly neglecting the Signified.

33. Joseph Smith, _Teachings of the Prophet Joseph Smith,_ comp. Joseph Fielding Smith (Salt Lake City: Deseret Book, 1938), 121.

34. See especially Richard Lloyd Anderson, _Investigating the Book of Mormon Witnesses_ (Salt Lake City: Deseret Book, 1981); Lyndon W. Cook, ed., _David Whitmer Interviews: A Restoration Witness_ (Orem, Utah: Grandin, 1991); Eldin Ricks, _The Case of the Book of Mormon Witnesses_ (Salt Lake City: Olympus, 1961); Milton V. Backman Jr., _Eyewitness Accounts of the Restoration_ (Orem, Utah: Grandin, 1983; Salt Lake City: Deseret Book, 1986) and Rhett Stephens James, _The Man Who Knew: The Early Years_ (Cache Valley, Utah: Martin Harris Pageant Committee, 1983).

The World and the Word: History, Literature, and Scripture

10

John S. Tanner

Scriptures are by nature preserved in words. Words alone, however, cannot contain the full reality of the worlds they represent. As sacred texts, our scriptures are overwhelmingly historical, presenting factual accounts of things that happened in time and space. But because they are written, scriptures are also inherently textual, possessing literary qualities that contribute to their witness. The aim of the writing of sacred history is different from that of history writing in general, because scripture seeks to bear testimony while it seeks to preserve events. To read the record without feeling the testimony is to misread. To be understood properly, scripture requires both the companionship of the Holy Ghost and a keen sensitivity to the inspired objectives of the author. Often those objectives are not seen fully without reading the scripture as sacred literature as well as history.

I have entitled my essay "The World and the Word" because I wish to focus on the relationship between sacred events and their representation in sacred script. My basic point is simple: scripture has textual as well as historical dimensions, and these twin aspects of scripture are not necessarily in opposition, although they are often complexly related. Sound scriptural exegesis should give due weight to both the historicity and textuality of the word of God.

Scripture is overwhelmingly historical, for the most part describing people and events that existed in time and space. When we speak of scripture's *historicity*, we refer to the truthfulness of its factual claims. Scripture is also inherently textual, consisting of words that inscribe sacred experience. When we allude to scripture's *textuality,* we refer to the attributes it possesses as a verbal artifact. Scripture's textuality may be appreciated in many ways, including through literary analysis. Whether, however, one attends to the historicity or textuality of scripture, due deference should be given to scripture's special authority. The proper way to read scripture is neither as history nor as literature alone, but as scripture. As Peter states, scripture is given to "holy men of God . . . as they were moved by the Holy Ghost" (2 Pet. 1:21). It should be read by the Spirit as well.

Res and *Verba*

My title "The World and the Word" recalls the ancient distinction between *res* and *verba*—between *things* and *words*. Words (*verba*) are not the things they stand for (*res*) but point beyond themselves. Thus I am not my name, but my name points to a real person. Language is representational; it re-presents the world in words. The distinction between *res* and *verba* (or signified and signifier) is a perennial and fundamental philosophical concern. It is, moreover, critical to any discussion of historicity, lest we mistakenly suppose that a verbal representation of the past is fully identical with the historical experience it describes.

Let me illustrate this point with an anecdote from *Gulliver's Travels.* When Gulliver journeys to the floating island of Laputa, he discovers a land populated by "natural philosophers" (or scientists), heirs of Sir Francis Bacon and, like Bacon, obsessed with the project of perfecting language. To this end, they concoct various madcap schemes. One is to "shorten discourse by cutting polysyllables into one, and leaving out verbs and participles, because in reality all things imaginable are but nouns."[1] An even more radical scheme is "for entirely abolishing all words whatsoever." "Since words are only the names for *things,*" these sages reason, "it would be more convenient for all men to carry about them such *things* as were necessary to express the particular business they are to discourse on."[2] Although this proposal did not catch on with the common people, Swift wryly notes that "many of the most learned and wise [did] adhere to the new scheme of expressing themselves by *things,* which hath only this inconvenience attending it, that if a man's business be very great, and of various kinds, he must be obliged in proportion to carry a greater bundle of *things* upon his back, unless he can afford one or two strong servants to attend him. I have often beheld two of those sages almost sinking under the weight of their packs, like pedlars among us; who when they met in the streets would lay down their loads, open their sacks and hold conversation for an hour together; then put up their implements, help each other to resume their burthens, and take their leave."[3]

Swift's satire serves to remind us that however fully and accurately language captures reality, it does not deliver up actual events or living authors but translates the world into words. We depend on words to communicate efficiently about even concrete "things," to say nothing of ideas, which require predicates and prepositions. Our access to the world is mediated through words.

This access, of course, is not perfect or complete because language can never be exact or full enough to convey the totality of our experience. Some find the incommensurability between the world and the word to be a cause for despair at being trapped in a "prison house of language." I find, rather, cause for wonder and gratitude that words, imperfect though they may be, allow us such remarkable windows not only into the past, but also into the thoughts and feelings of those with whom we share this divine gift of language. And I am persuaded that however darkly reality is refracted through the prism of words, language can, with the help of the Spirit, make us substantially present to each other and give us a foretaste of what it is to know even as we are known (cf. 1 Cor. 13:12).

For this to occur, the Spirit can and must enable the process of understanding. I believe that the Spirit is prerequisite to understanding all utterance,[4] but especially the inspired language of scripture (cf. D&C 50:17–22). Of course the Spirit, which has the power to reveal the meaning of all things (John 16:13; Moro. 10:5), can communicate directly to the soul without the medium of language. From this point of view, the written word may seem to be dispensable. But this is never the way the Lord perceives scripture. Rather, it is something precious to be examined, pondered, and preserved. The Lord regularly chooses to mediate his mind and will through the language of scripture, enfleshing the Word in words. He commands his prophets to record their witness in the written word and invites his children to read and ponder their words to gain access to inspired understanding. In the process, prophets become writers, their records become texts, and their audience becomes readers.

Given the textuality of their task, it is not surprising that scriptural authors are daunted by the same dilemmas that vex all writers. For example, the apostle John confesses that his subject, Jesus' life, is far more complex and full than he can portray—or than could ever be captured in print, even if he were to fill the whole world with books (John 21:25). Likewise, Book of Mormon historians frequently rue the fact that their narratives contain less than a "hundredth part" of the information available from what they have witnessed or what is reported in historical records (e.g., Jacob 3:13; W of M 1:5). They are overwhelmed by the challenge not only of selecting but also of structuring their material. Moroni seems to speak for every writer who has struggled over syntax when he laments, "When we write we behold our weakness, and stumble because of the placing of our words" (Ether 12:25). In a fallen world, ungraced by the Adamic tongue, the gap between *res* and *verba* provides ample occasion for such stumbling. Not even prophets attain such a fulness of utterance as to eliminate all traces of incommensurability between the truths they apprehend, feel, and experience, and the words they must use to represent this reality, even though their records best tell of "things as they really are" (Jacob 4:13) in language empowered to help us become who we really ought to be.

Reading Scripture Aright

So prophets are also writers and scriptures are also texts. Hence, while we must staunchly defend the historicity of scripture, we must not disregard its textuality. It is this quality that complicates the task of drawing clean, bright lines between even such useful and important dichotomies as fact/fiction or history/story. Such binary oppositions point to critical distinctions. Yet these minimal pairs are not mutually exclusive—even their etymologies attest to some continuity between categories. "Fiction," for example, derives from the Latin verb "to fashion." All texts, however, must be made, not only those one finds under the label "fiction." While not made up with the freedom of a novel, historical writing must mold the facts into intelligible forms, as anyone knows who has tried to set forth a coherent, orderly account of the past. Historical narratives thus require fashioning; they demand careful attention to structure, emphasis, significance, and the like. In this sense, factual writing is not unlike the writing of fiction. Similarly, "story" and "history" derive from the same root. This common etymology reminds us that a historian is, among other things, a storyteller who, while being faithful to the historical record, must make narrative choices about sequence, characterization, diction, significance, and so forth in order to make sense of the past. Thus, even factual writing inescapably entails fiction in the sense that it too must be fashioned (*fictio*); likewise, narrative history requires attention to the demands of a story. Hence, historical writing possesses not only the dimension of historicity but also of textuality, including qualities associated with literary texts.

The same general point applies not only to history but to every scriptural genre, such as preaching, prophecy, poetry, and even parable. The Sermon on the Mount, for example, may be analyzed as to both its historicity and its textuality. Thus one may properly, and with no contradiction, affirm the historicity of the sermon (e.g., its attribution to Jesus) as well as explicate its textuality (e.g., its rhetorical patterning, its hyperbole, and its intertextuality with the law of Moses or with other discourses within Matthew or across the entire canon). Similarly, an explicitly fictional genre, such as Zenos's allegory, not only invites literary interpretation but also makes numerous crucial claims to historicity. For example: there was a prophet Zenos; there were brass plates; an ancient Book of Mormon prophet named Jacob transcribed the allegory onto Nephi's small plates; Jacob's transcription was much later translated from gold plates by Joseph Smith; and Zenos's prophecies correlate to actual historical events. Any satisfactory reading of Zenos's allegory must be clear about its historicity *and* account for the verbal resources the author mobilizes to convey his meaning and make it resonate in our hearts.

Sound scriptural interpretation thus gives proper weight to both the historicity and the textuality of the word of God. As faith steers between the Scylla of skepticism and the Charybdis of credulity, Latter-day Saints should, on the one hand, resolutely resist the sophistry of those who describe miracles and revelations as fables or human invention, taking as our watchword Peter's testimony of the transfiguration: "For we have not followed cunningly devised fables, when we made known unto you the power and coming of our Lord Jesus Christ, but were eyewitnesses of his majesty" (2 Pet. 1:16); and, on the other hand, recognize that prophets characteristically record a particular kind of history. Scripture typically aspires to be more interpretive than mere chronicle and less comprehensive than the *Cambridge History of the World*. It aspires to the condition of testimony. Well does the Joseph Smith Translation retitle two of the Gospels "The Testimony of St. Matthew" and "The Testimony of John." As John freely admits, many details about Jesus' life are "not written in this book: but these are written, that ye might believe that Jesus is the Christ, the Son of God" (John 20:30–31). Scripture is best regarded as testament. Testaments are, to be sure, essentially and overwhelmingly historiographic, written by prophets and telling of events which not only can be coordinated with time and space but which often order and give meaning to time and space. At the same time, testaments are also the record of testators or witnesses, whose purpose is not merely to record facts but to bear witness. They bear the imprint of human testators and display the textual characteristics of all writing.

Hence, it is clearly a distortion to dismiss scripture's historical claims, as, for example, the Jesus Seminar does virtually wherever a Gospel describes supernatural events. Likewise, it is a mistake to deny scripture's textual qualities, as fundamentalists sometimes do when faced with evidence of rhetorical patterning in sacred texts. After all, there is no logical contradiction in believing simultaneously that scripture records the word of God and that the Lord reveals His word to his servants "in their weakness, after the manner of their language, that they might come to understanding" (D&C 1:24; cf. 29:33; 2 Ne. 31:3). Thus to read scripture aright is, as I noted at the outset, to give due weight to both the historicity and the textuality of the word of God.

Reading Scripture Amiss: The Liabilities of the Literary

Much contemporary scholarship reads scripture amiss by denying its fundamental historicity. Let me illustrate some of these errors by referring to modern biblical studies. As a Miltonist and erstwhile lecturer on "The Bible as Literature," I occasionally exploit biblical criticism to elucidate the Bible or Milton's works. This always requires special care because some scholars do not accept the historicity of essential biblical events, such as the Fall or the Resurrection.

For example, a few years ago in a leading journal of literary criticism I published an article on *Paradise Lost* that relied heavily on the work of the contemporary French philosopher Paul Ricoeur. Ricoeur is a brilliant thinker; his work develops trenchant insights into the symbolism of evil, insights that open up Milton's epic in truly remarkable ways. Nevertheless, for several years I sat on a draft of my essay, uncertain if and how to proceed, because Ricoeur's understanding of the Fall derives explicitly from the premise that the biblical story is unhistorical. Ricoeur asks, "What does it mean to 'understand' the Adamic myth?" He answers his own question thus: "In the first place, it means accepting the fact that it is a myth. . . . It must be well understood *from the outset* that, for the modern man who has learned the distinction between myth and history, this chronicle of the first man and the first pair can no longer be co-ordinated with the time of history and the space of geography. . . . It must be well understood that the question, Where and when did Adam eat the forbidden fruit?, no longer has meaning for us; every effort to save the letter of the story as a true history is vain and hopeless."[5]

Ricoeur thus brackets the "Adamic myth" from history. Although his intent is not to dismiss Genesis as fable but to honor and elucidate it as a richly symbolic myth that "has more meaning than a true history," he clearly does not believe in Adam the way a Latter-day Saint does.[6]

Consequently, it was troubling for me, as a believer, to ground my interpretation of *Paradise Lost* on Ricoeur—even though his disbelief in an actual Adam is utterly commonplace. (Indeed, critics tend to fault Ricoeur not for his skepticism but for his belief in such Christian "myths.") After much hesitation, I determined at last to send off my article with a caveat in my opening paragraphs proclaiming my own belief. "Too confessional," said the editor, and struck the offending passage. Try as I may, I could not prevail upon the journal to keep a direct disclaimer. Finally, I hit upon an indirect way to signal my convictions. I wrote a footnote citing a comment by the only other

Miltonist to refer to Ricoeur, William Kerrigan, in which he distances himself from Ricoeur's "faith in the Christian myth." I exploited this opening to insert my own demurral: "I share Kerrigan's indebtedness to Ricoeur, though not his skepticism about the Christian myth."[7] This note made it past the editor. But I wondered if it would sufficiently signal my belief to my readers. One of the more satisfying moments of my professional career occurred when a colleague I had never met approached me at a conference, complimented me on my Ricoeur article, and said, "I read your footnote. I am a believer, too."

This anecdote illustrates the difficulty of dealing seriously yet faithfully with modern biblical scholarship. I experienced similar difficulties as a doctoral candidate and newly minted Ph.D. assigned to teach courses in "the Bible as Literature" at two different state universities. These assignments pushed me toward taking a false position vis à vis scripture. As C. S. Lewis quipped, "Those who talk of reading the Bible 'as literature' sometimes mean . . . reading it without attending to the main thing it is about; like reading Burke with no interest in politics, or reading the *Aeneid* with no interest in Rome. That seems to me to be nonsense."[8] It did to me, too. Nor were my misgivings dispelled when I read the scholarship purporting to explicate scripture under the rubric of "the Bible as Literature." Until about twenty years ago, this approach yielded sorry and often trivial results. The deficiencies resulted in part from its practitioners' reluctance to engage seriously the truth claims made by the Bible and in part from their innocence of ancient languages, history, archaeology, theology, or other prerequisites of traditional Biblical studies.

"But," Lewis continues, "there is a saner sense in which the Bible, since it is after all literature, cannot properly be read except as literature."[9] For me, as for Lewis, the saner way is to read scripture first and foremost as scripture, attending to literary, historical, and even doctrinal matters as they constitute dimensions of the witness. The past couple of decades have witnessed the emergence of a number of truly noteworthy literary interpretations of scripture that do just this. Yet Latter-day Saint critics must consult even this scholarship warily because, like Ricoeur's work, much of it proceeds from premises that either deny or downplay the fundamental historicity of scripture.

The work of Robert Alter provides a case in point. Alter may be the single most significant contemporary literary critic of the Bible. His books on biblical narrative and poetry develop engaging, textured, telling readings of the Old Testament. Moreover, like Ricoeur, Alter is generally regarded as sympathetic to the Bible's truthfulness, if not to its literal truth. There is much to be admired in Alter. Nevertheless, his interpretive stance leans precariously toward denying the literal historicity of biblical narrative and narrators. For example, Alter famously asserts that "prose fiction is the best general rubric for describing biblical narrative."[10] This echoes the position of Herbert Schneidau, another contemporary critic, who similarly claims: "What we are witnessing in Genesis, and in parts of the David story, is the birth of a new kind of historicized fiction, moving steadily away from the motives and habits of the world of legend and myth."[11]

This fudging about the fundamental historicity of scripture is well answered by Meir Sternberg, an Israeli biblical scholar who, like Alter, deals very intelligently with the poetics of biblical narrative but expresses far firmer conviction as to its truth claims. Having roundly reproved Alter for denying the historicity of biblical narrative, Sternberg affirms his own position: "So does the Bible belong to the historical or the fictional genre? The mist enveloping the question once dissipated, . . . the answer becomes obvious. Of course the narrative is historiographic."[12] Sternberg continues: "Were the narrative written or read as fiction, then God would turn from the lord of history into a creature of the imagination, with the most disastrous results. The shape of time, the rationale of monotheism, the foundations of conduct, the national sense of identity, the very right to the land of Israel and the hope of deliverance to come: all hang in the generic balance. Hence the Bible's determination to sanctify and compel literal belief in the past."[13]

Few literary scholars of the Bible as intelligent as Sternberg argue as forthrightly for the "literal belief in the past" it records. Literary approaches to scripture still regularly downplay or deny its historicity. It is no wonder therefore (but it is also unfortunate) that literary readings are often regarded with suspicion by Latter-day Saints, who rightly insist on the literal truth of prophecy, miracles, and revelations. After my early experience in state universities, I too came to mistrust literary approaches to scripture, vowing not to teach another course in "The Bible as Literature." Since then, however, I have adopted a more conciliatory position, for the literal and the literary are not necessarily opposed to each other. Now I apply to my reading of biblical criticism the Lord's advice on reading the Apocrypha: "There are many things contained therein that are true. . . . There are many things contained therein that are not true. . . . Therefore, whoso readeth it, let him understand, for the Spirit manifesteth truth" (D&C 91:1–2, 4).

Reading Scripture Amiss: The Limits of the Literal

Just as literary interpretations of scripture can miss the mark by undervaluing the literal, so literalistic readings can miss the point by undervaluing the literary. The New Testament illustrates the latter peril in the encounter between Jesus and Nicodemus. When Jesus tells him, "Except a man be born again, he cannot see the kingdom of God," Nicodemus replies incredulously, "How can a man be born when he is old? can he enter the second time into his mother's womb, and be born?" (John 3:3–4). Of course reentering the womb is not what Jesus intends at all. The Savior rebukes Nicodemus' literalism as obtuse and wrongheaded: "Art thou a master of Israel, and knowest not these things?" (3:10).

This pattern persists throughout the Gospel of John. Jesus repeatedly describes Himself or His mission in metaphors that baffle His literal-minded interlocutors. For example, Jesus explains to the woman of Samaria that he would give her "living water"—to which she prosaically responds, "Sir, thou hast nothing to draw with, and the well is deep: from whence then hast thou that living water?" (John 4:10–11). Jesus later compares Himself to manna, telling the multitude: "I am the living bread which came down from heaven: if any man eat of this bread, he shall live for ever"—to which His hearers woodenly respond, "How can this man give us his flesh to eat?" (6:51–52). And Jesus informs His disciples, "Our friend Lazarus sleepeth; but I go, that I may awake him out of sleep"—to which His uncomprehending disciples answer, "Lord, if he sleep, he shall do well" (11:11–12). These and similar incidents remind us that scripture itself sometimes exposes a literal reading as spiritually myopic and insists on being read symbolically by those who have eyes to see and ears to hear (cf. Jer. 5:21; Matt. 13:13; 2 Ne. 9:31).

Yet knowing when and how to read symbolically is not easy. Moreover, the ontological status of figurative language in scripture is not always clear. It requires considerable tact—more than Nicodemus demonstrated—to know how to take the magnificent metaphors employed in the revelations. What does it mean, for example, that Christ is the light of the world? What looks like metaphor in the New Testament may encompass material realities according to modern revelation (e.g., D&C 88:6); in this case, the potential for misreading arises not from being too literalistic, like Nicodemus, but from not being literal enough (cf. 1 Ne. 22:1–3).

To cite another example of how complex the ontological status of figurative language can be, consider the passages in the Doctrine and Covenants in which the Lord indicates that the world groans under sin: "And the whole world lieth in sin, and groaneth under darkness and under the bondage of sin" (D&C 84:49); "the whole earth groans under the weight of its iniquity" (123:7). In these passages "groaning" appears figurative, personifying the earth as a sentient being with human feelings. Few readers, however, would likely stumble over the ontological status of this personification—which is not only unobtrusive but reprises a similar sentiment in Romans: "For we know that the whole creation groaneth and travaileth in pain" (8:22)—unless, that is, they read these verses in light of a remarkable colloquy between Enoch and Mother Earth in the Pearl of Great Price: "And it came to pass that Enoch looked upon the earth; and he heard a voice from the bowels thereof, saying: Wo, wo is me, the mother of men; I am pained, I am weary, because of the wickedness of my children. When shall I rest, and be cleansed from the filthiness which is gone forth out of me?" (Moses 7:48).

This passage never fails to move me deeply. Yet it also raises interesting questions about the nature of nature: How should we understand the ontological status of the voice? In what sense is the earth as a whole a sentient being? In what sense is the earth the "mother of men"? In what sense does it feel pain, become wearied, need rest, and require moral cleansing? And in what sense can the earth actually speak in an audible, presumably female voice? When metaphors come alive, as they appear to in Enoch's vision, we are compelled to reconsider the presumption that figurative language is only figurative and to open ourselves up to the possibility that "there are more things in heaven and earth . . . than are dreamt of in [our] philosophy."[14] This can be disorienting for modern readers, who are predisposed to regard both metaphors and miracles with coolly rational, naturalistic presumptions. Scriptures such as Enoch's vision of Mother Earth can and should make us skeptical of our skepticism; they should tune our ears to hear, with the ancients, the voice of the earth and open our eyes to see in the stars, sun, and moon "God moving in his majesty and power" (D&C 88:47; cf. 45–47).

At the same time, modern revelation may just as readily restrain readers from taking metaphors as more than metaphor. This can be seen in perhaps the most controverted, symbolic language in scripture, Jesus' famous invitation to His disciples at the Last Supper: "This is my body, take, eat" and "this is my blood, take, drink." Vast quantities of ink have been expended over just how to interpret these simple statements. Modern revelation makes it clear that the doctrine of transubstantiation takes them too literally. The Joseph Smith Translation and other Latter-day Saint scripture indicate that the copulative verb "is" does not establish identity but analogy between subject and predicate; that the bread and wine represent rather than become the Lord's body and blood; and that the sacrament is intended to memorialize rather than reenact the Atonement. Note how much hangs on what could be described as a literary question. In a sense, the great Reformation debates over the nature of the Eucharist centered on whether to take Christ's words as something more than metaphor or as something closer to simile.

Evidently, modern revelation provides no single rule for sorting the factual from the figurative. Indeed, it demonstrates that these are often deliberately and sometimes inextricably intertwined. Thus when Nephi's brothers ask if Isaiah's prophecies describe spiritual or temporal realities, Nephi responds that they are "both temporal and spiritual" (1 Ne. 22:3). Similarly, when the Saints asked the Prophet Joseph to interpret passages in the book of Revelation, the Prophet construed some images as literal, some as figurative, and some as both. It took revelation to understand Revelation. Hence, even for Latter-day Saints who accept without dispute the essential historicity of scripture, it is no easy task to disentangle the literary and the literal in scripture. Nor, I believe, is it wise to insist on sharply dualistic dichotomies between the literal and literary, historical and textual, world and word. To relentlessly pursue the "facts" behind the scriptural accounts of, for example, the Resurrection or First Vision, may be to look "beyond the mark" (Jacob 4:14) no less than to doubt that there were no miraculous events giving rise to the scriptural accounts.

Furthermore, rich meaning may inhere in factual events just as much as they do in literary inventions. I came to feel this keenly while writing a book on *Paradise Lost*. Too many critics presume that if something is symbolically significant it must be historically untrue. Not so. Adam and Eve's transgression can and does symbolize various aspects of human existence *even though it happened*. The literal may function symbolically without ceasing to be historical. "Can literary artifice be true?" asks an evangelical critic. "The answer is yes. To ask whether the Bible is literature or history is to set up a false dichotomy. The Bible is both—and much more."[15]

Let me illustrate this with a mundane example from the Gospel of John. When Judas leaves the Last Supper, John observes, "And it was night" (John 13:30). I assume that this is factually accurate reportage. On one level, this sentence is John's way of marking the time. But on another level, the words do more than tell the time. As Elder Talmage notes, this "terse" statement feels "ominous."[16] For the night into which Judas flees seems to foreshadow his dark deeds, express his moral condition, and presage the spiritual darkness toward which he and the narrative are moving. Furthermore, this sentence seems to signal a dramatic turn in the narrative, from darkness to light. When Judas leaves the room, something dark and sinister seems to have been cast out, enabling the Lord to speak more freely, intimately, and lovingly with the faithful followers who remain. The sublime discourses on discipleship that follow in John 14–17 stand in shining contrast to the tense table talk that had preceded them in John 13. Outside, Judas is mobilizing the forces of darkness. Inside the upper room, the remaining disciples are bathed in light and love. All these connotations and more are plausibly implied by the simple statement "And it was night." A novelist could not improve on this narrative detail, which, though prosaically true, is also pregnant with symbolic significance.

Concluding Coda: An Allegory of God's Love

As should be clear by now, my views on the subject of the historicity of scripture are complex. But I hope they are not ambiguous—especially as to the fundamental point. I unequivocally affirm the historicity of the miraculous events on which Christianity and the Restoration are founded. In doing so, I echo the words of an evangelical scholar who asserted, "As Christians we can never forget that ours is a historical faith, our salvation a salvation in history, and the written Word of God a collection of documents composed by prophets in specific times and places."[17] This assertion applies *a fortiori* to Latter-day Saints, who add modern revelation and acts of apostles to the canon. We proclaim that the voice of God has spoken not only to ancient prophets in Palestine but to other prophets, ancient and modern, at very specific times and places in the Americas. Hence, we testify that the Book of Mormon is a historical document. We believe that on 22 September 1827, an angel named Moroni gave gold plates to Joseph Smith declaring "glad tidings from Cumorah," and we bear record of "a voice of the Lord in the wilderness of Fayette, Seneca county, . . . [and] the voice of Michael on the banks of the Susquehanna. . . . [and] the voice of Peter, James, and John in the wilderness between Harmony, Susquehanna county, and Colesville, Broome county, on the Susquehanna river. . . . [and] the voice of God in the chamber of old Father Whitmer, in Fayette, Seneca county, and at sundry times, and in divers places" (D&C 128:20–21). I love the precise topicality of the Prophet Joseph Smith's exultant catalogue of theophanies. There can be no gainsaying that ours is gloriously and inescapably a historical faith.

At the same time that I celebrate the historicity of my faith, I revel in its textuality. I treasure the texts that preserve ancient and modern witnesses. These are of inestimable value. Not infrequently, I am absorbed by the verbal particularities of these witnesses—by their grammatical, rhetorical, and literary texture, which for me often appear inseparable from their meaning and message. Much insight comes from attending to scripture's textuality. Hence, my desire in this essay has been to articulate a measured "both/and" position with respect to the question of history vs. literature in understanding scripture.

In this spirit, let me conclude with one final example of how a literary reading of scripture can complement historically preoccupied interpretations and thereby open up a fuller, more complete appreciation of the text. My text is Zenos's Allegory of the Olive Tree, an explicitly literary genre whose literary quality, oddly, has been underappreciated. I have heard this allegory discussed in countless classes, sermons, and scholarly papers.[18] Almost always the interpretation focuses on working out correlations between the allegory and historical events. This seems a useful and important thing to do, but one that also risks missing the emotional center of the allegory, which is so moving and potentially redemptive for readers. Preoccupied with figuring out the allegory as a sort of literary puzzle, readers frequently seem to miss what Jacob implies they should feel from the experience of reading Zenos. Jacob points to the emotional heart of the text when he exclaims, "And how merciful is our God unto us, for he remembereth the house of Israel, both roots and branches; and he stretches forth his hands unto them all the day long; and they are a stiffnecked and a gainsaying people; but as many as will not harden their hearts shall be saved in the kingdom of God. Wherefore, my beloved brethren, I beseech of you in words of soberness that ye would repent, and come with full purpose of heart, and cleave unto God as he cleaveth unto you" (Jacob 6:4–5).

To feel what Jacob intends his people to feel, we must read this great allegory not only as a detailed prophecy of world history but as an allegory of God's love.[19] Jacob intends to move his readers to cleave unto a God who cleaveth unto His people, despite repeated provocations. Such an effect from reading is not only possible but more likely if the allegory is read as literature. A literary reading of the text attends to the characterization of the Lord of the vineyard as revealed in his repeated expressions of love. A literary reading cannot miss the Lord's repeated heartfelt, anguished cries of the Lord, which echo like a leitmotiv across the allegory, revealing the depths of desire in God's heart even for his backsliding chosen people: "It grieveth me that I should lose this tree." The Lord of the vineyard utters these words again and again, eight times over, building in intensity and cumulatively serving to characterize the astonishing loving-kindness of the God we worship. Let me cite these repetitions found in Jacob 5:

It grieveth me that I should lose this tree (7)
It grieveth me that I should lose this tree (11)
For it grieveth me that I should lose this tree (13)
And now it grieveth me that I should lose this tree (32)
And it grieveth me that I should lose them (46)
And it grieveth me that I should hew down all the trees of
  my vineyard, and cast them into the fire (47)
Yea, I will spare it a little longer, for it grieveth me that I
  should lose the trees of my vineyard (51)
For it grieveth me that I should lose the trees of my vineyard (66)

Woven throughout the allegory, this repeated emphasis on the Lord's grief reveals something unforgettable about the very character of God. The allegory functions like the parable of the Prodigal Son, vividly enacting the Lord's love for His errant children—in this case by comparing God not to a forgiving father but to a long-suffering gardener. Or, even more closely, it resembles Isaiah's "song of my beloved," testifying that the Lord does everything in His power to nurture his people, though they persist in bringing forth the bitter fruit of rebellion: "What could have been done more to my vineyard that I have not done in it?" asks the Lord through Isaiah (2 Ne. 15:4; Isa. 5:4). Likewise, Zenos records in Jacob 5:

And it came to pass that the Lord of the vineyard wept, and said unto the servant: What could I have done more for my vineyard? (41).

But, behold, they have become like unto the wild olive-tree, and they are of no worth but to be hewn down and cast into the fire; and it grieveth me that I should lose them. But what could I have done more in my vineyard? Have I slackened mine hand, that I have not nourished it? Nay, I have nourished it, . . . and I have stretched forth mine hand almost all the day long, and the end draweth nigh. And it grieveth me that I should hew down all the trees of my vineyard, and cast them into the fire that they should be burned (46–47).

And it came to pass that the Lord of the vineyard said unto the servant: Let us go to and hew down the trees of the vineyard and cast them into the fire, that they shall not cumber the ground of my vineyard, for I have done all. What could I have done more for my vineyard? But, behold, the servant said unto the Lord of the vineyard: Spare it a little longer (49–50).

These descriptions of a fictional character called the Lord of the vineyard conduct us, by means of allegory, into the heart of the Almighty himself. His tears remind us of other tender, sacred moments in scripture in which the Lord sorrows over his sinful people (e.g., Matt. 23:37; 3 Ne. 17:14; Moses 7:28). What is more, as we witness the juxtaposition of his tears and anger, we understand better that divine love is linked to divine punishment. In this sense, Zenos's allegory provides a more complex portrait of redemption than the Parable of the Prodigal Son, for the allegory's artistry, like Michelangelo's "Last Judgment," comprehends a righteous master, whose love prompts him at once to preserve and prune, save and burn his beloved vineyard.

In the same fashion, the servant's pleadings reveal much about the role of prophets, like Moses and the Savior Himself, who, like this servant, act as intercessors on behalf of a beloved but flawed and recalcitrant humanity. When the exasperated Lord first commands His servant to "pluck off the branches . . . and cast them into the fire," the servant responds, "Let us prune it, and dig about it, and nourish it a little longer, that perhaps it may bring forth good fruit" (Jacob 5:26–27). Similarly, when the Lord determines again to burn the vineyard, the servant pleads, "Spare it a little longer" (5:50). If the Lord is characterized by the refrain "it grieveth me that I should lose this tree," perhaps the servant may be typified by the words "a little longer."

By such literary means, Zenos helps us understand the character of God and His servants, feel their love for us, and resolve to cleave more fully unto the Lord who cleaves, so patiently, unto us. The meaning of the allegory's symbols is not exhausted once their correspondence to specific events in sacred history has been ascertained. Indeed, if history is all we learn from the allegory, we have learned little that could not be taught more directly and clearly by a straightforward synopsis of the dispensations. But we are meant to learn more and to feel more. We are meant to be supplied with a memorable way of conceptualizing God, His prophets, and ourselves—as a gardener, a servant, and a beloved tree—and with a moving narrative that dramatizes the Lord's persistent loving-kindness toward us and His servants' intercession on our behalf. We are meant to be the better from reading prophecy embodied in parable. For if we let the symbols work on our hearts, as well as inform our minds, we will feel truths that apply not only to particular historical moments but to all times, all places, and all people.

Thus in Zenos's allegory, as elsewhere in scripture, the literary must be appreciated with the literal, the textual with the historical, and the word with the world it represents. Both sides of these pairings are fundamental to the meaning of scripture. Surely to understand scripture aright is to give each its proper weight and due attention.

John S. Tanner is professor of English, Brigham Young University.

Notes

1. Jonathan Swift, *Gulliver's Travels and Other Writings,* ed. Louis A. Landa (Boston: Riverside, 1960), 150.

2. Ibid.

3. Ibid., 151.

4. I agree with George Steiner "that any coherent understanding of what language is and how language performs, that any coherent account of the capacity of human speech to communicate meaning and feeling is, in the final analysis, underwritten by the assumption of God's presence." *Real Presences* (Chicago: University of Chicago Press, 1989), 3.

5. Paul Ricoeur, *The Symbolism of Evil,* trans. Emerson Buchanan (New York: Harper & Row, 1967), 235.

6. Ibid., 236.

7. John S. Tanner, "'Say First What Cause': Ricoeur and the Etiology of Evil in *Paradise Lost,*" *PMLA* 103.1 (January 1988): 54 n. 3.

8. C. S. Lewis, *Reflections on the Psalms* (New York: Harcourt Brace, 1958), 2–3.

9. Ibid., 3.

10. Robert Alter, *The Art of Biblical Narrative* (New York: Basic Books, 1981), 24, and throughout chap. 2.

11. Herbert N. Schneidau, *Sacred Discontent: The Bible and Western Tradition* (Baton Rouge: Louisiana State University Press, 1976), 215.

12. Meir Sternberg, *The Poetics of Biblical Narrative: Ideological Literature and the Drama of Reading* (Bloomington: Indiana University Press, 1985), 30.

13. Ibid., 32.

14. William Shakespeare, *Hamlet* 1.5.166–67.

15. Tremper Longman III, "Storytellers and Poets in the Bible: Can Literary Artifice Be True," *Inerrancy and Hermeneutic: A Tradition, A Challenge, A Debate,* ed. Harvie M. Conn (Grand Rapids, Mich.: Baker, 1988), 149.

16. James E. Talmage, *Jesus the Christ* (Salt Lake City: Deseret Book, 1916), 599.

17. E. Earle Ellis, "Historical–Literary Criticism—After Two Hundred Years: Origins, Aberrations, Contributions, Limitations," *The Proceedings of the Conference on Biblical Inerrancy, 1987* (Nashville: Boardman, 1987), 415–16.

18. See *The Allegory of the Olive Tree: The Olive, the Bible, and Jacob 5,* ed. Stephen D. Ricks and John W. Welch (Salt Lake City: Deseret Book and F.A.R.M.S., 1994) for a fine collection of essays that greatly enrich our understanding of this remarkable allegory. My interpretation was stimulated many years ago in a class from Arthur Henry King and finds support in his essay in this collection entitled "Language Themes in Jacob 5: 'The vineyard of the Lord of hosts is the house of Israel (Isaiah 5:7),'" 140–73.

19. I briefly sketch this interpretation of the allegory in "Jacob and His Descendants as Authors," *Rediscovering the Book of Mormon,* ed. John L. Sorenson and Melvin J. Thorne (Salt Lake City: Deseret Book and F.A.R.M.S., 1991), 52–66.

The Historicity of the Book of Mormon

11

Elder Dallin H. Oaks

The issue of the historicity of the Book of Mormon highlights the difference between those who rely solely on scholarship and those who rely on revelation, faith, and scholarship. Those who rely solely on scholarship reject revelation and focus on a limited number of issues. But they can neither prove nor disprove the authenticity of the Book of Mormon through their secular evidence and methods. On the other hand, those who rely on a combination of revelation, faith, and scholarship can see and understand all of the complex issues of the Book of Mormon record, and it is only through that combination that the question of the historicity of the Book of Mormon can be answered.[1]

Some who term themselves believing Latter-day Saints are advocating that Latter-day Saints should "abandon claims that [the Book of Mormon] is a historical record of the ancient peoples of the Americas."[2] They are promoting the feasibility of reading and using the Book of Mormon as nothing more than a pious fiction with some valuable contents. These practitioners of so-called "higher criticism" raise the question of whether the Book of Mormon, which our prophets have put forward as the preeminent scripture of this dispensation, is fact or fable—history or just a story.

The historicity—historical authenticity—of the Book of Mormon is an issue so fundamental that it rests first upon faith in the Lord Jesus Christ, which is the first principle in this, as in all other matters. However, on the subject of the historicity of the Book of Mormon, there are many subsidiary issues that could each be the subject of a book. It is not my purpose to comment on any of these lesser issues, either those that are said to confirm the Book of Mormon or those that are said to disprove it.

Those lesser issues *are,* however, worthy of attention. Elder Neal A. Maxwell quoted Austin Farrer's explanation: "Though argument does not create conviction, the lack of it destroys belief. What seems to be proved may not be embraced; but what no one shows the ability to defend is quickly abandoned. Rational argument does not create belief, but it maintains a climate in which belief may flourish."[3]

In these remarks I will seek to use rational argument, but I will not rely on any proofs. I will approach the question of the historicity of the Book of Mormon from the standpoint of faith and revelation. I maintain that the issue of the historicity of the Book of Mormon is basically a difference between those who rely exclusively on scholarship and those who rely on a combination of scholarship, faith, and revelation. Those who rely exclusively on scholarship reject revelation and fulfill Nephi's prophecy that in the last days men "shall teach with their learning, and deny the Holy Ghost, which giveth utterance" (2 Ne. 28:4). The practitioners of that approach typically focus on a limited number of issues, like geography, horses, angelic delivery, or nineteenth-century language patterns. They ignore or gloss over the incredible complexity of the Book of Mormon record. Those who rely on scholarship, faith, and revelation are willing to look at the entire spectrum of issues—the content as well as the vocabulary, the revelation as well as the excavation.

Speaking for a moment as one whose profession is advocacy, I suggest that if one is willing to acknowledge the importance of faith and the reality of a realm beyond human understanding, the case for the Book of Mormon is the stronger case to argue. The case against the historicity of the Book of Mormon has to prove a negative. You do not prove a negative by prevailing on one debater's point or by establishing some subsidiary arguments.

For me, this obvious insight goes back over forty years to the first class I took on the Book of Mormon at Brigham Young University. The class was titled, somewhat boldly, the "Archaeology of the Book of Mormon." In retrospect, I think it should have been labelled something like "An Anthropologist Looks at a Few Subjects of Interest to Readers of the Book of Mormon." Here I was introduced to the idea that the Book of Mormon is not a history of all of the people who have lived on the continents of North and South America in all ages of the earth. Up to that time I had assumed that it was. If that were the claim of the Book of Mormon, any piece of historical, archaeological, or linguistic evidence to the contrary would weigh in against the Book of Mormon, and those who rely exclusively on scholarship would have a promising position to argue.

In contrast, if the Book of Mormon only purports to be an account of a few peoples who inhabited a portion of the Americas during a few millennia in the past, the burden of argument changes drastically. It is no longer a question of all versus none; it is a question of some versus none. In other words, in the circumstance I describe, the opponents of historicity must prove that the Book of Mormon has no historical validity for any peoples who lived in the Americas in a particular time frame, a notoriously difficult exercise. One does not prevail on that proposition by proving that a particular Eskimo culture represents migrations from Asia. The opponents of the historicity of the Book of Mormon must prove that the people whose religious life it records did not live anywhere in the Americas.

Another way of explaining the strength of the positive position on the historicity of the Book of Mormon is to point out that we who are its proponents are content with a standoff on this question. Honest investigators will conclude that there are so many evidences that the Book of Mormon is an ancient text that they cannot confidently resolve the question against its authenticity, despite some unanswered questions that seem to support the negative determination. In that circumstance, the proponents of the Book of Mormon can settle for a draw or a hung jury on the question of historicity and take a continuance until the controversy can be retried in another forum.

In fact, it is our position that secular evidence can neither prove nor disprove the authenticity of the Book of Mormon. Its authenticity depends, as it says, on a witness of the Holy Spirit. Our side will settle for a draw, but those who deny the historicity of the Book of Mormon cannot settle for a draw. They must try to disprove its historicity—or they seem to feel a necessity to do this—and in this they are unsuccessful because even the secular evidence, viewed in its entirety, is too complex for that.

Hugh Nibley made a related point when he wrote: "The first rule of historical criticism in dealing with the Book of Mormon or any other ancient text is, never oversimplify. For all its simple and straightforward narrative style, this history is packed as few others are with a staggering wealth of detail that completely escapes the casual reader. . . . Only laziness and vanity lead the student to the early conviction that he has the final answers on what the Book of Mormon contains."[4] Parenthetically, I would cite as an illustration of this point the linguistic, cultural, and writing matters described in support of the authenticity of the Book of Mormon in Orson Scott Card's persuasive essay, "The Book of Mormon—Artifact or Artifice?"[5]

I admire those scholars for whom scholarship does not exclude faith and revelation. It is part of my faith and experience that the Creator expects us to use the powers of reasoning He has placed within us, and that He also expects us to exercise our divine gift of faith and to cultivate our capacity to be taught by divine revelation. But these things do not come without seeking. Those who utilize scholarship and disparage faith and revelation should ponder the Savior's question: "How can ye believe, which receive honour one of another, and seek not the honour that cometh from God only?" (John 5:44).

God invites us to reason with Him, but I find it significant that the reasoning to which God invites us is tied to spiritual realities and maturity rather than to scholarly findings or credentials. In modern revelation the Lord has spoken of reasoning with His people (D&C 45:10, 15; 50:10–12; 61:13; see also Isa. 1:18). It is significant that all of these revelations were addressed to persons who had already entered into covenants with the Lord—to the elders of Israel and to the members of his restored Church.

In the first of these revelations, the Lord said that He had sent His everlasting covenant into the world to be a light to the world, a standard for his people: "Wherefore, come ye unto it," he said, "and with him that cometh I will reason as with men in days of old, and I will show unto you my strong reasoning" (D&C 45:10). Thus, this divine offer to reason was addressed to those who had shown faith in God, who had repented of their sins, who had made sacred covenants with the Lord in the waters of baptism, and who had received the Holy

Ghost, which testifies of the Father and the Son and leads us into truth. This was the group to whom the Lord offered (and offers) to enlarge their understanding by reason and revelation.

Some Latter-day Saint critics who deny the historicity of the Book of Mormon seek to make their proposed approach persuasive to Latter-day Saints by praising or affirming the value of some of the content of the book. Those who take this approach assume the significant burden of explaining how they can praise the contents of a book they have dismissed as a fable. I have never been able to understand the similar approach in reference to the divinity of the Savior. As we know, some scholars and some ministers proclaim Him to be a great teacher and then have to explain how the one who gave such sublime teachings could proclaim himself (falsely they say) to be the Son of God who would be resurrected from the dead.

The new-style critics have the same problem with the Book of Mormon. For example, we might affirm the value of the teachings recorded in the name of a man named Moroni, but if these teachings have value, how do we explain these statements also attributed to this man? "And if there be faults [in this record] they be the faults of a man. But behold, we know no fault; nevertheless God knoweth all things; therefore, he that condemneth, let him be aware lest he shall be in danger of hell fire" (Morm. 8:17). "And I exhort you to remember these things; for the time speedily cometh that ye shall know that I lie not, for ye shall see me at the bar of God; and the Lord God will say unto you: Did I not declare my words unto you, which were written by this man, like as one crying from the dead, yea, even as one speaking out of the dust?" (Moro. 10:27).

There is something strange about accepting the moral or religious content of a book while rejecting the truthfulness of its authors' declarations, predictions, and statements. This approach not only rejects the concepts of faith and revelation that the Book of Mormon explains and advocates, but it is also not even good scholarship.

Here I cannot resist recalling the words of a valued colleague and friend, now deceased. This famous law professor told a first-year class at the University of Chicago Law School that along with all else, a lawyer must also be a scholar. He continued: "That this has its delights will be recalled to you by the words of the old Jewish scholar: 'Garbage is garbage; but the *history* of garbage—that's scholarship.'"⁶ This charming illustration reminds us that scholarship can take what is mundane and make it sublime. So with the history of garbage. But scholarship, so-called, can also take what is sublime and make it mundane. Thus, my friend could have illustrated his point by saying, "Miracles are just a fable, but the history of miracles, that's scholarship." So with the Book of Mormon. Those who only respect this book as an object of scholarship have a very different perspective than those who revere it as the revealed word of God.

Scholarship and physical proofs are worldly values. I understand their value, and I have had some experience in using them. Such techniques speak to many after the manner of their understanding. But there are other methods and values too, and we must not be so committed to scholarship that we close our eyes and ears and hearts to what cannot be demonstrated by scholarship or defended according to physical proofs and intellectual reasoning.

To cite another illustration, history—even Church history—is not reducible to economics or geography or sociology, though each of these disciplines has something to teach on the subject. On the subject of history, President Gordon B. Hinckley commented on the critics who cull out demeaning and belittling information about some of our forbears: "We recognize that our forebears were human. They doubtless made mistakes. . . . But the mistakes were minor, when compared with the marvelous work which they accomplished. To highlight the mistakes and gloss over the greater good is to draw a caricature. Caricatures are amusing, but they are often ugly and dishonest. A man may have a blemish on his cheek and still have a face of beauty and strength, but if the blemish is emphasized unduly in relation to his other features, the portrait is lacking in integrity. . . . I do not fear truth. I welcome it. But I wish all of my facts in their proper context, with emphasis on those elements which explain the great growth and power of this organization."⁷

In the sixteenth chapter of Matthew, we read how Jesus taught Peter the important contrast between acting upon the witness of the Spirit and acting upon his own reasoning in reliance upon the ways of the world. "When Jesus came into the coasts of Caesarea Philippi, he asked his disciples, saying, Whom do men say that I the Son of man am? And they said, Some say that thou art John the Baptist: some, Elias; and others, Jeremias, or one of the prophets. He saith unto them,

But whom say ye that I am? And Simon Peter answered and said, Thou art the Christ, the Son of the living God. And Jesus answered and said unto him, Blessed art thou, Simon Bar-jona: for flesh and blood hath not revealed it unto thee, but my Father which is in heaven. . . . Then charged he his disciples that they should tell no man that he was Jesus the Christ" (Matt. 16:13–17, 20).

That was the Lord's teaching on the value of revelation by the Spirit ("Blessed art thou, Simon Bar-jona"). In the next three verses of this same chapter of Matthew we have the Savior's blunt teaching on the contrasting value of this same apostle's reasoning by worldly values: "From that time forth began Jesus to shew unto his disciples, how that he must go unto Jerusalem, and suffer many things of the elders and chief priests and scribes, and be killed, and be raised again the third day. Then Peter took him, and began to rebuke him, saying, Be it far from thee, Lord: this shall not be unto thee. But he turned, and said unto Peter, Get thee behind me, Satan: thou art an offence unto me: for thou savourest not the things that be of God, but those that be of men" (Matt. 16:21–23).

I suggest that we do the same thing and deserve the same rebuke as Peter whenever we subordinate a witness of the Spirit ("the things that be of God") to the work of scholars or the product of our own reasoning by worldly values (the things that "be of men").

Human reasoning cannot place limits on God or dilute the force of divine commandments or revelations. Persons who allow this to happen identify themselves with the unbelieving Nephites who rejected the testimony of the prophet Samuel. The Book of Mormon says, "They began to reason and to contend among themselves, saying: That it is not reasonable that such a being as a Christ shall come" (Hel. 16:17–18). Persons who practice that kind of "reasoning" deny themselves the choice experience someone has described as our heart telling us things that our mind does not know.[8]

Sadly, some Latter-day Saints ridicule others for their reliance on revelation. Such ridicule tends to come from those whose scholarly credentials are high and whose spiritual credentials are low.

The Book of Mormon's major significance is its witness of Jesus Christ as the only begotten Son of God the Eternal Father who redeems and saves us from death and sin. If an account stands as a preeminent witness of Jesus Christ, how can it possibly make no difference whether the account is fact or fable—whether the persons really lived who prophesied of Christ and gave eye witnesses of His appearances to them?

Professor John W. Welch pointed out to me that this new wave of antihistoricism "may be a new kid on the block in Salt Lake City, but it has been around in a lot of other Christian neighborhoods for several decades." Indeed! The argument that it makes no difference whether the Book of Mormon is fact or fable is surely a sibling to the argument that it makes no difference whether Jesus Christ ever lived. As we know, there are many so-called Christian teachers who espouse the teachings and deny the teacher. Beyond that, there are those who even deny the existence or the knowability of God. Their counterparts in Mormondom embrace some of the teachings of the Book of Mormon but deny its historicity.

Recently, as I was scanning the magazine *Chronicles,* published by the Rockford Institute, I was stopped by the title of a book review, "Who Needs the Historical Jesus?"[9] and by the formidable reputation of its author. Jacob Neusner, who is Dr., Rabbi, and Professor, reviewed two books whose titles both include the phrase "the historical Jesus." His comments are persuasive on the subject of historicity in general.

Neusner praises these two books, one as "an intensively powerful and poetic book . . . by a great writer who is also an original and weighty scholar"[10] and the other as "a masterpiece of scholarship."[11] But notwithstanding his tributes to their technique, Neusner forthrightly challenges the appropriateness of the effort the authors have undertaken. Their effort, typical in today's scholarly world, was to use a skeptical reading of the scriptures rather than a believing one, to present a historical study that would "distinguish fact from fiction, myth or legend from authentic event." In doing so, their "skeptical reading of the Gospels"[12] caused them to assume that the Jesus Christ of the Gospels was not the Jesus who actually lived. It also caused them to assume that historians can know the difference.

I now quote Neusner's conclusions:

No historical work explains itself so disingenuously as does work on the historical Jesus: from beginning, middle, to end, the issue is theological.[13]

Surely no question bears more profound theological implications for Christians than what the person they believe to be the incarnate God really, actually, truly said and did here on earth. But historical method, which knows nothing of the supernatural and looks upon miracles with unreserved stupefaction, presumes to answer them.[14]

But statements (historical or otherwise) about the founders of religions present a truth of a different kind. Such statements not only bear weightier implications, but they appeal to sources distinct from the kind that record what George Washington did on a certain day in 1775. They are based upon revelation, not mere information; they claim, and those who value them believe, that they originate in God's revelation or inspiration. Asking the Gospels to give historical rather than gospel truth confuses theological truth with historical fact, diminishing them to the measurements of this world, treating Jesus as precisely the opposite of what Christianity has always known Him to be, which is unique.

When we speak of "the historical Jesus," therefore, we dissect a sacred subject with a secular scalpel, and in the confusion of categories of truth the patient dies on the operating table; the surgeons forget why they made their cut; they remove the heart and neglect to put it back. The statement "One and one are two," or "The Constitutional Convention met in 1787," is simply not of the same order as "Moses received the Torah at Sinai" or "Jesus Christ is Son of God."

What historical evidence can tell us whether someone really rose from the dead, or what God said to the prophet on Sinai? I cannot identify a historical method equal to the work of verifying the claim that God's Son was born to a virgin girl. And how can historians accustomed to explaining the causes of the Civil War speak of miracles, or men rising from the dead, and of other matters of broad belief? Historians working with miracle stories turn out something that is either paraphrastic of the faith, indifferent to it, or merely silly. In their work we have nothing other than theology masquerading as "critical history." If I were a Christian, I would ask why the crown of science has now to be placed upon the head of a Jesus reduced to this-worldly dimensions, adding that here is just another crown of thorns. In my own view as a rabbi, I say only that these books are simply and monumentally irrelevant.[15]

Please excuse me for burdening you with that long quote, but I hope you will agree with my conclusion that what the rabbi/professor said about the historical Jesus is just as appropriate and persuasive on the question of the historicity of the Book of Mormon.[16]

To put the matter briefly, a scholarly expert is a specialist in a particular discipline. By definition, he knows everything or almost everything about a very narrow field of human experience. To think that he can tell us something about other scholarly disciplines, let alone about God's purposes and the eternal scheme of things, is naive at best.

Good scholars understand the limitations of their own fields, and their conclusions are carefully limited to the areas of their expertise. In connection with this, I remember the reported observation of an old lawyer. As they traveled through a pastoral setting with cows grazing on green meadows, an acquaintance said, "Look at those spotted cows." The cautious lawyer observed carefully and conceded, "Yes, those cows are spotted, at least on this side." I wish that all of the critics of the Book of Mormon, including those who feel compelled to question its historicity, were even half that cautious about their "scholarly" conclusions.

In this message I have offered some thoughts on matters relating to the historicity of the Book of Mormon.

1. On this subject, as on so many others involving our faith and theology, it is important to rely on faith and revelation as well as scholarship.

2. I am convinced that secular evidence can neither prove nor disprove the authenticity of the Book of Mormon.

3. Those who deny the historicity of the Book of Mormon have the difficult task of trying to prove a negative. They also have the awkward duty of explaining how they can dismiss the Book of Mormon as a fable while still praising some of its contents.

4. We know from the Bible that Jesus taught His apostles that in the important matter of His own identity and mission they were "blessed" for relying on the witness of revelation ("the things that be of God"), and it is offensive to Him for them to act upon worldly values and reasoning ("the things . . . that be of men") (Matt. 16:23).

5. Those scholars who rely on faith and revelation as well as scholarship, and who assume the authenticity of the Book of Mormon, must endure ridicule from those who disdain these things of God.

6. I have also illustrated that not all scholars disdain the value of religious belief and the legitimacy of the supernatural when applied to theological truth. Some even criticize the "intellectual provincialism" of those who apply the methods of historical criticism to the Book of Mormon.

I testify of Jesus Christ, whom we serve, whose Church this is. I invoke his blessings upon you, in the name of Jesus Christ, amen.

Elder Dallin H. Oaks is a member of the Quorum of the Twelve Apostles, The Church of Jesus Christ of Latter-day Saints.

Notes

1. This paper was originally presented 29 October 1993 at the Annual Dinner of the Foundation for Ancient Research and Mormon Studies, Provo, Utah, and was available as a typescript from F.A.R.M.S. The valuable suggestions of Professor John W. Welch, Brigham Young University Law School, are gratefully acknowledged.

2. Anthony A. Hutchinson, "The Word of God Is Enough: The Book of Mormon as Nineteenth-Century Scripture," *New Approaches to the Book of Mormon: Exploration in Critical Methodology,* ed. Brent Lee Metcalfe (Salt Lake City: Signature Books, 1993), 1.

3. Austin Farrer, "The Christian Apologist," in *Light on C. S. Lewis,* ed. Jocelyn Gibb (New York: Harcourt, Brace & World, 1965), 26.

4. Hugh Nibley, *Lehi in the Desert, The World of the Jaredites, There Were Jaredites,* The Collected Works of Hugh Nibley: Volume 5, The Book of Mormon (Salt Lake City: Deseret Book and the Foundation for Ancient Research and Mormon Studies, 1988), 237.

5. Orson Scott Card, *A Storyteller in Zion: Essays and Speeches by Orson Scott Card* (Salt Lake City: Bookcraft, 1993), 13–45.

6. Paul M. Bator, "Talk to the First Year Class," *The Law School Record* 35 (spring 1989): 7.

7. Gordon B. Hinckley, *Conference Report,* October 1983, 68.

8. Harold B. Lee, *Stand Ye in Holy Places* (Salt Lake City: Deseret Book, 1974), 92.

9. Jacob Neusner, "Who Needs the Historical Jesus?" review of *A Marginal Jew: Rethinking the Historical Jesus,* by John P. Meier and *The Historical Jesus: The Life of a Mediterranean Jewish Peasant,* by John Dominic Crossan, published in *Chronicles,* July 1993, 32–34.

10. Ibid., 34.

11. Ibid., 33.

12. Ibid., 32.

13. Ibid., 34.

14. Ibid., 32.

15. Ibid., 32–33.

16. Neusner apparently agrees. See his letter to the editor in *Sunstone,* July 1993, 7–8.